Foreknowledge and
Social Identity in 1 Peter

Foreknowledge and Social Identity in 1 Peter

PAUL A. HIMES

☙PICKWICK *Publications* · Eugene, Oregon

FOREKNOWLEDGE AND SOCIAL IDENTITY IN 1 PETER

Copyright © 2014 Paul A. Himes. All rights reserved. Except for brief quotations in critical publications or reviews, no part of this book may be reproduced in any manner without prior written permission from the publisher. Write: Permissions. Wipf and Stock Publishers, 199 W. 8th Ave., Suite 3, Eugene, OR 97401.

Pickwick Publications
An Imprint of Wipf and Stock Publishers
199 W. 8th Ave., Suite 3
Eugene, OR 97401

www.wipfandstock.com

ISBN 13: 978-1-62564-362-9

Cataloguing-in-Publication Data

Himes, Paul A.

Foreknowledge and social identity in 1 Peter / Paul A. Himes.

xvi + 224 p. ; 23 cm. Includes bibliographical references.

ISBN 13: 978-1-62564-362-9

1. Bible. Peter, 1st—Criticism, interpretation, etc. 2. Bible. Peter, 1st—Social scientific criticism.. 3. Group identity. 4. God (Christianity)—Omniscience. I. Title.

BS2795.52 H52 2014

Manufactured in the U.S.A.   08/13/2014

Scripture quotations marked (ESV) are from The Holy Bible, English Standard Version® (ESV®), copyright © 2001 by Crossway Bibles, a publishing ministry of Good News Publishers. Used by permission. All rights reserved.

The lexical searches utilized in this study, as well the Greek text from those searches, are from the following sources: *Accordance 8.4*, OakTree Software, copyright © 2009, and *Thesaurus Linguae Graecae*, University of California, copyright © 2009 by *TLG* and the Regents of the University of California.

To Bethany Hills Baptist Church in Raleigh, NC (Fall 2008 to Fall 2013): thanks for being my friends and helping me keep my sanity!

To my parents, John Rice Himes and Patty Lynn Himes: you're my role models, and all that I've accomplished pales in significance to your thirty-plus years service as missionaries.

Contents

Foreword by David Alan Black | ix
Preface | xi
Acknowledgments | xiii
Abbreviations | xv

1 Thesis and Survey of Scholarship, and Methodology | 1
2 Displacement Terminology and Social Identity in 1 Peter | 38
3 The Significance of Semantic Range and Context for Interpretation | 74
4 The Semantic Range of Πρόγνωσις and Προγινώσκω | 99
5 The Concept of Foreknowledge in Three Key Texts in First Peter (1:2; 1:10–12; and 1:20) | 131
6 The Significance of Foreknowledge for a New Social Identity in 1 Peter | 162
7 Conclusion | 180

Bibliography | 189
Index of Scripture and Other Ancient Works | 209
Index of Subject Matter | 219
Index of Authors | 221

Foreword

It was my privilege and joy, as Paul Himes's major professor in his PhD program, to have read his doctoral dissertation, and it is now my great pleasure to commend it to other readers. What I find most appealing about Dr. Himes' book is his handling of the biblical text. His exegetical acumen is apparent on every page, no less when he is handling a Greek lexeme as when he is delving into deep theological questions. Of particular significance is his treatment of the concept of "foreknowledge" in Peter's writings and, by extension, in New Testament theology. Dr. Himes's conclusion may not be unique to him—he is quick to acknowledge his indebtedness to John Elliott—but it is one that demands our attention.

I am more than grateful to Dr. Himes for this significant contribution to biblical theology. It will undoubtedly fill an important gap in the literature. More significantly, perhaps it will serve as a salutary reminder that we Christians are little more than pilgrims and strangers—resident aliens—whose main concern ought to always be to interpret the gospel of salvation in ways that are relevant to the surrounding culture. Paradise Lost will one day become Paradise Gained. Until then, Christians have no reason to evade their responsibility to proclaim the gospel to the utmost of their power while being prepared to live it and, if necessary, die for it.

If this book plays even a small role in calling the church back to it primary task of evangelism, it will have served a useful purpose indeed.

David Alan Black
M. O. Owens, Jr., Chair in New Testament
Southeastern Baptist Theological Seminary

Preface

Ever since I took a particular theology class my junior year in college, I have been fascinated with the concept of divine foreknowledge, especially as it is discussed in the New Testament. I observed that while much had been written on πρόγνωσις and προγινώσκω in the New Testament, very little original research had been done on how these words were used within the Koine era. Pursuing a PhD under Greek scholar David Alan Black presented the perfect opportunity to pursue this area of research.

Halfway through my doctoral studies, I had the privilege of taking a distance-ed course on 1 Peter with Dr. Gene L. Green from Wheaton College. Dr. Green introduced me to the works of John H. Elliott, especially his monumental work *A Home for the Homeless*. Here I discovered social-scientific criticism and how it could be used within New Testament studies. I soon resolved that my dissertation would fuse both lexical semantics and social-scientific criticism into a study of foreknowledge and social-identity in 1 Peter.

I greatly benefited from the comments of Dr. Black, Dr. David Beck, and Dr. Gene Green in my dissertation defense. In particular, the comments of Dr. Green have formed the basis for the vast majority of revisions for this book. I hope that my efforts in this study do tribute to the amount of time those three scholars have put into critiquing my work. Most of all, I hope that this study on foreknowledge and social identity benefits both academia and the church. If this work can generate greater interest in the excellent scholarship surrounding 1 Peter, or, even more importantly, if this work can point the reader to the powerful theological truths of this epistle, then I trust that I have done my duty.

Acknowledgments

The journey from prospectus to dissertation to actual book has been a long one, but I am grateful to be at the finish line. First and foremost, I am grateful to my Lord Jesus Christ for his mercy and grace. May this study of 1 Peter be a tribute to his finished work.

Second, I am grateful especially to my brothers and sisters in Christ at Bethany Hills Baptist Church, Raleigh, NC, from August 2008 to the present day (November 2013). You have been my family and my home. When I was lonely, you befriended me. When I was hungry, you fed me. When I was discouraged, you prayed for me. When I was bored, you gave me ministry opportunities. May the Lord bless you all for your kindness and friendship.

To my parents, you have always believed in me and supported me. You were my first Bible teachers, and if I have made it this far it is only because you set a godly example. Thank you for all you've done for me.

Thanks to all my good friends for your prayers and encouragement. Thanks especially to Mark Farnham, Michael and Jessica Stover, and Kevin and Brooke Miner for your support and friendships in my doctoral studies and the months immediately after. You all went above and beyond the call of duty!

A number of scholars have contributed to the formation of this book in one way or another. I am grateful to Dr. David Black for advising me and pushing me to excel, to Dr. Andreas Köstenberger for advising me to broaden my thesis, to Dr. David Beck for contributing as my secondary reader and to Dr. Gene Green, my outside reader whose distance-ed class on 1 Peter was very beneficial to my research and my thesis. I would like to especially thank Dr. Green for his excellent comments on how I could improve my dissertation, comments which formed the basis for my revision for Pickwick.

I also give thanks to my three proofreaders: Chuck Bumgardner, Joe Green, and John Himes. I give further thanks to Dr. Stephen Stout, whose work as the official SBL style checker has also been invaluable. I am also grateful to David and Gabbi Barnhart for help with some of the more difficult German sources. You all made my life much easier!

Finally, I am grateful to Pickwick Publications for providing me with the opportunity to contribute to scholarship on 1 Peter. Thanks especially to Dr. K. C. Hanson for providing assistance and answering my questions.

Abbreviations

1 Clem	1 Clement
1 Chron	1 Chronicles
1 Pet	1 Peter
2 Pet	2 Peter
AB	Anchor Bible
Ag. Ap.	Against Apion
ANF	The Ante-Nicene Fathers
Ant.	Jewish Antiquities
BBR	Bulletin for Biblical Research
BibSac	Bibliotheca Sacra
BTB	Biblical Theology Bulletin
CBQ	Catholic Biblical Quarterly
Confusion	On the Confusion of Tongues
Def. orac.	The Obsolescence of Oracles
DGRBM	Dictionary of Greek and Roman Biography and Mythology
Div.	De divinatione
ESV	English Standard Version
Herm.	Shepherd of Hermes
ISBE	International Standard Bible Encyclopedia
JBL	Journal of Biblical Literature
Jdt	Judith
JSNT	Journal for the Study of the New Testament

JSNTSup	Journal for the Study of the New Testament Supplements
J.W.	*Jewish War*
LCL	Loeb Classical Library
LXX	The Septuagint
Nat. D.	*De natura deorum*
NDBT	New Dictionary of Biblical Theology
Nestle-Aland	The *Novum Testamentum Graece* edited by Barbara Aland, et. al.
NIB	The New Interpreter's Bible
NPNF1	*The Nicene and Post-Nicene Fathers*, Series 1
NPNF2	*The Nicene and Post-Nicene Fathers*, Series 2
NTS	New Testament Studies
PG	J.-P. Migne's Patrologia Graeca
Pyth. Orac.	*The Oracles at Delphi No Longer Given in Verse*
Rom	Romans
SSC	Social Scientific Criticism
TLG	*Thesaurus Linguae Graecae*
Wis	Wisdom of Solomon

1

Thesis, Survey of Scholarship, and Methodology

The context of 1 Peter must, to a certain degree, be viewed through the lens of interaction, even "conflict," between the Christian community and the society around it.[1] Yet this conflict in 1 Peter is tied to the "otherness" of believers, i.e., their status as strangers and their distinction from those outside of their group.[2] For such strangers, their own lack of social status always lurks at the door, threatening to overwhelm them with despair. To this community of strangers, however, Peter offers the following word of hope: despite their sense of physical and spiritual displacement, their new social identity is forever bound up in the foreknowledge of God. Who they were, who they are, and who they are becoming is no surprise, but rather part of the cosmic master plan, tied inseparably to their identity in Christ.[3]

---

1. As Leonhard Goppelt, *Der erste Petrusbrief*, 56, states, "The historical situation of the churches [communities], which this letter responds to, is prominently marked by their conflict with society" ("Die geschichtliche Situation der Gemeinden, die der Brief anspricht, ist entscheidend durch ihren Konflikt mit der Gesellschaft gekennzeichnet"). All translations are the work of this writer unless otherwise stated.

2. See Elliott, *Home for the Homeless*, 75. Cf. also Goppelt, *Der erste Petrusbrief*, 77, who further notes, "1 Peter characterizes them, at a glance, in a horizontal relationship with their environment: they are separated out of the people of the world through election and live under it scattered as strangers, strangers who have no homeland here" ("Der 1 Petr kennzeichnet sie in der Horizontalen im Blick auf das Verhältnis zu ihrer Umwelt: Sie sind aus der Völkerwelt durch die Erwählung ausgesondert und leben unter ihr zerstreut als Fremde, die hier keine Heimat haben").

3. The matter of authorship will not factor significantly into this study's thesis. For the sake of convenience, the epistle's author will be referred to simply as "Peter." See

2   Foreknowledge and Social Identity in 1 Peter

The concepts of church, community, and social identity have, of course, been thoroughly explored in the Petrine literature of the past few decades. Indeed, fortunately gone are the days when John Elliott could sadly point out that "1 Peter suffers second-class status in the estimation of modern NT exegetes . . . [I]t is generally treated as one of the step-children of the NT canon."[4] First Peter is no longer the "exegetical stepchild" it once was. It now sits in the banquet hall with the other epistles, though still, perhaps, at a somewhat lower seat than its Pauline cousins.

Yet a few gaps remain in Petrine scholarship. While social identity in 1 Peter has been explored, virtually no one has yet to link the social identity of the Petrine audience with the concept of foreknowledge in 1 Peter, despite the fact that the latter plays a prominent role in the first major section of the epistle. This study will attempt to demonstrate just how foreknowledge functions in 1 Peter's discussion of the audience's social identity. In the process, this study will challenge the scholarly consensus on two items: first, it will argue that foreknowledge in 1 Peter primarily possesses *sociological*, rather than strictly *soteriological*, significance. Secondly, this study will argue that foreknowledge in 1 Peter (both the concept and the terminology) should be viewed strictly in prescient or mantic terms rather than being considered synonymous with foreordination (determining something ahead of time) or loving beforehand. Ultimately, the prescient terminology in 1 Pet 1:2; 1:10–12; and 1:20 functions as a word of encouragement to the believers and plays a major role in explaining the "how" and "why" of their new social identity in Christ.

THE PROBLEM STATED

That 1 Peter deals with the concept of believers as a community is not debated. Indeed, as Theophil Spörri noted almost one hundred years ago, despite the lack of the specific term ἐκκλησία, 1 Peter still remains a fruitful ground for an investigation of early Christian ecclesiology and community.[5] Furthermore, to a certain degree, this development of a theology of

---

below for further discussion.

4. Elliott, "Rehabilitation of an Exegetical Step-Child," 243.

5. Spörri, *Der Gemeindegedanke im ersten Petrusbrief*, 12. It should be stressed here that the German term *Gemeinde*, while literally "community," nevertheless is often used as the common term for "church." Thus it must be acknowledged that frequently the German term will not always have the same force as this writer's use of "community," being more theologically/ecclesiologically oriented. Nevertheless, a study of *Gemeinde*, even in an ecclesiological sense, necessarily means a study of "community." Thus German discussions of "Gemeinde" in 1 Peter remain extremely relevant to this study.

church/community relies on Old Testament terminology.⁶ Thus the study of *Gemeindegedanke* in 1 Peter is intertwined with the study of 1 Peter's use of the Old Testament, including its discussion of OT prophets and their foreknowledge of future events (incomplete though that might have been).

Furthermore, 1 Peter exists as a "letter of consolation" (5:12) designed to help Christians experiencing hostility from those around them.⁷ The believers are in dire straits. Consequently, William Kirkpatrick paints the following picture:

> Adverse social conditions threatened to undermine the faith of these new converts. At the same time, these same conditions called into question the meaning and relevance of the church as a divinely initiated community. However, the circumstances of these chosen immigrants, who are expected to live as strangers in the world, as well as that of the church as a gathered community, has not been left to chance, nor is their circumstance of suffering an accident of history.⁸

Despite the above statement, surprisingly little work has been done linking either foreknowledge or Old Testament prophecy with that sense of community that 1 Peter develops, even though both foreknowledge and prophecy (the prophets in 1:10–12; foreknowledge in 1:1 and 1:20) play a prominent role in 1 Peter's opening discourse. Furthermore, prophecy is, by its very nature, related to the concept of foreknowledge in the ancient biblical world (note, for example, Josephus, *J.W.* 8.231–234 and Judith 11:16–19), and 1 Pet 1:2 and 1:20 contain the noun πρόγνωσις and the verb προγινώσκω respectively, effectively bracketing the discussion of prophecy in 1:10–12. Thus the concept of foreknowledge must play some role in the early stages of 1 Peter's discourse. Nevertheless, to this writer's knowledge, no work has been done that explores the connection between the concept of foreknowledge and social identity (or ecclesiology, *Gemeindegedanke*, social displacement, etc.).

Furthermore, when scholars discuss foreknowledge in 1 Peter, they overwhelmingly (with a few key exceptions) discuss it in terms of (1) God's foreordination and/or "loving beforehand," and (2) soteriology. In other words, scholars almost universally see foreknowledge in 1 Peter as closely tied to God's salvific work, referring to the act of God whereby he foreordains a person's destiny and/or loves them intimately beforehand (resulting in eternal choice). While foreknowledge is, to some degree, tied to God's

6. Schröger, *Gemeinde im 1. Petrusbrief*, 7.
7. Richard, "Honorable Conduct among the Gentiles," 414.
8. Kirkpatrick, "Theology of First Peter," 64–65.

salvific word, those who discuss foreknowledge in such terms often neglect the lexical meaning of the terminology in Koine Greek as well as the context of the first section of 1 Peter. In this writer's opinion, sufficient work has not been done on either the semantics of foreknowledge or its context in 1 Peter. As a result, foreknowledge in 1 Peter has been misunderstood and forced to play a role it was never meant to play in the theology of the letter.

METHODOLOGY AND CHAPTER LAYOUT

Ultimately, this book is concerned with the concept of foreknowledge in 1 Pet 1:2, 10–12, and 20. Yet because foreknowledge plays a prominent role in the development of 1 Peter's ecclesiology, this study will necessarily focus on social displacement and social identity from 1:1 to 2:11. While extensive exegetical work will mostly be limited to the first chapter of the epistle, specifically the verses dealing with foreknowledge, the overall theme and rhetoric of the first major section of 1 Peter (1:3—2:10) will also be examined.

In order to prove the proposed thesis (stated below), this study will pay special attention to the following two areas of scholarship: social-scientific criticism and lexical semantics. Early on, this study will explore various social-scientific views on 1 Peter, especially the theme of displacement and how 1 Peter offers a word of comfort to all displaced believers. This will require both a general overview of social-scientific criticism as well as an examination of the specific application of that methodology to 1 Peter. The latter will require an analysis of John H. Elliott's monumental *A Home for the Homeless* as well as the various responses to his work and alternate views on the social status of the recipients.[9]

Later, in order to demonstrate why πρόγνωσις and προγινώσκω should be taken in a prescient or mantic sense, this study will examine lexical semantics and its application to exegesis. At that point, we will also discuss why it is beneficial to examine a word's extra-biblical usage in order to assist with determining a word's biblical meaning; this study will then provide a comprehensive lexical analysis of πρόγνωσις and προγινώσκω. This study will also examine how those words function within the context of 1 Peter. Of necessity, we will also examine the terms παρεπίδημος and πάροικος, although much lexical work has already been done on these words by scholars (in contrast to the lack of original scholarly work on πρόγνωσις and προγινώσκω).

9. Elliott, *Home for the Homeless.*

The remainder of this current chapter will provide a thesis statement together with definitions of key terms, briefly discuss the background and structure of 1 Peter (paying special attention to the position of 1:1—2:10/11 within the overall outline of the epistle), and then provide a survey of scholarship on the nature of community and social identity in 1 Peter, the use of foreknowledge in 1 Peter, and the general meaning of foreknowledge in the NT. The two final sections of this chapter will briefly examine the concept of foreknowledge within first-century thought (both Jewish and Greco-Roman) and provide a brief introduction to social-scientific criticism before concluding.

The second chapter will focus on the social identity of the recipients of 1 Peter (with an emphasis on the concepts of displacement and communal identity) in an attempt to lay the groundwork for a discussion of how the concept of foreknowledge might relate to social identity. In this second chapter, special attention will be given to John Elliott's work in addition to the various responses to Elliott and alternate views on the social and spiritual status of the audience of 1 Peter.[10] The last section of this chapter will analyze displacement terminology in 1 Peter (terminology such as παρεπίδημος) and draw some conclusions regarding the status of the recipients of the epistle.

The third chapter will deal with lexical semantics and offer a defense as to why semantic range is helpful for determining a word's meaning in a NT text. In other words, justification will be provided as to why the texts of the day (AD 1–100 and the Septuagint) should be examined in addition to a word's context in a particular NT passage.

Chapter four, then, will examine how exactly the specific terms πρόγνωσις and προγινώσκω were used in the literature of the day. This chapter will analyze every single usage of these terms in the Greek literature from AD 1–100 and in the LXX. Some conclusions will be drawn regarding their general use within the Greco-Roman world of NT times.

The fifth chapter will analyze the specific texts of the first section of 1 Peter that relate to foreknowledge, specifically 1 Pet 1:2, 10–12, and 20. Each section will be examined in light of its relation to the social status of the epistle's recipients and how foreknowledge can here function as a word of comfort.

The sixth chapter will then examine how both foreknowledge and social identity function within the broader theology and argumentation of 1 Peter. The fifth and sixth chapters will be the key chapters of the study and

---

10. As noted above, Elliott's *Home for the Homeless* will be the primary focus, but other works will also be examined.

will attempt to integrate all of the above research into a coherent theory regarding the roles of foreknowledge and social identity in the epistle.

The final chapter will conclude by summarizing this study's findings, offering responses to potential objections, and discussing possible opportunities for further research.

THESIS STATEMENT AND CLARIFICATION OF TERMINOLOGY

The thesis of this study is that *from the introduction to the beginning of the second major section of the epistle, 1 Peter uses the concept of "foreknowledge" as a word of comfort to offset his readers' status as socially-displaced strangers and to thus emphasize their new-found social identity in Christ.*

As mentioned above, this thesis assumes that "foreknowledge" should be thought of as a prescient term with sociological significance (in the context of 1 Peter). The term "foreknowledge," for the sake of this study, is defined simply as "the act or state of knowing something ahead of time." As such, the term naturally encompasses everything that is foreordained, but the converse (i.e., that foreordination necessarily encompasses all that is foreknown) should not *necessarily* be assumed true.[11] Furthermore, as will be demonstrated, conceptually foreknowledge can be possessed either by God or by men and women. Theologically, of course, one may argue that the foreknowledge of the former is qualitatively superior to that of the latter, but this is irrelevant to this study.

"Prescience," then, is synonymous with foreknowledge as defined above. The term "mantic," however, is somewhat narrower and is related to prophecy and divination. Consequently, "mantic" is an appropriate term when describing some passages that include foreknowledge (e.g., 1 Pet 1:10–12), but not all passages.[12]

---

11. This is a purely theological discussion and quite out of the scope of this study. This writer will, however, strongly argue that to automatically *assume* that foreknowledge must equal foreordination, especially in the Petrine passages, is to allow one's predetermined theology to dominate one's exegesis. However, even *if* all that the Father foreknows is necessarily foreordained (a theological argument that is mostly irrelevant to the message of 1 Peter), this still does not mean that Peter cannot use the term "foreknowledge" in a strictly mantic or prescient sense. Consider the following semantic analogy: one may argue that all clean-up hitters in baseball are necessarily power hitters. However, one can still discuss the concept of "clean-up hitter" without necessarily concerning oneself with the concept of "power hitter" (the ability to drive in runs is not necessarily determined by how far one can hit a home run). The two terms may overlap, but they may also be discussed as representing two distinct concepts.

12. See "Mantic," *Merriam-Webster*, n.p. Online.

"Social identity" in this study is defined as how a person or group views themselves in light of their surrounding society and culture, and how one fits or fails to fit into the social, ethnic, economic, and religious groups that make up that society. As such, there are similarities between this term and the German *Gemeinde* (church/community), though the latter seems to be geared more towards ecclesiology in German theological works whereas this writer is also concerned with sociology (though obviously the two overlap in 1 Peter). The term "social identity" in reference to 1 Peter is not original to this writer, though its use in discussions of 1 Peter is surprisingly rare.[13]

"Displacement" refers to that condition whereby a person or group finds himself, herself, or themselves in an unfamiliar and/or hostile social context, perhaps as a result of political exile, forced relocation, idealistic change, colonization, etc. This study will view the readers of 1 Peter primarily through the lens of displacement. In other words, the readers of 1 Peter are experiencing a sense of displacement, possibly due to factors such as having been relocated into a new geographical and social context, having experienced conversion (and thus a radical ideological change), or perhaps a combination of both (the various views will be discussed in the next chapter). As such, "displacement" will be viewed as a negative social concept.

BACKGROUND AND RECIPIENTS OF 1 PETER

Before continuing onto a survey of scholarship, at least some attention must be given to the general circumstances and structure of 1 Peter. To begin with, this study will assume Petrine authorship, often referring to the author as "Peter" rather than the awkward and wordy "Petrine author" or "Petrine community." Ultimately, however, the authorship of the epistle is irrelevant to this study.[14]

---

13. Yet see, among others, Fagbemi, "Living for Christ in a Hostile World," 7, where he states, "In the interaction between the theological and *social identity* of the people . . ." (emphasis added). The term "social identity" was used in a broader sense years earlier by Judge, "The Social Identity of the First Christians," 201–17.

14. For the classic defense of Petrine authorship, see Selwyn, *First Epistle of St. Peter*, 7–38 (Selwyn also argues that Silvanus played a major role in the epistle's composition; see esp. 17 and 27). For a more modern defense, see Schreiner, *1, 2 Peter, Jude*, 21–36. For a technical, indirect defense of Petrine authorship through an examination of the Greek of 1 Peter, see Jobes, "The Syntax of 1 Peter," 159–73. For alternate views on Petrine scholarship, see Elliott, *I Peter*, 124–30; and Horrell, "The Product of a Petrine Circle?" 29–60.

The ethnic identity of the recipients is more important to this writer's thesis. Unfortunately, providing a definitive answer to the question is beyond the scope of this study. The majority of scholars seem to hold to a mixed Jewish-Gentile audience. Edward Selwyn, for example, argues, "It is doubtful, indeed, whether there were many Churches in the first century outside Palestine, at any rate in the larger centers of population, of which the members were wholly Jewish or wholly Gentile."[15] Some scholars, however, see either a primarily Jewish or primarily Gentile audience.[16] For the sake of this study, a mixed audience will be presumed with no preconceived notions regarding Jewish or Gentile predominance. As Stephen Fagbemi aptly notes, "The text is far from precise about the racial origin of its recipients ... [A]s evidence abounds in the text to support both positions [i.e., primarily Jewish vs. primarily Gentile], it seems reasonable to argue that the church was a mixture of both Gentile and Jewish Christians" (especially when one considers Acts 2:9–10).[17] Furthermore, this study's thesis should remain coherent regardless of the ethnic makeup of the epistle's audience, for both Jews and Gentiles were quite likely to suffer a sense of displacement in the Roman-controlled Asia Minor of the first century.[18]

The geographical locations of the recipients, on the other hand, are made explicitly clear by the introduction to the letter, which addresses believers in the regions of Pontus, Galatia, Cappadocia, Asia, and Bithynia. By the time of 1 Peter, this portion of the Middle East possessed a complicated history and ethnic makeup, especially due to the presence of Celts and Gauls. Beginning in 280 BC, Greece herself had experienced a massive military migration of Celts.[19] As a direct consequence of this, Asia Minor

---

15. Selwyn, *First Epistle of St. Peter,* 44; cf. Achtemeier, *1 Peter,* 50–51; Elliott, *I Peter,* 96.

16. For an argument for a primarily Gentile audience, see Green, "The Use of the Old Testament for Christian Ethics in 1 Peter," 276–77, and Schreiner, *1, 2 Peter, Jude,* 51. For an argument for a primarily Jewish audience, see Liebengood, "'Don't Be Like Your Fathers,'" esp. 1–14; and Harmon, "Peter," 35.

17. Fagbemi, *Who Are the Elect in 1 Peter?*, 68. The reader should also note Preston Duane Warden, "Alienation and Community in 1 Peter," 12–13, where he argues that one should be careful to not generalize the background of 1 Peter's audience in Asia Minor, for "1 Peter is addressed to a very large geographical area, encompassing many different cultural and social situations. References to 'Anatolian Christians' or to social situations faced by 'Christians in Asia Minor' encompass such territorial and cultural diversity as to make suspect any conclusions with respect to the specific social situation of the addressees of 1 Peter."

18. For a discussion of the geographical situation of the letter's addressees, the article by Hemer, "Address of 1 Peter," 239–43, is very helpful.

19. Mitchell, *The Celts and the Impact of Roman Rule,* 13–15 (Mitchell, on p. 15, states, "The Greek world was clearly facing a whole nation on the move"). Mitchell's

saw an influx of Gauls and Celts. Approximately 10,000 civilian Gauls accompanied the fighting men into Asia Minor, and approximately 60 years later Attalus I sent more Celts to the region, "accompanied by their families and a baggage train."[20] They were not necessarily the dominant power in Anatolia, of course. Antiochus' defeat of the Gauls around 268 BC had major repercussions on where these invading races could settle and live.[21] Yet clearly the Gauls and Celts forged a new destiny for many of their ethnicity among the others of Asia Minor, heavily impacting the various regions to which 1 Peter was written (especially Galatia, Bithynia, and Pontus).[22]

The rise of Roman power, of course, would have significantly impacted the socio-political makeup of Asia Minor. The Romans first began to take a major role in Anatolian affairs with the battle of Magnesia (190 BC) and the defeat of the Seleucids.[23] Later, Roman military influence in Asia Minor seemed all but certain with the assimilation of Pergamum as "the core of the Roman province of Asia."[24] Anatolia was not, however, always an easy conquest. Of the various regions 1 Peter addresses, Pontus is notable for becoming the focal point of Mithridates Eupator's violent opposition to Rome. Yet the eventual defeat of Mithridates represented both the first and the last "great nationalist movement" of the area against Roman power.[25] After Mithridate's defeat in 73 BC, Bithynia soon became part of the empire, for "Nicomedes had, perhaps in emulation of the last Attalid ruler of Pergamum, bequeathed his country to the Romans . . ."[26] Cappadocia, on the other hand, had become a province of Rome during the early part of Tiberius' reign. However, "The subsequent history of Cappadocia is obscure and, in view of its character as a frontier-province, largely military. Its fortunes were much influenced by political vicissitudes, connected with the perpetual struggle to maintain a Roman client-ruler in neighboring Armenia."[27]

---

two-volume work, together with the ancient Greek and Latin authors, should be considered the starting point for all research concerning this point of Asia Minor's history.

20. Ibid., 15.

21. See the discussion in Mitchell, *The Celts and the Impact of Roman Rule*, 18–19.

22. See Mitchell, *The Celts and the Impact of Roman Rule*, 24–29 regarding Gaul influence in Galatia. Mitchell discusses the Gaul's relationships with Bithynia, Pontus, and Cappadocia (ibid., 19).

23. Ibid., 23.

24. Howard, *History of Turkey*, 28–29.

25. Lloyd, *Ancient Turkey*, 175, 177.

26. Ibid., 178.

27. Ibid., 203–4; cf. Howard, *History of Turkey*, 28–29

Galatia represented a significant part of Rome's strategy while existing as a remarkably diverse province. Early on it represented one of the bricks in a "wall of *imperial* provinces with armies guarding the inner frontier" against the threat of Persia.[28] Galatia was incorporated into the Roman empire soon after the death of her king Amyntas (25 BC).[29] Yet even by this time Galatia was already "the largest of all the vassal-kingdoms."[30] By the time Galatia became a Roman province, the newcomer Gauls and the older Phrygians and Cappadocians "had begun to intermarry and otherwise adapt their ways to local conditions, but their national idiosyncrasies and distinctive social customs gave a peculiar twist of character to the mixed race which resulted."[31] Upon these diverse races of Galatia, Rome "imposed a unity which must always be artificial; small wonder, then, that the boundaries of Galatia were so frequently altered."[32]

Ultimately, "The appearance of Anatolia changed fundamentally between the second century BC and the second century AD . . . Roman rule brought a network of all-weather roads, which transformed overland communications; permanent garrisons guarded the eastern frontier, and the Roman soldiers became a common sight on the roads and in the small towns . . . Roman power was acknowledged everywhere."[33] Hand-in-hand with this overt display of transcendent Roman rule, however, was a strong sense of patriotism within the key cities themselves.[34] It was to this social-political and ethnic situation that 1 Peter was written.

THE THEMES AND STRUCTURE OF 1 PETER

Many scholars have written on the major themes of 1 Peter. Some have correctly noted the prominent role of suffering and persecution in the epistle.[35] Different scholars, however, debate the degree of persecution implied in 1 Pet 2:20; 3:9–19; and 4:12–19. Many argue that the persecution is local

---

28. Moffett, *History of Christianity in Asia*, 1:8.
29. Levick, *Roman Colonies*, 29; Lloyd, *Ancient Turkey*, 197.
30. Lloyd, *Ancient Turkey*, 201–2.
31. Ibid., 202.
32. Levick, *Roman Colonies*, 121.
33. Mitchell, *The Celts and the Impact of Roman Rule*, 241.
34. Ibid., 206.
35. See, for example, Wikenhauser and Schmid, *Einleitung in das Neue Testament*, 590. They state, "The theme of 1 Peter is the testing of the Christian faith and life in suffering and persecution" ("Das Thema des 1 Petr ist die Bewährung des christlichen Glaubens und Lebens in Leiden und Verfolgungen").

and thus downplay any official imperial connection.[36] Yet Duane Warden argues against the consensus, declaring that ". . . one ought not to dismiss too quickly the role of provincial and city governments in opposing the new religion."[37] Warden further argues, "The role of official political powers in the persecutions addressed in 1 Peter was substantial."[38] Though relevant to this study (since the recipients were, quite clearly, suffering), a thorough examination of the nature of persecution is beyond the scope of this study. Whether or not the persecution of 1 Peter's audience was local, imperial, physical, psychological, or a combination of all of the above, the fact remains that the believers were under incredible social pressure for various reasons (including displacement and conversion). Warden says it best: "1 Peter evidences the perceived alienation of the believers from official society, indeed from all society which had not embraced the message heralded by the community of believers."[39]

Much more could be said about the other themes of 1 Peter, yet such a discussion is beyond the scope of this study. The reader should note that the point of this study is not to argue that displacement, community, foreknowledge, or ecclesiology are necessarily the primary topics of the epistle, but only that they play an important role in 1 Peter's argument and theology.

Regarding the literary nature of 1 Peter, this study will agree with James W. Thompson that "1 Peter is a rhetorical unity," for "it has an introduction, a body, and a conclusion."[40] Similarly, Earl J. Richard states, "The document is a real letter, for it retains the basic characteristics of the genre, especially a standard opening and closing."[41]

Modern scholarship has produced various outlines of 1 Peter, yet the majority seems to hold that 1:3—2:10 constitutes the first major section of the epistle (some, of course, include the first two verses within that unit). Thus Ervin Ray Starwalt, who has done more work on the matter than most, argues that all of 1:3—2:10 is "the body introduction" (with 2:1—4:11

---

36. See, for example, Elliott, *1 Peter*, 98–103; Moule, "Nature and Purpose of 1 Peter," 8.

37. Warden, "Imperial Persecution and the Dating of 1 Peter and Revelation," 209.

38. Warden, "Alienation and Community," 51.

39. Ibid., 187. Another possibility to consider is that, as Alan Bandy argues, "Most opposition to the Christian faith in the Roman Empire transpired through the means of the lawcourt" (Bandy, "Persecution and the Purpose of Revelation," 395). In his article, Bandy is specifically discussing those churches in Asia Minor to which Revelation was written.

40. Thompson, "Rhetoric of 1 Peter," 240.

41. Richard, "Honorable Conduct among the Gentiles," 414.

being "the body middle").[42] A substantial number of commentators are in agreement that 2:10/2:11 represents a break and transition from the first major section of 1 Peter to the second major section, though they would not necessarily follow Starwalt's terminology.[43] The reader should especially note Max-Alain Chevallier's article where he views that entire section (up to 1 Pet 2:10) as one distinct unit that makes use of deliberate literary devices and techniques that seem to be lacking in the rest of the epistle (except for 4:12 to the end).[44] For alternate outlines, the reader should note the commentaries by Achtemeier, Selwyn, and Ben Witherington III, as well as the article by Tommy Lea.[45] It is significant, however, that even those commentators with different outlines still see 2:10 as the end of a major section. This study will, however, briefly take note of 2:11, since 1:1 and 2:11 are the only places in 1 Peter where the term παρεπίδημος occurs (and, together with Heb 11:13, the only occurrences in the entire NT).[46] This study, then, will treat 1:3—2:10 as one section but will also discuss 2:11, treating it as a transition verse and the introduction to the next major section.[47]

SURVEY OF SCHOLARSHIP

In order to demonstrate the need for the present study, this study will examine how both ancient and modern scholarship has viewed foreknowledge

---

42. Starwalt, "Discourse Analysis of 1 Peter," 33.

43. See, for example, Elliott, *I Peter*, 82; Goppelt, *Der erste Petrusbrief*, 89 (Goppelt calls 1:3—2:10 the "erster hauptteil"); Jobes, *1 Peter*, 56; McKnight, *1 Peter*, 34; Michaels, *1 Peter*, xxxvii; Schelkle, *Die Petrusbriefe, der Judasbrief*, 68 (1 Pet 2:11 begins the "Zweiter Teil"); Spicq, *Les Épitres de Saint Pierre*, 37; Usteri, *Wissenschaftlicher und Praktischer Commentar*, vii.

44. Chevallier "1 Pierre 1/1 à 2/10," 129–42, esp. 138–40.

45. Achtemeier, *1 Peter*, 73, for example, sees 2:10/2:11 as the transition between the 3rd and 4th sections (the "body opening" and the "body middle"), though this includes the two-verse introduction. For Selwyn, *First Epistle of Peter*, 4–5, 1 Pet 1:3–12 is the "first doctrinal section," 1:13—2:3 is the "first hortatory section," 2:4–10 is the "second doctrinal section," and 2:11—3:12 is the "second hortatory section." Witherington, *Socio-Rhetorical Commentary on 1-2 Peter*, 47–49, follows the non-rhetorical outline of J. N. D. Kelly, but offers his own rhetorical outline where 1:3–12 is the "exordium," 1:13–16 is the "propositio," 1:17—2:10 is "argument 1," and 2:11—3:12 is "argument 2." Finally, Lea, "Outline and Exposition of First Peter," 17–18, views 1:3–12 as the "first teaching section," 1:13—2:3 as the "first preaching section," 2:4–10 as the "second teaching section," and 2:11 as the introduction to the "second preaching section."

46. Lexical search done via *Accordance Bible Software* 8.4.

47. Regarding the textual situation, an examination of Metzger, *Textual Commentary*, 616–19, as well as the Nestle-Aland *Novum Testamentum Graece* (28th ed.), indicates no major textual variants that would impact this study's argument.

and social identity in the first section of 1 Peter. Since discussions on "social identity" *per se* in 1 Peter are rare in the patristics, much of the following section will focus on the church fathers' treatment of the identity of the church in 1 Peter 2 (as well as their treatment of foreknowledge).

The Early Church Fathers on the Church in 1 Peter 2

The patristic works include a number of references to 1 Peter that simply cite the epistle in passing. For this reason, it is difficult to see what most of the earliest of the church fathers would have thought about this study's thesis. It is especially difficult to discover any discussions on the role of foreknowledge in 1 Peter. Nevertheless, quite a few early Christians use 1 Peter 2 to discuss the identity of the church. These and other key citations will be examined.

In general, the early church often applied key passages in 1 Peter 2 to the identity of the community of believers. Thus, in his *Epistle to the Ephesians*, Ignatius cites 1 Pet 2:9 as an encouragement to those who follow Christ in contrast to unbelievers.[48] Likewise, in his *Epistle to the Philadelphians*, within the context of a discussion on the universal church, he gives specific instructions to husbands, wives, single women, etc. and admonishes them to act correctly in light of their status designated in 1 Pet 2:9.[49]

Similarly, Clement of Alexandria takes a very general approach in his citation of 1 Pet 2:5, discussing how believers constitute a new temple for God.[50] Tertullian, however, in his *Answer to the Jews*, cites 1 Pet 2:10 and/or Hosea 1:10 (he does not explicitly say which) in order to contrast Christians with Jews, arguing that this text demonstrates how Christians have become God's people.[51]

Interestingly, Origin at one point applies 1 Pet 2:9 to the nation of Israel in the midst of a discussion of the believers' refusal to acknowledge Greek gods.[52] Elsewhere, however, he cites 1 Pet 2:5 specifically in reference to believers being built up as a new temple to replace the old, devastated temple.[53]

Methodius basically incorporates 1 Pet 2:9 into a hymn that glorifies the universal church, thus providing the reader with a formal celebration of

---

48. Ignatius, *Epistle of Ignatius to the Ephesians* 9 (*ANF* 1.53).
49. Ignatius, *Epistle of Ignatius to the Philadelphians* 4 (*ANF* 1.81).
50. Clement of Alexandria, *Fragments of Clemens Alexandrinus* 12.3 (*ANF* 2.585).
51. Tertullian, *An Answer to the Jews* 3 (*ANF* 3.155).
52. Origin, *Against Celsus* 5.10 (*ANF* 4.546–47).
53. Origin, *Against Celsus* 8.19 (*ANF* 4.646).

the identity of believers.[54] Yet, interestingly, 1 Pet 2:9 could also be used in very practical contexts, as when the *Constitution of the Holy Apostles* uses the text in its instruction for a bishop anointing women for baptism.[55] The *Constitution* also uses the same text in the midst of a sample prayer, thus demonstrating, together with Methodius, the strong liturgical force of the text.[56]

Years later, Augustine cites 1 Pet 2:9 in passing as referring to all Christians, not just the clergy.[57] He also cites 1 Pet 2:9-10 in his *Reply to Faustus the Manichæan*, this time in the context of his assertion that the Old Testament prophecies apply to the Gentiles.[58] Elsewhere, Augustine discusses Christ as the cornerstone and the Christian's role in the building up of a new, holy city, citing 1 Pet 2:5 in the process.[59] In his discussion of Psalm 122, he continues that analogy, stressing the fact that believers are the stones that the Lord uses to build a future city (and a temple).[60] While Augustine is departing somewhat from the original scriptural analogy of a simple building, as opposed to an entire city, the sense remains essentially the same, and Augustine is clearly treating the text as a reference to the universal Church, a community of believers.

Like Augustine in *City of God*, Jerome applies 1 Pet 2:9 to the church in general. In fact, Jerome actually uses the text to equate the layman with the clergy, arguing that what is not permitted to the one should not be permitted to the other.[61] Thus early on there was a recognition that 1 Pet 2:9 has a universal force that applies to the entire Christian community, clergy as well as laity.

Cyril of Jerusalem devotes an entire lecture to 1 Peter where he compares and contrasts Israel in the Exodus with Christians of his present time.[62] The sermon as a whole, however, is mostly concerned with instructions for baptism and has little to say on either foreknowledge or Christian communal identity.

Eventually, the terminology of 1 Pet 2:9 began to be used in a "grander" sense to refer to the church more as a corporate entity than as a community

---

54. Methodius, *Oration Concerning Simeon and Anna* (ANF 6. 392–93).
55. *Constitution of the Holy Apostles* 3.2 (ANF 7.431).
56. Ibid., 2.7 (ANF 7.422).
57. Augustine, *City of God* 20.10 (NPNF1 2.432).
58. Augustine, *Reply to Faustus* 22.89 (NPNF1 4.309).
59. Augustine, *Expositions on the Psalms* 87.3 (NPNF1 8.421).
60. Ibid., 122.4 (NPNF1 8.593–94).
61. Jerome, *Dialogue against the Luciferians* 3–4 (NPNF2 6.321).
62. Cyril of Jerusalem, *Catechetical Lectures* 19 (NPNF2 7.144–46).

of believers. Thus Gregory of Nazianzen alludes to 1 Pet 2:9 when, in *The Panegyric on S. Basil*, he describes Basil as essentially coming to the rescue of the Church; the focus here is on the Church as a corporate (almost nationalistic) entity, rather than made up of "average" believers.[63] Leo the Great likewise downplays the individual Christian in his allusion to 1 Pet 2:9. In referring to the Apostles and Rome, he declares, "These are they who promoted thee to such glory, that being made a holy nation, a chosen people, a priestly and royal state, and the head of the world through the blessed Peter's holy See thou didst attain a wider sway by the worship of God than by earthly government."[64] Thus it is the apostles, not the community of believers, who become the focus of the text. Leo also seems to be one of the first to explicitly discuss the order of prepositions in 1 Pet 1:2, indicating that the 3rd preposition describes the means by which the Spirit's work takes place (though, unfortunately, he does not seem to discuss what "according to the foreknowledge of God" modifies).[65]

Like Leo, Gregory the Great cites 1 Pet 2:9 specifically in reference to the priests and/or leaders of the church (significantly, he does not cite the rest of the verse that mentions a "holy nation"). The context of his citation is actually a reference to the color of the priest's robe and how it should reflect the following: "The priest's heart, while hoping for the high things which he preaches, should repress in itself even the suggestion of vice." This is in light of the priest's relationship to the "heavenly kingdom."[66] In this way one can note how, to a certain degree, there seems to have been a shift away from the focus on believers in general to a focus on the corporate church and her leaders.

As seen above, quite a few patristic citations exist that discuss the identity of the church in 1 Peter 2. Patristic discussions on the passages concerning foreknowledge (1 Pet 1:2, 10–12, 20), however, are much more difficult to find. Nevertheless, a few key texts must be noted. Although he does not spend much time on foreknowledge in this passage, Chrysostom phrases his discussion on 1 Pet 1:18–21 in terms of social identity, specifically the buying and selling of slaves and a slave's identity in reference to his or her master. God is portrayed as a benevolent master, yet, through the act

---

63. Gregory of Nazianzen, *Orations* 43.41 (*NPNF2* 7.409). According to Gregory, Basil saw ". . . the holy nation, the royal priesthood, in such evil plight that it was torn asunder into ten thousand opinions and errors . . ." (trans. Charles Gordon Browne and James Edward Swallow).

64. Leo the Great, *Sermons* 82.1 (*NPNF2* 12.195), trans. Charles Lett Feltoe.

65. Leo the Great, *Letters* 29.5 (*NPNF2* 12.42).

66. Gregory the Great, *Book of Pastoral Rule* 2.3 (*NPNF2* 12.11), trans. James Barmby.

of sinning, humans have become the property of the devil ("For the devil gained you; you are the possession of that one") and have become strangers to God. Yet Christ bought believers with his blood and thus creates an "excellent people" (λαὸς περιούσιος [apparently drawing from the terminology of Titus 2:14]).[67]

Didymus the Blind seems to view πρόγνωσις in 1 Pet 1:2 as a prescient term, mostly (*Præscientia enim nihil aliud est putanda, quam contemplatio futurorum;* . . .).[68] However, it should be noted that Didymus does link the text to Eph 1:4 and 5, and that Didymus clearly sees "according to the foreknowledge" as modifying election in this text.[69]

Years later, Venerable Bede also links "according to the foreknowledge" in 1 Pet 1:2 to "elect" in the previous verse, although he gives no syntactical reason. He also links this context in 1 Peter to Rom 8:29.[70] Regarding the identity of the strangers in 2:11, Bede takes a strictly metaphorical view: "He suitably calls them *newcomers and strangers* that they may the less subject their mind to earthly affairs the more they remember that they have a fatherland in heaven."[71]

The Early Church Fathers on Foreknowledge in General

The discussion of foreknowledge within the context of 1 Peter itself is sadly scarce within the earliest patristic writings. Yet since a major argument of this paper is that "foreknowledge" (as the concept "knowing something ahead of time") must not be automatically equated with "foreordination," it is necessary to survey what the early church fathers said about the concept in general. Such a survey, of course, must give pride of place to Augustine of Hippo, who quite possibly had more to say on the topic than the rest of the early church combined. Significantly, Augustine's conception of foreknowledge, even divine foreknowledge (despite his staunch views on unconditional election), differs radically from any position that is quick to equate the concept with foreordination. In fact, one sees very little suggestion in the early church that God's foreordination was necessarily equated

---

67. Chrysostomus, *In Primam S. Petri Epistolam* 1 (PG 64.1053.c). Translation by this writer.

68. Didymi Alexandrini, *Epistolam S, Petri Primam Enarratio* 1.2 (PG 39.1755–56).

69. As seen in Didymi Alexandrini, *Epistolam S, Petri Primam Enarratio* 1.2. (PG 39.1756), where he states, "Κἄν τοίνυν κατὰ πρόγνωσιν ἐκλεκτοὶ ἦσαν.'"

70. Bede the Venerable, *Commentary on the Seven Catholic Epistles* (trans. Dom David Hurst), 70.

71. Ibid., 89.

with his foreknowledge, and thus it is unlikely that the early church would have necessarily interpreted 1 Pet 1:2 or 1:20 in that way.

To begin with, one must point out that in *Against Celsus* 2.20, Origin gives an extended argument of why foreknowledge is not to be equated with foreordination, even arguing that Judas, despite being foreknown by Jesus that he was a traitor, nevertheless could have acted otherwise than he did.[72] Later, in *Against Celsus* 4.96, he argues that foreknowledge itself is not strictly a divine attribute ("... ὅτι τὸ τὰ μέλλοντα προγιγνώσκειν οὐ πάντως θεῖον ἐστί ..."), but is rather a neutral ("μέσον") attribute that exists among all sorts of men.[73]

Elsewhere, the *Clementine Homilies* likewise discuss both divine and human foreknowledge, arguing that since God gave foreknowledge to Moses, how could God himself not have had it?[74] In his "Exposition of the Orthodox Faith," when stressing how evil comes about through free will, John of Damascus speaks of God's foreknowledge of the future in prescient terms, clearly stating, "Knowledge is of what exists and foreknowledge is of what will surely exist in the future."[75]

Clement, when discussing the Apostles' appointment of church leaders, says that the Apostles had "received perfect foreknowledge" (*1 Clement* 44.2—"πρόγνωσιν εἰληφότες τελείαν").[76] *Shepherd of Hermas* 31.4 uses the term in a theological context with God as the subject, but still seems to use it in a prescient sense because the context discusses the evil that is in men's heart (ὁ κύριος καὶ πάντα προγινώσκων, ἔγνω τὴν ἀσθένειαν τῶν ἀνθρώπων) and the Lord's compassion on creation despite the plans of the devil to corrupt humanity.[77] In *Herm*. 66.5, the protagonist is told that God has blessed him by allowing him to have foreknowledge (the participle of προγινώσκω) about future trials so that he can "bear them [the trials] with strength."[78]

72. Origin, *Against Celsus* 2.20 (ANF 4.440). Indeed, Origin states, against the argument of Celsus, φαμὲν οὐχὶ τὸν θεσπίσαντα αἴτιον εἶναι τοῦ ἐσομένου ... ("We are not saying that prophecy is the cause of what will happen, ... "). The reader should note that θεσπίσαντα (whether or not one translates it as "prophecy") in this text clearly refers to the act of knowing something ahead of time. The Greek text is taken from Origin, *Contra Celsum* 2.20 (PG 11.836b), and the translation is this writer's own.

73. Origin, *Contra Celsum* 4.96 (PG 11.1173d).

74. *Clementine Homilies* 3.44 (ANF 8.246–47). See also 3.43 (ANF 8.246) and 3.11–15 (ANF 8.240–41) for further discussions of foreknowledge.

75. John of Damascus, *Exposition of the Orthodox Faith* 21 (NPNF2 9.94), trans. S. D. F. Salmond.

76. Greek text taken from Holmes, ed., *Apostolic Fathers*; the translation from Greek is this writer's own.

77. Greek text taken from ibid.

78. Greek text taken from ibid.; the translation is this writer's own.

Apparently Augustine has the most to say about foreknowledge. Often his statements are in the context of a theodicy. In *City of God*, in opposition to Cicero (who feared that divine foreknowledge meant the loss of free will), Augustine argues, "To confess that God exists, and at the same time to deny that He has foreknowledge of future things, is the most manifest folly."[79] Indeed, "One who is not prescient of all future things is not God."[80] Furthermore, at least in *City of God*, Augustine believed that free will was compatible with foreknowledge and that the actions of human free will could be known by God (though most likely Augustine's views would be more in congruence with modern compatibilism than libertarianism).[81]

Within the same discussion, we see Augustine differentiate between (prescient) foreknowledge and foreordination. He states,

> For a man does not sin because God foreknew that He would sin. On the contrary, there is no doubt that the man himself sins when he sins. For He Whose foreknowledge cannot fail foresaw not that fate or fortune or something else would sin, but the man himself. If a man chooses not to sin, he certainly does not sin; but if he chooses not to sin, this also was foreknown by God.[82]

Even more clearly, in his "Homilies on John," Tractate 53.4, Augustine states,

> The Lord, in His foreknowledge of the future, foretold by the prophet the unbelief of the Jews; *He foretold it, but did not cause it. For God does not compel anyone to sin simply because He knows already the future sins of men.* For He foreknew sins that were theirs, not His own; sins that were referable to no one else, but to their own selves. Accordingly, if what He foreknew as theirs is not really theirs, then had He no true foreknowledge: but as His foreknowledge is infallible, it is doubtless no one else, but they themselves, whose sinfulness God foreknew, that are the sinners. The Jews, therefore, committed sin, with no compulsion to do so on His part, to whom sin is an object of displeasure; but He foretold their committing of it, because nothing is concealed from His knowledge. And, accordingly, had they wished to do good instead of evil, they would not have been hindered; but in this which they were to do they were foreseen of Him who

---

79. Augustine, *City of God* 5.9 (*NPNF*1 2.90), trans. Marcus Dods.
80. Ibid. (*NPNF*1 2.92), trans. Marcus Dods.
81. Ibid., 5.9–10 (*NPNF*1 2.91–93).
82. Ibid., 5.10 (Cambridge Texts in the History of Political Thought), trans. R. W. Dyson.

knows what every man will do, and what He is yet to render unto such an one according to his work.[83]

Elsewhere, we see Augustine discussing God's foreknowledge in light of man's initial fall in the Garden of Eden. Here, once again, there is no hint that Augustine equated foreknowledge with foreordination. Indeed, Augustine indicates that God works good *in spite of* his foreknowledge that man would commit evil.[84] In Augustine's discussion of baptism, we see further indication that Augustine thought of foreknowledge in prescient terms.[85] All this must be considered in light of the fact that Augustine did *not* believe that "foreseen faith" (or "foreseen goodness") was the cause of election; i.e. (if the reader will pardon an anachronism), Augustine was clearly not an Arminian.[86] The point, then, is that one can hold to a deterministic or compatibilist view of election without redefining the concept of "knowing something ahead of time" to equal that of "determining something ahead of time."

From what this writer has seen, very little evidence exists to demonstrate that the early church merged the concepts of foreknowledge with either foreordination or the state of knowing intimately beforehand. Rather, the early church (including Augustine) saw foreknowledge as a distinct (though often interrelated) concept when compared to foreordination.

83. Augustine, *Homilies on the Gospel of John* 53.4 (*NPNF*1 7.292), trans. John Gibb and James Innes; emphasis is this writer's. The reader should note that Augustine's view on free will is probably very much in line with compatibilism, since he places an emphasis on doing what one desires, yet the point remains that he treats "foreknowledge" as a prescient term.

84. Augustine, *Enchiridion* 104 (*NPNF*1 3.271), and *Catechising of the Uninstructed* 18 (*NPNF*1 3.302).

85. Augustine, *On Baptism, Against the Donatists* 4.3 (*NPNF*1 4.448). The discussion here concerns the fact that only God truly knows the heart (who is regenerate and who is not), and only God knows what a person will be like in the future. We also see in this passage a strong sense of God's foreordination, in addition to his intimate knowledge of those that are his. Nevertheless, Augustine's concept of "foreknowledge" seems to be strictly mantic/prescient, even though it is tied closely to election (simply because one concept is used in close proximity to another concept does not make the two identical).

86. Augustine, *Homilies on the Gospel of John* 86.2 (*NPNF*1 7.353). Even here, however, Augustine is not arguing that foreknowledge equals foreordination, but simply declaring that "here surely is at fault the vain reasoning of those who defend the foreknowledge of God in opposition to His grace" (trans. John Gibb and James Innes). Cf. James Jorgenson, "Predestination According to Divine Foreknowledge," in *Salvation in Christ*, 161, who notes, "For Saint Augustine, God's foreknowledge of human merits and sins was not the cause of predestination. The sovereign and non-frustratable will of God was the basis of predestination." For further discussion on Augustine's view of foreknowledge, the reader should note den Bok, "In vrijheid voorzien," 40–60.

Indeed, Augustine, as noted above, goes to great lengths in his theodicy to distinguish divine foreknowledge from divine foreordination.

Thus the view that the terminology for "foreknowledge" equals the concept of "knowing something ahead of time" has its roots in the early church. Conceivably, then, this writer's view that foreknowledge in 1 Peter functions in a prescient sense would have been acceptable to the early Christian writers, even those with a more deterministic outlook.[87]

Modern Scholarship on Foreknowledge in 1 Peter

By the dawn of the Reformation, scholars were devoting considerable more time to discussing the meaning of foreknowledge in 1 Peter. Thus Desiderius Erasmus, for example, links foreknowledge in 1 Pet 1:2 closely to election and foreordination (though his primary emphasis seems to be to point out that God's decrees do not occur by chance).[88] John Calvin clearly views "according to the foreknowledge" as modifying "elect" in the same passage and stresses that election ultimately finds its root cause in God Himself.[89] Regarding 1 Pet 1:20, προγινώσκω is translated in a deterministic sense (*quae praeordinatus fuerat*, or "what was preordained") and is definitely viewed in terms of divine council.[90] Clearly, then, the conceptual equation of "foreknowledge" with "foreordination" existed during the Reformation period.

In the modern era, this writer was unable to find a single article, essay, dissertation, or book that focused on foreknowledge specifically in 1 Peter. Yet the following key articles and essays do discuss foreknowledge (specifically the terms πρόγνωσις and προγινώσκω) in the New Testament, dealing with 1 Peter in the process. To begin with, in the 1800s an unidentified author wrote an article in the *Methodist Review* that delves into such issues as the relationship between volition and responsibility, God's relationship to time (i.e., whether or not God can truly be said to possess future knowledge in the strictest sense), and whether or not God's foreknowledge in and of itself *necessitates* what he foreknows. As for 1 Pet 1:2, the author offers the now standard argument that foreknowledge implies divine determination

---

87. It must be acknowledged that some Patristic occurrences of "foreknowledge" are difficult to analyze and are somewhat ambiguous. See, for example, Justin Martyr, *The First Apology of Justin* 45, who speaks of ὁ ἀριθμὸς τῶν προεγνωσμένων αὐτῷ ("The number of those foreknown by him"; the Greek text is taken from Justinus Martyr, *Apologia Prima Pro Christianis* 45 [PG 6.396d]). Foreknowledge, however, is not a main point of Justin's discussion here.

88. Erasmus, *Galatians to the Apocalypse*, 745.

89. Calvini, *Epistola ad Hebraeos. Epistolae Petri, Ioannis, Iacobi et Iudae*, 202.

90. Ibid., 217.

(arguing from the use of "to know" in such passages as Amos 3:2, Matt 25:12, etc.).[91]

Over a hundred years later, John W. Cobb wrote a short article on foreknowledge, stating that "God has foreseen those who could be saved to his glory, and he set out on an eternal purpose to save them." At the same time, he argued that it was "untenable" to hold that ". . . God elected certain individuals to be saved without regard for human freedom."[92] In contrast, a few years later Edgar C. James wrote an article on foreknowledge where he argued that mere prescient knowledge is not enough to account for the use of the terminology in the NT.[93]

More recently, S. M. Baugh has contributed to the discussion with arguments similar to those of James.[94] Later, Tom McCall and Keith Stanglin wrote their own article in response to Baugh's essay.[95] Oddly enough, even though McCall and Stanglin argue against Baugh's perspective on the key passages, they still concede his point regarding the meaning of the words: "Baugh's word studies seem to us to be quite clear and indeed helpful."[96] In other words, they concede Baugh's view of the meaning of the terms, but not his view of their significance. Thus they are able to declare that ". . . to say that God foreknows a person's response of faith that results in mutual and deeply relational, committed love does not contradict the meaning of πρόγνωσις, that is, God's personal, eternal commitment to that person."[97] In addition, Robert H. Lescelius has written a recent article that interacts with the key Scriptural passages but does not contribute much that cannot be found in the arguments by James and Baugh.[98]

Finally, C. Gordon Olson provides a rare discussion of the lexical background of the terminology. Olson's presentation begins with a lexical discussion rather than a theological discussion and strongly argues that foreknowledge is a prescient term.[99] Nevertheless, even Olson relies mostly on secondary literature (lexicons, wordbooks, etc.) when discussing πρόγνωσις and προγινώσκω.[100] Thus no scholar, to this writer's knowledge,

---

91. "Thoughts on the Fore-Knowledge of God," 11–14; 49–53..
92. Cobb, "Election Is Based on Foreknowledge," 28.
93. James, "Is Foreknowledge Equivalent to Foreordination?," 215–19.
94. Baugh, "The Meaning of Foreknowledge," 183–200.
95. McCall and Stanglin, "S. M. Baugh and the Meaning of Foreknowledge," 19–31.
96. Ibid., 22.
97. Ibid., 31.
98. Lescelius, "Foreknowledge," 25–39.
99. Olson, "Lexical Study of Foreknowledge and Predestination."
100. Ibid.; see especially pp. 3–4. I.e., for the most part Olson (like others) does not

has provided anything close to an adequate examination of how the words were used in the Greek of AD 1–100.

In the modern era, the commentaries overwhelmingly hold to both a deterministic sense and a soteriological emphasis for foreknowledge in 1 Peter. In 1 Pet 1:2, the majority of commentators hold that "according to the foreknowledge of God" modifies election. This goes at least as far back as Wilhelm Steiger.[101] In the years since then, the majority of commentators have followed suit.[102] J. N. D. Kelly is typical of this position when he states, "If these clauses [the three prepositional phrases] are linked, as in the translation, with chosen, the first affirms that the Asian Christians' election has come about as a result of, i.e., is grounded in, God the Father's foreknowledge."[103] Along the same lines, Goppelt also argues for tying the three prepositional phrases closely to election.[104]

A few older commentators, however, suggest that "according to the foreknowledge of God" actually modifies "apostle" in addition to other words (for example, Hort and Selwyn).[105] A few of the above commentators, such as Steiger, Schreiner, and Goppelt, at least interact with this idea yet quickly dismiss it.[106]

Interestingly, Wayne Grudem suggests that the three prepositional phrases should be taken as modifying "the whole situation of the readers described in the first verse."[107] Grudem argues that the English translations become awkward when ἐκλεκτοῖς alone is viewed as the focus of the three

---

seem to interact directly with the primary texts, but relies on the secondary sources (e.g., lexicons) for his information.

101. Steiger, *Der erste Brief Petri*, 37.

102. Achtemeier, *1 Peter*, 86; Bartlett, "First Peter," 12:247; Brox, *Der Erste Petrusbrief*, 57; Charles, "1 Peter," 13:298; Davids, *First Epistle of Peter*, 47–48; Buit, "Voici votre vocation," in *La Première Epître de Saint Pierre*, 42; Elliott, *I Peter*, 317; Feldmeier, *Der erste Brief des Petrus*, 35; Goppelt, *Der erste Petrusbrief*, 83; Jobes, *1 Peter*, 66–67; Kelly, *Commentary on the Epistles of Peter and Jude*, 42; Kistemaker, *James, Epistles of John, Peter, and Jude*, 35; Marshall, *1 Peter*, 31; McKnight, *1 Peter*, 53 (McKnight is much more tentative in his conclusions); Michaels, *1 Peter*, 3–4; Schreiner, *1, 2 Peter, Jude*, 52–53; Usteri, *Commentar über den Ersten Petrusbrief*, 7 (Usteri sees it as modifying "ἐκλεκτοῖς παρεπιδήμοις," but seems to especially apply it to ἐκλεκτοῖς); and Witherington, *Socio-Rhetorical Commentary on 1–2 Peter*, 69.

103. Kelly, *Epistles of Peter and Jude*, 42.

104. Goppelt, *Der erste Petrusbrief*, 83.

105. Hort, *First Epistle of Peter: I.1–II. 17*, 18; Selwyn, *First Epistle of Peter*, 119.

106. Steiger, *Der erste Brief Petri*, 37; Schreiner, *1, 2 Peter*, 52–53; and Goppelt, *Der erste Petrusbrief*, 83 n34.

107. Wayne Grudem, *1 Peter* (TNTC; Grand Rapids, Mich.: Eerdmans, 1988), 50–51.

prepositions.[108] Douglas Harink comes close to Grudem's position, arguing that seeing foreknowledge directly tied to election

> tend[s] to leave the last two phrases of 1:2 dangling on their own and theologically separated from 1:1. However, the Greek text may well be read as drawing all of 1:1 into the theological reality described in the three phrases of 1:2 . . . In other words, the church just is what it is, "elect exiles of the Diaspora," because of the foreknowing, sanctifying, and justifying action of God the Father, Spirit, and Son.[109]

Similarly, Wolfgang Schrage argues that the three prepositions refer to "the addresses and their appointment to their status as strangers."[110] Indeed, "according to the foreknowledge" is seen as applying to the "beginning and basis of the Christ-path."[111] Although Schrage still holds to a deterministic sense for the term "foreknowledge" (as noted below), his view on the prepositional phrase is significantly closer to Grudem's (and this writer's) because he does not seem to apply it strictly to "election." Schelkle, on the other hand, argues that the verse as a whole points to the phrase ἐκλεκτοῖς παρεπιδήμοις, but his emphasis nevertheless seems to be on the concept of election ("erwählung").[112]

Nevertheless, Grudem and the others are by far the minority. Most scholars automatically assume that the phrase modifies "elect" and leave it at that. Francis H. Agnew, for example, devotes a total of two lines to this topic in an article that deals almost exclusively with 1 Pet 1:2.[113] Almost nobody that this writer could find deals with the possibility that the phrase specifically modifies either the dative παρεπιδήμοις or the genitive διασπορᾶς. Hort at least mentions the possibility but inexplicably states, "We may pass over παρεπιδήμοις διασπορᾶς as evidently inadequate to carrying the contents of v. 2."[114]

As for the meaning of foreknowledge in 1 Peter, the vast majority of commentators see something beyond a strictly prescient sense. Regarding

---

108. Ibid., 51.

109. Harink, *1 and 2 Peter*, 39. The classic commentator Francis Wright Beare, in *First Epistle of Peter*, holds to a similar position (p. 49).

110. Schrage, "Der erste Petrusbrief," 10:67 ("Die drei Bestimmungen von V.2 beziehen sich sämtlich auf die Adressaten und ihre Erwählung zu Fremden"). Translation is this writer's own.

111. Ibid.

112. Schelkle, *Die Petrusbriefe—der Judasbrief*, 20.

113. Agnew, "1 Peter 1:2—An Alternative Translation," 69.

114. Hort, *First Epistle of Peter*, 18.

24 Foreknowledge and Social Identity in 1 Peter

1 Pet 1:2, Kelly is typical when he argues that this foreknowledge "is much more than knowing what will happen in the future; it includes, as it does in the language of the LXX (e.g., Num. xvi. 5; Jdt. ix. 6; Am. iii.2) and in the thought of the Qumran sect, His effective choice."[115] Goppelt and Spicq argue for a similar sense.[116] The majority of scholars follow suit, preferring at least some emphasis on divine determination, though some emphasize the concept of intimate knowledge, concern, and/or love (with some overlap between all four concepts).[117]

Regarding 1:20, Kelly argues, "We have already noticed . . . that for him God's foreknowledge includes His creative will and determination."[118] Similarly, Jobes states, "The foreknowledge of Christ's redeeming death [1:19-20] corresponds to God's electing foreknowledge of those who would be redeemed by it (1:20)."[119] Once more, Goppelt and Spicq also emphasize a sense of determined action in this verse.[120] A plethora of other scholars (with one notable exception) similarly see at least some sort of deterministic sense as intrinsic to the word.[121] While Scripture clearly teaches that Christ's

---

115. Kelly, *Commentary on the Epistles of Peter and Jude*, 42–43.

116. Goppelt, *Der erste Petrusbriefe*, 85, declares, "Gottes πρόγνωσις, sein 'Vorhererkennen,' ist schon nach dem AT nicht Vorauswissen, sondern Vorherbestimmen, das als erwählendes Handeln wirksam wird" ("God's πρόγνωσις, his 'precognition,' is not the same as the OT concept of foreknowledge, but rather refers to predetermination, which takes effect as his chosen act." Similarly, Spicq, *Les Épîtres de Saint Pierre*, 42, states, "Plus qu'un discernement, la *prognosis* pétrinienne est un choix et une décision" ("More than discernment, Petrine 'prognosis' is a choice and a decision").

117. Achtemeier, *1 Peter*, 86; Beare, *First Epistle of Peter*, 50 (for Beare, the term "always applies primarily to persons and includes the thought of the divine Providence and of the divine Will for human life"); Brox, *Der Erste Petrusbrief*, 57; Davids, *First Epistle of Peter*, 48; Elliott, *I Peter*, 318; Feldmeier, *Der erste Brief des Petrus*, 36–37; Grudem, *1 Peter*, 50; Hort, *First Epistle of Peter*, 20; Jobes, *1 Peter*, 68; Kistemaker, *Epistles*, 35; Leighton, *A Practical Commentary*, 24. Marshall, *1 Peter*, 31; McKnight, *1 Peter*, 53 (McKnight sees the word "as determinative rather than confirmative of human choice"); Michaels, *1 Peter*, 10; Reicke, *Epistles of James, Peter, and Jude*, 77; Schelkle, *Die Petrusbriefe, Der Judasbrief*, 20; Schrage, NTD 10:67; Schreiner, *1, 2 Peter, Jude*, 53–54; Schweizer, *Der erste Petrusbrief*, 17; Selwyn, *First Epistle of St. Peter*, 119; Steiger, *Der erste Brief Petri*, 37; Usteri, *Commentar über den Ersten Petrusbrief*, 8.

118. Kelly, *Commentary on the Epistles of Peter and Jude*, 76.

119. Jobes, *1 Peter*, 119.

120. Goppelt, *Der erste Petrusbrief*, 125, and Spicq, *Les Épîtres de Saint Pierre*, 69.

121. Achtemeier, *1 Peter*, 131; Beare, *First Epistle of Peter*, 80; Brox, *Der erste Petrusbrief*, 83; Davids, *First Epistle of Peter*, 73–74; Feldmeier, *Der erste Brief des Petrus*, 79; Grudem, *1 Peter*, 85; Hort, *First Epistle of Peter*, 80; Kistemaker, *Epistles*, 67; Leighton, *Practical Commentary*, 165; Marshall, *1 Peter*, 56; Michaels, *1 Peter*, 66; Schelkle, *Die Petrusbriefe, der Judasbrief*, 50; Schreiner, *1, 2 Peter, Jude*, 87; Steiger, *Der erste Brief Petri*, 180. A few scholars emphasize both foreknowledge *and* foreordination in this passage (such as Elliott, *I Peter*, 376). The one major exception who emphasizes the

death was foreordained as opposed to simply foreknown, it is this writer's contention that 1 Pet 1:20 deals strictly with the issue of foreknowledge and thus should be taken on its own terms. Foreordination may be implied, but it is not the main point of 1 Pet 1:20.

A few sources beyond the commentaries deal specifically with the prophets in 1:10–12.[122] Nevertheless, very few of them connect the role of prophecy in 1:10–12 with foreknowledge in 1:2 and 1:20. It is this writer's contention that all three passages tie in with the concept of the social identity of believers in 1 Peter.

A number of sources deal with the concepts of community and identity in 1 Peter, the most significant, perhaps, being Elliott's *A Home for the Homeless*.[123] Furthermore, this is an area where German scholarship has contributed greatly over the past 100 years. Theophil Spörri was possibly one of the first of any nationality to focus extensively on the concept of church/community in 1 Peter.[124] Indeed, modern scholar Horst Goldstein is quick to point out the importance of Spörri's work for today and how it set the groundwork for many of the modern studies on ecclesiology in 1 Peter.[125] The many years since Spörri's work have seen a number of other significant German sources. Friedrich Schröger, for example, launches his substantial work by arguing that 1 Peter drew from Old Testament terminology to develop the concept of "community-church" and in the process discarded the Pauline "antithesis" of Israel vs. the Church.[126] Similarly, Joseph B. Soucek, in a more recent article, while acknowledging that neither ἐκκλησία nor κόσμος occur in the epistle, argues that 1 Peter nevertheless evidences a "very distinctive understanding of the nature, the peculiarity, the independence of the communal-brotherhood of faith . . . of the people of God within the world."[127]

---

prescient sense of the word as primary is Ben Witherington (see his *Socio-Rhetorical Commentary on 1–2 Peter*, 108). Sadly, Witherington represents the minority.

122. See, for example, Love, "First Epistle of Peter," 69; Warden, "Prophets of 1 Peter 1:10–12," 5–6

123. Elliott, *A Home for the Homeless*.

124. Spörri, *Der Gemeindegedanke im ersten Petrusbrief*. Note especially p. 8 of his introduction.

125. Goldstein, "Das Gemeindeverständnis des ersten Petrusbriefs," 16, states, "Spörri's investigation is considered fundamental to this very day" ("Spörris Untersuchung gilt bis heute als grundlegend").

126. Friedrich Schröger, *Gemeinde im 1. Petrusbrief*, 7–8.

127. Soucek, "Das Gegenüber von Gemeinde und Welt nach dem ersten Petrusbrief," 199.

Horst Goldstein has written one of the more significant dissertations on *Gemeinde* ("church" or "community") in first Peter. He provides a comprehensive, epistle-wide analysis of the concept, arguing that the Petrine author describes the Christian community/church (*Gemeinde*) as ". . . the anthropological-corporative application of the soteriologically-elevated Christology."[128]

A few other significant dissertations and monographs should be noted. Recently, Eric James Gréaux has emphasized the role of 1 Peter "as a diaspora letter" with the "metaphorical use of diaspora language."[129] Stephen Ayodeji A. Fagbemi, in his monograph, focuses on "the social context of the original readers" while ultimately applying it to modern-day Nigeria.[130] Benjamin H. Dunning's *Aliens and Sojourners: Self as Other in the Rhetoric of Early Christianity* deals with the concepts of "alien" and "stranger" from a broader perspective (all of Greco-Roman culture), but he does deal specifically with 1 Peter.[131] Pierre Francois Steenberg devotes his dissertation to a discussion of how Peter, in the face of the social pressures facing his readers, set about persuading them to remain in the faith.[132] Elsewhere, Chu Luan Eileen Poh provides a thorough discussion of the social background of 1 Peter, especially regarding the nature of social relationships between believers and non-believers.[133]

FOREKNOWLEDGE AND PROPHECY IN JEWISH AND GRECO-ROMAN THOUGHT OF THE FIRST CENTURY AD

Space prohibits a comprehensive discussion of all references to the concept of "knowing something ahead of time" either in or leading up to the first century. Nevertheless, a few key texts must be pointed out. To begin with, the concept of "knowing something ahead of time" is represented mostly by prophecy and the prophetic role within Jewish thought. In Deut 18:21–22, for example, the test of a prophet's legitimacy as an emissary of God is

---

128. Goldstein, "Das Gemeindeverständnis des ersten Petrusbriefs," 17 ("Der Vf. des 1 Pt beschreibt die christliche Gemeinde als anthropologisch-korporative Applikation soteriologsicher Erhöhungschristologie").

129. Gréaux, "'To the Elect Exiles of the Dispersion . . . from Babylon,'" 59, 75.

130. Fagbemi, *Who Are the Elect in 1 Peter?*, 3.

131. Dunning, *Aliens and Sojourners*, see esp. 25–26.

132. Steenberg, "The Reversal of Roles as the Reasoning for Remaining Christian," 14.

133. Poh, "The Social World of 1 Peter," 8–9.

tied to his mantic trustworthiness. It would, of course, be overly simplistic to suggest that foretelling was the *primary* role of a prophet, or even that foreknowledge was a *necessary* characteristic of an Old Testament prophet. A. B. Davidson, for example, suggests, "The chief activity of the prophets was directed towards realizing the theocratic union of man and God," and certainly this task does not *necessitate* mantic utterances.[134] Nevertheless, the concepts are linked, and many of the Old Testament prophets engaged in foretelling. This, as we shall later argue, forms the basis for the theology behind 1 Pet 1:10-12.

Second Temple Jewish literature also deals with prophecy and foreknowledge. Thus Philo, in *Heir* 260-261, explicitly links status as a prophet to the ability to know the future.[135] Similarly, "Josephus presents prophets as those who frequently interpret events or declare the will of God in particular situations."[136] In the Dead Sea Scrolls, 4Q339, we have a list of "False Prophets in Israel," though what exactly made these prophets "false" is either lost or not discussed. More significantly, 4Q410 (a document entitled "An Unknown Prophecy") is actually a curse on a group of people with the author claming he's seen a vision, or "oracle," about this particular group. Here, in the last line of that text, we have a clear example of an author claiming foreknowledge.[137] It is worth mentioning, however, that much Rabbinic literature of the Second Temple period viewed the actual class of "prophets" as having ceased to exist.[138] However, foreknowledge of the future, even supernatural foreknowledge, could still occasionally manifest itself in the post-prophetic era, as Josephus suggests in *J.W.* 1.68-69. Clearly, then, the concept of "supernaturally knowing something ahead of time" was not foreign to Jews of the Second Temple era.

Within the Greco-Roman literature of the time, the nature of prophecy and divination were the center of an intense debate.[139] Within this debate, Epicurean Greek philosophy is portrayed as advocating a complete rejection

---

134. Davidson, *Old Testament Prophecy*, 10.

135. As L. Stephen Cook states, "For Philo, this prophetic ecstasy (as experienced by the biblical prophets) consistently manifests itself in a prophet's ability to predict the future." (*On the Question of the "Cessation of Prophecy,"* 92)].

136. Cook, *On the Question of the "Cessation of Prophecy,"* 123; see, for example, *Ant.* 3.60, 8.405-7

137. Trans. by Michael Wise, et al.

138. Cook, *On the Question of the "Cessation of Prophecy,"* 150

139. Green, "'As for Prophecies,'" 108-17. I am grateful to Dr. Gene L. Green (the outside reader for my study) for strongly suggesting that I explore the issues discussed in the following paragraphs.

of the possibility of legitimate prophecy (μαντική).¹⁴⁰ Marcus Tullius Cicero also opposed the concept of prophecy and divination of the future. In *De divinatione*, he portrays a dialogue between himself (against divination) and the Stoic Quintus (pro divination). At one point he quotes favorably the classic line from Euripides, "The best diviner I maintain to be/ The man who guesses or conjectures best)."¹⁴¹ Since his brother's definition of foreknowledge involves "chance" (i.e., as opposed to scientific predictions), Cicero declares, "Hence, it seems to me that it is not in the power even of God himself to know what event is going to happen accidentally and by chance. For if He knows, then the event is certain to happen; but if it is certain to happen, chance does not exist. And yet chance does exist, therefore there is no foreknowledge of things that happen by chance." Cicero also mocks specific types of divination, and in 2.57.117 goes after the Delphic oracles: "However, the main question is this: why are Delphic oracles (of which I have just given you examples) not uttered at the present time and have not been for a long time? And why are they regarded with the utmost contempt? . . . When did the virtue disappear? Was it after men began to be less credulous?"¹⁴² Thus, as Gene Green writes, "Much of Cicero's argument was framed within the current debates between the Stoics and the Epicureans. While the Stoics affirmed both fate and divination, the Epicureans denied them both."¹⁴³ The Epicureans often pointed to "unfulfilled prophecy" as evidence "against foreknowledge (providence) of the affairs of the world."¹⁴⁴

In the later half of the first century, however, the act of mantic divination received a prolific defender in the form of Plutarch. As Dominique Jaillard notes, "With Plutarch, we have the emergence of a new type of figure, the 'philosopher priest.'"¹⁴⁵ Plutarch took a special interest in defending mantic occurrence at the Oracle of Delphi, for he himself served as a priest there. Indeed, "Delphi seems to have become a second home to Plutarch . . . All his life he was anxious that the prestige of Delphi should be restored, . . ."¹⁴⁶ At Delphi, "Plutarch discussed philosophy with students and eminent visitors, and he made Delphi the scene and subject of some of his best

---

140. Diogenes Laertius, *Epicurus* 135. Marcus Tullius Cicero, *Nat. d.* 2.3. For further discussions of Greco-Roman philosophy on foreknowledge and oracles, see Green, "'As for Prophecies,'" 107–22, and Neyrey, "Form and Background of the Polemic," 407–431.

141. *Div.*, 2.4.12; trans. Falconer.

142. Ibid., 2.57.117.

143. Green, "'As for Prophecies,'" 113–14.

144. Neyrey, "Form and Background of the Polemic," 409.

145. Jaillard, "Plutarque et la divination," 169 ("Avec Plutarque, nous saisissons l'émergence d'une figure neuve, celle d'un philosophe prêtre, . . .)"

146. Barrow, *Plutarch and His Times*, 31.

dialogues. His religious conviction was as prominent a characteristic of him as his commitments to politics and was translated into his priesthood at Delphi just as his political interests were expressed in his role as magistrate and diplomat."[147]

Plutarch spends much of his time speculating on the nature of divination and communication between the divine and the human. Indeed, to a certain degree, his "rational discourse . . . is commentary and exegesis on what happens in the rite of divination with its various mantic phenomena."[148] In the process, Plutarch attempts to defend traditional piety against the opposing forces of both atheism and superstition.[149] In *The Oracles at Delphi No Longer Given in Verse*, Plutarch presents a dialogue between the skeptical Boëthius, in the process of converting to Epicureanism, and others. Boëthius no longer takes the Delphic oracle seriously, basically suggesting that its human proclaimers simply get lucky when they seemingly predict something that actually happens. Sarapion, however, counters that prophecy regarding specific events, rather than general and vague events, can justify the legitimacy of an oracle. (*Pyth. orac.* 396–399). In *The Obsolescense of Oracles*, Plutarch provides (once again in the form of dialogue) discussions regarding the nature of prophecy itself and its relation to both the divine and the seer (*Def. orac.*, see esp. 8–9, 40–41). From reading Plutarch, "We are left with the impression that concern about the oracles' continued validity was both wisespread and well known."[150] Nevertheless Plutarch is firm in his admonition that "fulfillment of those things that were previously foretold stands as proof of divine inspiration . . ."[151]

Thus the concept of foreknowledge was a hotly debated topic within the first century, and Christians themselves may have struggled with whether or not divine foreknowledge and/or divinely inspired prophecy was even a viable concept.[152] First Peter, however, seems to assume the validity of both divine foreknowledge and human prophecy, and, as will be argued later, the author integrates both concepts into the epistle's theology.

---

147. Jones, "Plutarch," 2:962.

148. Jaillard, "Plutarque et la divination," 164 ("Le discours rationallel, . . . est *commentaire et exégèse* sur ce qui se passe dans le rite, sur les divers phénomènes mantiques: . . ." (emphasis is Jaillard's)..

149. Jaillard, "Plutarque et la divination,"159

150. Green, "'As for Prophecies,'" 115

151. Ibid., 116

152. See Green, "'As for Prophecies,'" 117–21.

SOCIAL-SCIENTIFIC CRITICISM AND ITS RELEVANCE FOR 1 PETER

Since this study concerns itself with the social identity of the audience of 1 Peter, the discipline known as social-scientific criticism (hereafter referred to as SSC) will play a major role in the development of this paper's thesis. The following discussion will introduce the reader to the history and scope of SSC, as well as its relevance for New Testament studies.

At the most basic level, SSC attempts "to find out what an initial audience understood when it heard some person read a given document aloud."[153] When applied to the NT, SSC assumes "that the NT texts have lying behind them an unspoken context which, if it can be filled in, will help in understanding the passages themselves."[154] That "unspoken context," of course, primarily involves the development of a body of believers around the Gospel of Jesus Christ, a fact that, in of itself, may be viewed within the larger social context.[155] In other words, the events of the NT did not happen in either a historical or social vacuum. As Philip F. Elser aptly notes, "The New Testament writings manifest a complex interpenetration of society and Gospel, of context and *kerygma* ('the proclamation of faith'), and . . . we cannot hope to understand either without an appropriate methodology for dealing with the social side."[156]

SSC focuses on the social context of the New Testament and is thus intimately connected to the exegesis of the New Testament; consequently, it may be defined as *"that phase of the task which analyzes the social and cultural dimensions of the text and of its environmental context through the utilization of the perspectives, theory, models, and research of the social sciences."*[157]

History of SSC

SSC has its roots in anthropology and other social sciences. In the late 1800s and early 1900s, theologians began to evidence an awareness of the value of social perspectives for exegesis. Adolf von Harnack, for example, began to

---

153. Malina, "Rhetorical Criticism and Social-Scientific Criticism," 6.
154. Kenneth Berding, "The Hermeneutical Framework of Social-Scientific Criticism," 7.
155. Elliott, *What Is Social-Scientific Criticism?*, 7.
156. Esler, *The First Christians in Their Social Worlds*, 2.
157. Elliott, *What Is Social-Scientific Criticism?*, 7 (emphasis added).

concentrate more and more on social issues in his writings, and Adolf Deissman's monumental *Light from the Ancient East* interacted not only with the literary aspects of the documents it examined but also with the social aspects as well.[158] Furthermore, Adolf Deissman's work on form criticism served as an impetus into the investigation of "the social dimensions of early Christianity."[159] To a certain degree, this interest in the social dynamics of the New Testament arose due to a dissatisfaction with the scholarly status quo regarding historical issues in exegesis.[160]

Ultimately, however, the close of World War I saw a sudden lack of interest in the topic (Ernst Lohmeyer and the "Chicago School" being a couple of the exceptions).[161] Indeed, the next fifty years or so saw an overall dearth of scholarship in proto-SSC.[162]

Yet in 1972, at the AAR/SBL meeting in Los Angeles, Wayne Meeks led a new discussion among scholars under the title "Experiments toward a Social Description of Early Christianity." A similar meeting was held the next year, led by Meeks and Leander Keck, and this follow-up conference saw substantially more participation, including contributions by NT scholars Paul Achtemeier and John Elliott.[163] Also in 1973, German scholar Gerd Theissen published a major work that focused on Jesus' words ". . . from the perspective of a sociology of literature."[164] Within a few years, German biblical scholars became interested in *Sozialgeschichte* and held an important meeting on the topic in Villigst, Germany, in 1977.[165]

The year 1981 saw both John Elliott and David Balch publish significant works on SSC (works that were, in fact, "diametrically opposed" to each other).[166] In 1986, "The Context Group" was created, and around that time the term "social-scientific criticism" itself was coined by John Elliott.[167] Since then, SSC has taken its place alongside other disciplines as an acknowledged part of critical biblical scholarship.

---

158. Van Aarde, "Inleiding tot die sosiaal-wetenskaplike kritiese eksegese van Nuwe-Testamentiese tekste," 51.
159. Horrell, "Social-Scientific Interpretation of the New Testament," 4.
160. Malherbe, *Social Aspects of Early Christianity*, 2.
161. Ibid., 4.
162. Horrell, "Social-Scientific Interpretation of the New Testament," 5.
163. Elliott, "From Social Description to Social-Scientific Criticism," 26.
164. Elliott, *What Is Social-Scientific Criticism?*, 21.
165. Elliott, "The History of a Society of Biblical Literature Section," 27.
166. Ibid., 28.
167. Ibid., 29.

The Application of SSC to New Testament Studies

SSC is, of course, intrinsically linked to both social and historical studies. The whole point of SSC is to utilize "the resources which the social sciences offer, alongside the other methods of textual and historical criticism . . . " so that one may develop "a fuller and better appreciation of the biblical texts and communities within their historical, social, and cultural setting."[168] Yet SSC must not be thought of as identical to any purely historical or social study. As Philip Esler points out, SSC fills a role that strictly historical studies cannot manage by themselves:

> Given its emphasis on the novel, the unique and the particular, history (at least to the extent that it does not employ social-scientific perspectives) cannot hope to supply all the questions which must be put to the New Testament if we are to penetrate the ordinary and everyday . . . interrelationships, values, and symbols which characterized the early Christian communities.[169]

In other words, the historian generally deals with the unique—the hero, the great battle, the economic collapse—rather than the mundane issues such as how a slave viewed his or her role in relation to his or her master.[170] It should be emphasized, however, that historical and social studies exist to complement, rather than oppose, each other.[171] Nevertheless, in

---

168. Horrell, "Social-Scientific Interpretation of the New Testament," 3.

169. Esler, *The First Christians*, 2.

170. There is, of course, a sense in which the examination of the norm must not be conducted completely apart from the examination of the unique, even within SSC. Thus Malherbe, *Social Aspects*, 12, when discussing the study of a community, points out that "given the importance ancient communities attached to their founders, the question of how a community understood itself can often only be established by examining its relationship to its founders or elders as well as the philosophical or theological teaching it received from him." Consequently, Malherbe stresses the need to "balance" a study of a community with a study of its founders/leaders, taking care not to overemphasize either. Malherbe's cautions are well stated, yet there may certainly be times when the role of a leader or founder is less prominent than at other times. The various communities addressed by 1 Peter, for example, do not seem to have any key figure that plays a prominent role in their current social status, other than the two opposing figures in the form of the emperor and King Jesus.

171. The reader should especially note the discussion by Craffert, "Towards an Interdisciplinary Definition," 123–44. Craffert strongly argues against creating an "either-or" fallacy with history and SSC (pp. 126, 128). He argues that an "antithetical relationship between history and the social sciences" is "neither a logical necessity imposed by the material . . . nor the only viable option" (p. 126). Craffert provides a fruitful discussion of how SSC and historical sciences should work together (128, 139–40).

a general sense, one may perhaps say that SSC concerns itself with *norms* more than *exceptions*.

By the same token, SSC should not be confused with mere social description. The latter does not build theories or models and is content merely to observe customs, institutions, etc. Furthermore, social description focuses on primary source material such as coins and art.[172] Of course, social description and simple observation are absolutely necessary for SSC. Indeed, one "should strive to know as much as possible about the actual social circumstances of those communities before venturing theoretical descriptions or explanations of them."[173] Even theoretical models in SSC should always be grounded on emic data; i.e., data-gathering will precede and assist in the formation of any legitimate model.[174]

Yet ultimately, "a genuine social-scientific approach operates on a different level from that of social description," for "a social-scientific analysis *abstracts* data in the sense of unearthing, making explicit what is buried and implicit in the narrative discourse."[175] Thus, as Elliott notes, "A study is not sociological (or social-scientific) unless and until it presents a hypothesis concerning a relationship of some social phenomena, a hypothesis that guides a collection of data that are then used to illustrate and explain the relation, meaning and function of the social phenomena."[176]

New Testament SSC, then, takes the raw social data, builds various theories and models around that data, and then applies this to the study of Scripture. Thus, for example, archaeologists might unearth a series of coins depicting the relationship of a slave to his or her master. The SSC scholar then takes that raw data (i.e., what is depicted on the coins) and builds a theory and/or a model around the social significance of the data. He or she then might apply that to any relevant New Testament texts dealing with slaves and masters (a strictly historical study, of course, would perhaps be more concerned with whether or not the coins depict an actual *event* rather than a social custom, or whether or not the minting of such a coin resulted

---

172. Osiek, *What Are They Saying about the Social Setting of the New Testament?*, 4.

173. Malherbe, *Social Aspects of Early Christianity*, 20.

174. Elliott, *What is Social-Scientific Criticism?*, 49. "Emic" may be defined, according to *Merriam-Webster*, as the following: "Of, relating to, or involving analysis of cultural phenomena from the perspective of one who participates in the culture being studied." See "Emic," *Merriam-Webster*, n.p. Online.

175. Van Staden and van Aarde, "Social Description or Social-scientific Interpretation?," 57–59.

176. Elliott, "History of a Society of Biblical Literature Section," 30. Cf. Craffert, "Towards an Interdisciplinary Definition," 131–35, for more discussion of the differences between social description and SSC.

from a key event). Naturally, care must be taken that theories and models are not developed that have little concern for accuracy. Indeed, as Malina emphasizes, a fair application of SSC must ultimately "allow for validation, testing."[177] In this way, SSC would be held to the same scientific standards as any other discipline. Furthermore, the final arbitrator of meaning is the text, not the model.[178]

For many proponents of SSC, the use of models to interpret and apply the raw data is key. As Elliott explains, "Put simply, a model is like a metaphor. Both model and metaphor compare similar properties and stimulate imagination in order to advance understanding from the more well known to the lesser known . . . , [but] a model differs from a metaphor in terms of its comprehensiveness and complexity and often its intended function."[179] Elliott, drawing on the work of T. F. Carney, Bruce Malina, and others, defines a model as follows:

> Models are thus conceptual vehicles for articulating, applying, testing, and possibly reconstructing theories used in the analysis and interpretation of specific social data . . . [a model] is *consciously structured* and *systematically arranged* in order to serve as a *speculative instrument* for the purpose of organizing, profiling, and interpreting a complex welter of detail.[180]

Carolyn Osiek adds that truly effective models should be "verifiable" while giving the scholar "some measure of predictability about how the particular aspect of the social system works."[181]

Yet David Horrell, for one, argues that the use of artificial models can prove harmful. He states,

---

177. Malina, "Why Interpret the Bible with the Social Sciences?," 129–30. The reader should also note Malina's helpful "four principles" for SSC on these pages: 1. "The approach must be cross-cultural" (i.e., it must allow for "comparison between alien groups"). 2. "The approach must be historical." 3. "The approach must focus on the world, geographical and social, depicted in the texts and inhabited by the texts' original audience." 4. "It should allow for validation, testing." Regarding the first point, however, see Crook, "Reflections on Culture and Social-Scientific Models," 515 and 520, where he discusses the dangers of simply forcing models developed in our modern culture onto ancient cultures.

178. Esler, *The First Christians*, 12–13.

179. Elliott, "Social-Scientific Criticism of the New Testament," 4.

180. Ibid., 5–6. Emphasis is Elliott's.

181. Osiek, *What Are They Saying?*, 109. Key to this view of SSC is the argument that everybody uses models, whether they realize it or not (see Elliott, "Social-Scientific Criticism," 6; Esler, *The First Christians*, 12).

> Not the least of these problems, it seems to me, is the way in which a model-based approach can lead to historically and culturally variable evidence being interpreted through the lens of a generalized model of social behaviour. The rich diversity of human behaviour is thereby homogenized and explained in terms of what is "typical"—which can actually be no real explanation at all.[182]

Craffert concurs, noting that the use of models might cause one to fail to see how divergent culture can be.[183]

Elsewhere, Horrell further argues, "The problem with starting with a model is that . . . it can lead the researcher to view the evidence in a particular way, or to assume that a certain pattern of conduct must be present."[184] Once again Craffert parallels Horrell, similarly arguing that the danger with models is that "one's methodology is predetermined by the aim of interpretation which is, at the bottom, a philosophical choice."[185] Indeed, "It is no secret that . . . almost any text or data set can be shaped to fit a theory."[186]

Horrell, Craffert, and others offer some valid critiques and cautions on the use of models. A few remarks may be offered in response, however. While the use of models may indeed over-generalize the evidence and ignore diversity, nevertheless one cannot deny that certain broad and general social concepts exist in each culture. Indeed, 1 Peter's use of παρεπίδημος and πάροικος, regardless of whether the terms are used literally, metaphorically, or both, presupposes some sort of shared sociological understanding between Peter and his readers; otherwise the words themselves would be meaningless (in this way lexical semantics, to a certain degree, is intertwined with a culture's shared social concepts). Naturally, the underlying sense behind the terms must not be forced into duty as an explanation for all social phenomena spoken of in 1 Peter, lest the concerns of Horrell and Craffert ring true. Nevertheless, society's role in shaping world-view and, consequently, terminology must not be overlooked.[187]

Indeed, this principle naturally exists in the present age as well. In Japan, where this writer grew up, the term *tate-mae* (literally "that which

182. Horrell, "Models and Methods," 84.
183. Craffert, "More on Models and Muddles," 232. Cf. Berding, "Hermeneutical Framework," 13.
184. Horrell, "Models and Methods," 90–91.
185. Craffert, "More on Models and Muddles," 218.
186. Ibid., 233.
187. The reader should note Esler's response to Horrell, "Models in New Testament Interpretation,"107–13, esp. 110–11, where he states, "Horrell seems to leave little room at all for cultural influences on individuals."

is set before"), for example, represents a concept that influences cultural behavior. *Tate-mae* refers to the act, when interacting with others, of showing the other person what one believes they wish to see, thus avoiding giving offense and allowing one to "save face." As a result, speaking one's mind may be frowned upon (depending upon the context). Indeed, teacher-parent meetings in Japanese schools have traditionally consisted of an obligatory time of *sake* (rice wine) consumption before the participants are allowed to express their true views (the logic being that one cannot be held as accountable for what is said under the influence of alcohol). Furthermore, the word *tatemae* functions in the language only because a shared social concept, that of "saving face," exists in Japanese culture. Thus it would not necessarily be inaccurate to view certain parts of Japanese society through the "lens" of *tate-mae*. The danger, of course, would stem from the temptation to make all parts of Japanese culture fit one's understanding of *tate-mae*, or to automatically make *tate-mae* the interpretive crux behind a particular individual's actions.

Secondly, it must be acknowledged that a model may force evidence to fit its mold as, for example, when the actions of an individual are viewed in light of a sociological model.[188] Yet in the case of 1 Peter, the audience consists of a group of people covering a wide geographical territory subservient to the Roman Empire. Thus, if the model is kept general and not used to explain the sociological worldview of individual recipients of the letter, this fallacy may be avoided. As far as 1 Peter is concerned, the author is merely drawing on generally accepted sociological concepts (in this case, concepts such as "displacement," "community," and "social identity") and allowing them to influence his rhetorical strategy. The formation of a model, then, can proceed cautiously in ch. 2.[189]

A major part of this study's thesis argues that 1 Peter is written to an audience suffering from a sense of displacement (whether physical/geographical, spiritual, or both). Since "displacement" and its converse, "social identity" (or, to a certain degree, "nationality"), are both social concepts, SSC becomes an important tool for this study. It must be stressed once more, however, that SSC is only used to explain the *general* concepts that would have been familiar to 1 Peter's audience; SSC is not meant to explain individual motivations beyond those of the author interacting with his audience.

188. Horrell, "Models and Methods," 91–92.

189. For other helpful critiques of SSC, including its use of models, see the following sources: Berding, "The Hermeneutical Framework," 3–22; Dvorak, "John H. Elliott's Social-Scientific Criticism," 251–78; Barton, "Historical Criticism and Social-Scientific Perspectives," 61–89, and Mulholland, "Sociological Criticism," 170–86.

CONCLUSION

This study argues that 1 Peter uses the concept of foreknowledge as a word of comfort to offset his readers' status as socially displaced strangers and to emphasize their new-found social identity in Christ. As has been demonstrated, no scholar has yet provided an adequate lexical and conceptual examination of the use of foreknowledge in 1 Peter. Furthermore, scholars generally treat "foreknowledge" in 1 Pet 1:2 and 1:20 in such a way that stresses the *soteriological* implications, whereas this study will place more stress on the *sociological* implications of the relevant passages. Finally, only a few deal with the connection between the discussion of prophets in 1:10–12 and the discussion of foreknowledge in 1:2 and 1:20.

In the following chapter, this study will examine and analyze John Elliott's and others' SSC treatment of 1 Peter and then attempt to develop a lens of "displacement" through which to view 1 Peter. This will then help set the stage for the subsequent discussion of foreknowledge's connection with social identity.

2

Displacement Terminology and Social Identity in 1 Peter

In the classic story *The Man Without a Country*, Edward Everett Hale narrates how the fictional Philip Nolan curses his own homeland and is consequently exiled from her forever, living off her shores on a naval ship with all his companions forbidden from even mentioning his country's name ever again in his presence. Truly homeless, an exile, Nolan suffers from loneliness and depression due to his outcast status yet eventually repents of his actions, feeling genuine affection for his country once again (although never allowed to step foot on her).[1]

Throughout history, the homeless and displaced have suffered anguish at their displacement and have often been shunned by those around them for their strangeness. In order to understand the significance of foreknowledge in 1 Peter, one must first examine the "homelessness" of the recipients, i.e., the negative social situation that they, like Nolan, found themselves in. The recipients are described as being "sojourners" and "exiles" (1 Pet 1,1; 2:11), going about their "exile" in the land (1 Pet 1:17).[2] Clearly Peter's choice of this terminology (παρεπίδημος, πάροικος, and παροικία) was deliberate, yet significant debate exists over both the meaning and the significance of the words, especially whether or not they should be viewed literally or metaphorically.

The majority view has been that such displacement terminology refers to the Christians' status as strangers on earth, pining for a heavenly home.

1. Hale, *Man Without a Country*.
2. Scripture is taken from the English Standard Version unless otherwise noted.

Yet in 1981 John Elliott challenged that view by arguing that the terminology in 1 Peter refers to the literal social and legal circumstances of the recipients and has little to do with a "heaven is my home" theology.[3] Scholars reacted in a variety of ways—some positively, yet most negatively. Certainly some of the critiques of Elliott may be legitimate, and this writer will disagree with Elliott somewhat on the semantics of the terminology. Yet this writer will contend that to a certain degree Elliott is correct. The displacement terminology in 1 Peter is not concerned with a *vertical* "earth vs. heaven" theology but rather a *horizontal* sense. The recipients are displaced from their homes, suffering from the lack of a literal homeland (at the national level, not simply "earth" in general), yet able to find a new community and social identity in the church. Furthermore, Peter's use of the terminology assumes that the readers genuinely knew what constitutes a literal πάροικος. Thus a literal sense, to some degree, cannot be denied.

Yet there is no need to posit a false dichotomy between literal and spiritual. Some or most believers may have been experiencing a literal, social state of displacement, yet Peter can by extension apply the terminology to all believers as he points to the literal πάροικοι as the image of what believers truly are. Once again, however, the concept is not "strangers in this world vs. citizens in heaven," but "strangers in Asia Minor vs. citizens in the church with fellow believers."[4] Social identity, then, abides in the church, that "holy nation" (1 Pet 2:9), rather than heaven, and the prescient terminology of chapter 1 functions as the bridge of hope between the despair of social displacement and the new "home" found within the Christian *Gemeinde*. The first section of this chapter will examine the traditional view, Elliott's view, reactions to Elliott, and alternate views. The second section will provide a background study and lexical examination of the displacement terminology in 1 Peter, while the third section will analyze the arguments of Elliott and his critics (for the most part defending Elliott) and offer a suggestion

---

3. Elliott originally published his work in 1981, but this study will be interacting with his revised work, *Home for the Homeless*, published in 2005.

4. This argument does *not* mean, however, that the concept of "strangers on earth with a home in heaven" does not exist elsewhere in Scripture, e.g., Hebrews 11:10–16. Even Elliott, *Home for the Homeless*, 99 n79, argues that in Hebrews (in contrast with 1 Peter), "Estrangement is to be viewed not simply as a social but ultimately as a cosmological phenomenon. God's faithful people are not simply aliens in society but strangers 'on earth'... Whereas 1 Peter stresses the need for Christian community here and now as the answer to social alienation, Hebrews directs attention away from the hopeless earthly scene to the heavenly home which awaits those who remain steadfast in faith." Yet this study, like Elliott's *Home for the Homeless*, is concerned with social identity in 1 Peter rather than Hebrews, despite the fact that both letters make equally essential contributions to our understanding of the Christian life.

for interpretation. The chapter will then conclude with a brief discussion of how this links to the concept of foreknowledge in 1 Peter.

DISPLACEMENT TERMINOLOGY AND THE SOCIAL CIRCUMSTANCES OF 1 PETER: VARIOUS VIEWS

The Majority View: Displacement in a Primarily Metaphorical Sense

The majority view on the significance of πάροικος, etc., emphasizes a pilgrim theology, namely that Christians are but temporary residents on earth, looking forward to a permanent home in heaven. According to this view, Christians "are called 'the exiles of the dispersion' because they are a small Christian minority scattered throughout a largely pagan world."[5] Applying this same line of thought to 1 Peter's ecclesiology, Friedrich Schröger argues, "According to the understanding of 1 Peter, a parish is a group of people who find themselves a society of strangers in this world, whose true home is in heaven."[6] Indeed, as Norbert Brox notes, the "otherness" of Christians ultimately stems from the "otherness" of Christ and its manifestation within the community of believers. It is the Christian life itself, then, that causes the "strangeness" and "isolation."[7]

M.-A. Chevallier, for one, explicitly rejects a literal sociological emphasis for the terminology. Chevallier argues that, since all Christians are in the *diaspora*, the displacement terminology (πάροικος, παρεπίδημος, etc.) applies equally to all Christians. Thus, for Chevallier, the displacement terminology must be viewed in light of salvation history (Chevallier links 1 Pet 2:11 to the LXX Gen 23:4 and Psalm 38:12, for example). As a result, the use of "stranger" in 1 Peter does not necessarily entail a literal sociological condition.[8]

---

5. Filson, "Partakers with Christ," 402.

6. Schröger, *Gemeinde im 1. Petrusbrief*, 130 ("Eine Pfarrei ist nach dem Verständnis des 1. Petrusbriefes demnach eine Gruppe von Menschen, die sich in dieser Welt in Fremdlingschaft vorfindet, deren wahre Heimat im Himmel ist." Unless otherwise noted, all German, French, and Italian translations are the work of this writer). Cf. also Schröger's discussion on p. 129.

7. Brox, "Situation und Sprache," 7.

8. Chevallier, "Condition et vocation des chrétiens en diaspora," 394 ("En réalité, la qualité de residents étrangers définit pour lui la condition commune de *tous* les chrétiens parce que, pour lui, comme nous l'avons vu, tous les chrétiens sont en diaspora.

Similarly, Christian Wolff, in his extensive study of the theological concept of "strangeness," focuses on the theme that all Christians are, by virtue of their theological orientation, strangers. Indeed, "Christians are of another parentage than their environment."[9] Furthermore, as Theophil Spörri notes, the status of Christians as "exiles of the dispersion" (1 Pet 1:1) stems directly from the will of God.[10]

Victor Paul Furnish provides one of the more thorough treatments of the topic from the traditional, metaphorical perspective. Furnish argues that the phrase "elect sojourners of the diaspora . . . introduces a major and pervasive conception in I Peter: Christians are the elect of God and thus only temporarily in this present world."[11] Thus "for a time" Christians "are in the world and beset by its claims and contingencies, transitory as those are," and this fact remains "a fundamental aspect of the Christian view of the life of faith."[12] Furnish also emphasizes the contrast between the temporary state of displacement and the timeless future awaiting Christians. They are "destined for a salvation beyond time and history but temporarily subject to the dangers and deceits of their own passions and of society's."[13] Ultimately, for Furnish, the entirely of 1 Pet 1:1-12 represents "*the worldly sojourn of God's elect people, what their election promises for them and demands of them.*"[14]

Norbert Brox follows a similar position to Furnish, arguing that the displacement terminology in 1 Peter consists of "metaphors for religious existence." In addition, Brox also emphasizes the "*self-designation*" of the title of "stranger" in relation to the Christian community; indeed, "they estranged *themselves*."[15] For Brox, early Christians embraced the term; they "wanted to be strange" and found that it was "a satisfying and even sectarian pleasure to be the stranger, the 'other.'"[16]

Au reste, en appliquant aux chrétiens ce nom d'etrangers, il ne s'agit pas de donner d'eux une caractéristique sociologique. S'ils méritent ce tire, c'est dans la perspective proper de l'historie du salut" [emphasis is Chevallier's]).

9. Wolff, "Christ und Welt," 335 ("Die Christen sind anderer Herkunft als ihre Umwelt").

10. Ibid., 334. Cf. Spörri, *Der Gemeindegedanke im Ersten Petrusbrief*, 25 ("Erscheint 2,9 ausdrücklich die Gemeinde als Gegenstand der göttlichen Auswahl, nämlich als auserwähltes Geschlecht").

11. Furnish, "Elect Sojourners in Christ," 3.

12. Ibid., 4.

13. Ibid., 4-5.

14. Ibid., 10. Emphasis is Furnish's.

15. Norbert Brox, "Stranger in Early Christianity," 47-48 (emphasis mine).

16. Ibid., 47-48.

Thus, for many scholars, the social aspect of the displacement terminology in 1 Peter is mostly irrelevant, for Peter's audience were not necessarily *literal* παρεπίδημοι or πάροικοι (whatever a literal meaning might entail). Rather, Peter uses the terminology *metaphorically* to refer to their "homeless" state while on earth. The audience of 1 Peter may or may not have suffered literal legal and/or cultural isolation. Regardless, the designation πάροικος is self-designated and applicable only because of their status as Christians.

For these scholars, some social interaction is still in view, yet the focus is primarily on social interaction with others in light of one's status as Christians, not social status in relation to the state or local government. Charles Talbert, for example, argues that 1 Peter's recipients " . . . had a religious experience so radical (conversion) that it involves a break with one's past and that the Christian community is composed exclusively of those who have had such an experience. This gives the group social cohesion, which is necessary for the group to survive as a group."[17] C. L. E. Poh summarizes, "It is in the realm of their social relationships with non-Christians after conversion that Peter addresses his readers figuratively as πάροικοι and παρεπίδημοι."[18] Similarly, for Stephen Fagbemi, the term παρεπίδημοι "reflects on the theological and spiritual identity of the world" yet also "gives an indication of the likely experience and social situation of the readers."[19] Furthermore, Peter, through use of displacement terminology, provides "a spiritual foundation to the believers' social status whilst also appealing for an ethical outlook and life-style that is consistent with their religious identity." This social status, however, can only be truly comprehended through the spiritual designation of "election" in 1 Peter.[20]

This metaphorical sense has more or less been the dominant paradigm for studying the social status of 1 Peter's readers.[21] To be fair, this perception of 1 Peter's audience as "strangers on earth" does seem to be reflected elsewhere in the New Testament. Yet others have been dissatisfied with this treatment of the terminology, and consequently alternate theories on Peter's audience have been advanced.

---

17. Talbert, "Plan of 1 Peter," 147–48.
18. Poh, "Social World of 1 Peter," 23.
19. Fagbemi, "Living for Christ in a Hostile World," 5.
20. Ibid., 12.
21. The metaphorical sense is followed by quite a few modern commentaries. See, for example, Davids, *First Epistle of Peter*, 46–47; Feldmeier, *Der erste Brief des Petrus*, 10–11; Grudem, *1 Peter*, 48–49; Michaels, *1 Peter*, 116; Schreiner, *1, 2 Peter, Jude*, 40.

Literal Strangers and Their New Home: John H. Elliott and the Alternate Interpretation of the Displacement Terminology in 1 Peter

The 1981 publication of John H. Elliott's *A Home for the Homeless* represents a major break with the traditional theory of the "earthly pilgrims on their way to heaven" model. Yet not only did Elliott challenge the consensus on 1 Peter, he simultaneously introduced New Testament scholarship to a paradigm of research that relied heavily on social-scientific criticism (SSC). While SSC had made inroads in NT scholarship decades before, Elliott brought it to the forefront.[22]

At the heart of Elliott's thesis stands a rejection of a *primarily* metaphorical sense for παρεπίδημος and πάροικος. Indeed, Elliott goes to great lengths to both discuss and emphasize the literal use of the displacement terminology. For example, when discussing 1 Pet 1:17 and 2:11, Elliott states, "The *actual political and social condition* of the addressees as *paroikoi* is used as an occasion to encourage their religious peculiarity and strangeness."[23] Indeed, much of the emphasis of 1 Peter concerns itself with that very literal social status. Hence, the audience of 1 Peter consists of

---

22. Immediate reaction to *Home for the Homeless* in the book review section of academic journals was mixed. Paul Achtemeier (Review of *Home of the Homeless*, 130–33), for example, praises Elliott for his solid research and genuine contribution, yet strongly disagrees with Elliott's central thesis, arguing that "Elliott is so intent upon denying 'a theology of an earthly pilgrimage of God's people' . . . that he never considers the possibility that the letter is in fact addressed to precisely the *social* problems that have come upon people who *became paroikoi* with their conversion" (p. 132; emphasis is Achtemeier's). Likewise, Christian Wolff (Review of *Home for the Homeless*, 443–45) praises the book for its "conceptual unity" and its "abundance of new interpretive suggestions," etc., yet ultimately remains unconvinced of its central thesis (p. 445; "Gleichwohl haben mich die Hauptthesen . . . E.s. nicht überzeugt"). Colin Hemer (Review of *A Home for the Homeless*, 120–23), recognizes that Elliott's work is a significant contribution and offers "sympathy for its general aims" (121), yet also strongly criticizes both the scope of Elliott's research and his methodology (the reader might be interested and perhaps somewhat amused to see Hemer refer to *Home for the Homeless* as " . . . a very American book in the methodological confidence of an opening chapter which somehow provokes rather than allays doubts!" [p. 123]). On the other hand, Stanley B. Marrow (Review of *Home for the Homeless*, 483–84) provides a much more favorable review, saving his negative critique mostly for the process of sociology rather than Elliott himself. He states, "If the book under review remains a mixture of sociology and exegesis, the fault is not the author's but that of the sociological component itself. The significant conclusions reached in the study can arguably stand on the solid ground of good exegesis, *sans phrase*; and the best parts of this book are just that" (p. 484).

23. Elliott, *Home for the Homeless*, 35–36; emphasis added. Cf. also *Home for the Homeless*, p. 42.

> *aliens permanently residing in (paroikia, paroikoi)* or *strangers temporarily visiting or passing through (parepidemoi)* the four provinces of Asia Minor named in the salutation (1:1) . . . The central focus of 1 Peter concerns the interaction of Christians and society, the social contrasts and conflicts which have created a crisis for the Christian movement in Asia Minor. 1 Peter is a letter addressed to resident aliens and visiting strangers who, since their conversion to Christianity, still find themselves estranged from any place of belonging. They are still displaced *paroikoi* seeking an *oikos*.[24]

Consequently, Elliott reacts strongly against the "heaven is our home" perspective of much of scholarship. He argues,

> The addresses of 1 Peter were *paroikoi* by virtue of their social condition, not by virtue of their "heavenly home." The alternative to this marginal social condition of which 1 Peter speaks is not an ephemeral "heaven is our home" form of consolation but the new home and social family to which the Christians belong here and now; namely, the *oikos tou theou*.[25]

Furthermore, while Elliott fully admits to an eschatological emphasis within 1 Peter, he argues that "the achievement of that future reward (5:4) is everywhere linked to, and dependent upon, the believers' maintenance of the bonds of their brotherhood here and now."[26] Elliott disagrees specifically with the work of both Chevalier and Wolff, arguing that "in 1 Peter the addressees were not being told that they had been made strangers by God's election but that they could find strength *to remain* strangers in the conviction of their divine election."[27]

The emphasis and contrast regarding social identity put forth by the first section of 1 Peter, then, does not concern itself with a "pilgrims on earth vs. at home in heaven" dichotomy. Rather, "The fundamental contrast in 1 Peter is not a cosmological but a sociological one: the Christian community set apart from and in tension with its social neighbors." Indeed, even the emphasis on 1 Pet 1:4 ("to an inheritance . . . kept in heaven for you") is more of a "temporal" rather than a "spatial" concern. In other words, the contrast is not "heaven vs. earth" but rather past status as unbelievers versus

---

24. Ibid., 48–49; emphasis is Elliott's.

25. Ibid., 130.

26. Ibid., 130. The reader should note that both Elliott and his critics emphasize that 1 Peter concerns itself with interaction within the Christian community. That issue, then, is not part of the debate.

27. Ibid., 131.

current state as believers possessing a new inheritance.²⁸ Similarly, in 1 Pet 1:17 ("the time of your exile"), Elliott argues that "the actual contrast, however, is not between a 'time of pilgrimage on earth' and a future 'abode in heaven' but rather between the different types of behavior and associations which characterize the present and past stages of the readers' lives."²⁹

Elliott also goes to great pains to argue that, since the displacement terminology should be taken in a primarily literal sense, the literal πάροικοι to which 1 Peter is addressed were necessarily strangers/foreigners *before* their conversion.³⁰ For Elliott, then, Christianity offered a degree of attraction for these "homeless."³¹ Yet those who converted still found themselves treated as outcasts and ostracized.³² Thus 1 Peter offers an encouraging word to such Christian strangers, emphasizing holiness, election, and community.³³

Responses to Elliott's Views on the Displacement Terminology of 1 Peter

While initial journal reviews of *A Home for the Homeless* were mixed (as noted above), much (although not all) of Petrine scholarship since then has reacted negatively. Below is a discussion of the main objections brought against Elliott's central thesis (lexical considerations will be discussed in the next section).

To begin with, J. De Waal Dryden argues that Elliott's focus is skewed because "the letter seeks to transform *individual* lives within the community. As is often the case with social-scientific approaches, individual and transcendental elements tend to become eclipsed by or subsumed under social realities."³⁴ Dryden further argues that Elliott fails to see that the displacement terminology was meant "as an identity to be *embraced*," and that 1 Peter provides these titles as "central identity markers which are

---

28. Ibid., 42–43. Cf. Elliott's discussion in *1 Peter*, 336, where he focuses on the contrast between national Israel's longing for the return of their geographical territory with the "transcendent and permanent" inheritance gained by the believers of 1 Peter. Indeed, "For strangers and resident aliens who would also be ineligible to inherit land where they currently reside, this promise of an inheritance preserved in heaven thus had a double appeal" (ibid.).

29. Elliott, *Home for the Homeless*, 44.
30. Ibid., 49, 78.
31. Ibid., 122.
32. Ibid., 79.
33. Ibid., 121, 126, 188.
34. Dryden, *Theology and Ethics in 1 Peter*, 42–43. Emphasis is Dryden's.

prescribed for the community to embrace in its relation to pagan culture."[35] In contrast to Elliott's paradigm of "conflict" in regards to social identity in 1 Peter, Dryden argues that the terminology "strangers and aliens" is meant to draw unbelievers in, not create an exclusive sect.[36]

C. L. E. Poh, in her dissertation, suggests that Elliott's position "downplays the radical change" of conversion on the recipients since, if they were already alienated, the effect of conversion would not have been as significant. Furthermore, Poh suggests that " . . . the addressees do not all seem to have been socially and economically deprived. Rather they were apparently of varied social and economic status."[37] Similarly, William Schutter suggests that Elliott, in responding to objections that minimize the social aspect of "alienation," actually "goes to the other extreme, however, by minimizing the effects of conversion on alienation."[38]

Like others, Stephen Fagbemi suggests that "Elliott underestimates the significance of individual Christians." He further argues,

> Elliott's analysis risks defining the church as consisting of only socially deprived people without the rich and upper class people. This will be sending a wrong signal, as the message of scripture itself was addressed to all of them. This risks making the church basically that of the "disinherited" or socially marginalized, which it was not.[39]

Ultimately, for Fagbemi, there is "no clear evidence to argue that the people were necessarily social aliens or strangers," and if the recipients of 1 Peter truly "were social aliens, it must have been because of their Christian faith or identity."[40] In his 1996 commentary, Achtemeier parallels Fagbemi by arguing that "it is . . . unlikely that one can deduce anything about the prior political status of the readers by the use of these terms in 1 Peter."[41]

---

35. Ibid., 135 (emphasis is Dryden's).

36. Ibid., 138.

37. Poh, "Social World of 1 Peter," 23.

38. Schutter, *Hermeneutic and Composition*, 10 n44.

39. Fagbemi, *Who Are the Elect in 1 Peter?*, 54. Cf. also Fagbemi, "Living for Christ in a Hostile World," 3–4, where he argues that Elliott's " . . . position is problematic, as it also tends to suggest that the membership is entirely within the socially marginalized group. The position lacks any concrete evidence for the reason of their displacement if it were not religious . . . to refer to them as representing the pre-conversion political status of the people is no more than mere conjecture. And it would further undermine the theological or spiritual message that is implied in the text" (here Fagbemi cites 1 Pet 2:13–17 as an example).

40. Fagbemi, *Who Are the Elect?*, 70.

41. Achtemeier, *1 Peter*, 56; cf. also p. 71.

The most direct and significant criticism of Elliott's work comes from Moses Chin's 1991 article entitled "A Heavenly Home for the Homeless: Aliens and Strangers in 1 Peter."[42] Chin argues against Elliott's views on πάροικος and παρεπίδημος at both the lexical and the theological level. At the theological level, Chin draws especially from the Old Testament usage of displacement terminology to bolster his argument. He notes that in the LXX, "God's people were consistently known as πάροικοι," yet the term "was not just an identifying mark of their nomadic way of life, but more importantly, marked their theological and covenantal status."[43]

Furthermore, Chin argues that the significance of the LXX usage is that the Abrahamic covenant initiates and encapsulates a relationship with God that

> is most aptly described by the "sojourning language," so much so that the whole national thinking and philosophy displays for us "a nation on the move." Its social and religious outlook reflects that of travelers journeying towards a land they can call their home. Nationalism is equated with the cessation of the journey, and yet ironically the nation was formed only because it was on the journey. To be driven out of the Land then, as during the post-Canaan era more specifically the exilic period, is to be on sojourn again.[44]

Chin further points to 1 Chr 29:14–15; Pss 38 [39]:13–14; and 118 [119]:19 as clear examples of displacement terminology with a primarily spiritual sense.[45] Thus, in 1 Peter, just as in the OT, the use of displacement terminology "is tied up with the sojourning as God's covenantal people"; indeed, "the readers of 1 Peter are bound by something more significant than their immediate social setting. They were chosen on a cosmological journey."[46]

A few others, however, have followed Elliott's interpretation. Fika van Rensburg, for example, argues that the audience 1 Peter addresses as πάροικοι held that status both before and after their conversion. The audience of 1 Peter had already been experiencing persecution prior to conversion due to its social status, but "since becoming Christians, their situation had become more difficult." Thus, "The first readers/hearers of 1 Peter were

---

42. Chin, "Heavenly Home for the Homeless," 96–112.
43. Ibid., 102.
44. Ibid., 104.
45. Ibid., 105–6.
46. Ibid., 111–12.

aliens, not merely in a metaphoric figurative way, but in the literal sociopolitical sense of the word."[47]

Scott McKnight offers a substantial defense of the basic premise of Elliott's view by examining what exactly would be required for the terminology to be considered metaphorical rather than literal. Following the work of G. B. Caird in *The Language and Imagery of the Bible*, McKnight observes that "when an expression shows a high correspondence between the term and the reality, the term is more likely to be literal; . . . Christians of Asia Minor may well be socially marginalized; indeed, many, if not most, were."[48] McKnight further argues, "It is clear that 1:1, taken at face value, is literal: we are talking about 'exiles' in the (literal) Dispersion in (literal) Pontus and Galatia, etc."[49] As for 1 Pet 1:18 and 2:11, McKnight once again applies the principles of Caird: "Do we not need explicit evidence, or at least strong logical argument, to suggest that either of these terms is a metaphor for 'life on earth as a pilgrimage'?" For McKnight, such evidence is not forthcoming, while a literal, social context for the terminology makes the most sense.[50]

Alternate Views on the Displacement Terminology in 1 Peter

The traditional metaphorical view and Elliott's literal view are not the only possibilities, however. Alternatives exist (with some overlap among all the views).[51] Torrey Seland argues that both designations παρεπίδημος and πάροικος should be viewed positively, and that the terms in the expression ἐκλεκτοῖς παρεπιδήμοις διασπορᾶς "probably represent a typical description of the recipients; [sic] not something occasional or temporary but typical and enduring." For Seland, the author "seems to locate the beginning of the

---

47. Van Rensburg, "Christians as 'Resident and Visiting Aliens,'" 579–80; cf. 576–79 for Rensburg's own survey of scholarship on the various views of the displacement terminology in 1 Peter.

48. McKnight, "Aliens and Exiles," 382.

49. Ibid., 383.

50. Ibid.

51. See, for example, Achtemeier, *1 Peter*, 82, where, in reference to the use of παρεπίδημος in 1 Pet 1:1, he argues that the term "refers . . . less to the notion of Christians disdaining the temporal because of their longing for their eternal, heavenly home, with its implications of withdrawal from secular society, than to the notion that despite such treatment, they must nevertheless continue to practice their faith in the midst of those who abuse them." In this way Achtemeier, who as noted above is critical of Elliott's view, nevertheless cannot be totally classified as holding to the traditional view.

recipients' situation at the time of God's election."⁵² Thus the audience of 1 Peter became "strangers" upon conversion. Yet for Seland,

> it is probable that the author of 1 Peter did not envisage his readers as actual (former) proselytes but that their social condition was considered by the author to be comparable with the social condition of Jewish proselytes. Accordingly, the descriptions should not be read in light of an ideology of heavenly pilgrimage on earth or of a socially deprived situation of aliens and temporary residents in general but in light of descriptions of the social situation of diaspora Jewish proselytes.⁵³

In this way Seland clearly sees his thesis as an alternative to both Elliott's view and the traditional view.

Karen Jobes prefers to see the terminology as literal, like Elliott, but from a different perspective. Jobes theorizes that the πάροικοι 1 Peter writes to were actually the result of Claudius' expulsion of the Christians from Rome and were Christians who were non-citizens.⁵⁴ Thus

> Because Peter's original readers were not citizens of the dominant power, they had been displaced and consequently found themselves outsiders both in Rome and in their new location. In effect, they were outsiders in their world, which is exactly the point that allows the metaphorical interpretation of Christians as sojourning pilgrims to emerge.⁵⁵

Nevertheless, in objection to the strictly metaphorical view, Jobes argues,

> It seems odd that the entire book of 1 Peter is both framed (1:1; cf. 5:13) and saturated with the terms of exile and foreignness (e.g. the extensive use of Ps. 33 LXX [34 Eng.], a psalm of deliverance from sojourning as a foreigner). Moreover, 1 Peter is the only NT book to use the motif of foreignness to explain the life of the Christian with respect to society... The nature and extent of the "foreigner" metaphor in 1 Peter are better explained if it

---

52. Seland, "πάροικος καὶ παρεπίδημος," 256–57.

53. Ibid., 257.

54. Jobes, 1 Peter, 32–33. Jobes, drawing on the work of V. M. Scramuzza, suggests that the "Jews" Suetonius mentions were actually Christians because Christianity was still considered a part of Judaism at this point.

55. Ibid., 38.

was triggered by a real event or experience instead of just being pulled out of thin air.[56]

Thus Jobes both agrees with Elliott (that the designations are primarily literal) while substantially differing from him (in that the readers were πάροικοι after conversion, not before).

In order to understand and trace the connection between the themes of "stranger" and "foreknowledge" in 1 Peter, one must come to a decision regarding how to view the former. Before analyzing the various views, however, it is essential to examine both the background and the lexical range of the terminology in Koine Greek.

THE STRANGER IN THE FIRST CENTURY: BACKGROUND AND LEXICAL EXAMINATION

The concepts of "home" and "stranger," of course, are basically universal to any culture.[57] Furthermore, within a social context, the concept of "identity" remains supremely important for both groups and individuals. As Fagbemi aptly notes, "Identity is a vital aspect of human culture and institution . . . [It] informs character and character defines identity."[58] In order to understand the significance of these themes for 1 Peter, this study will briefly examine the basic historical and social background of the concepts of home vs. homelessness in the first-century Roman empire before proceeding to a lexical study of παρεπίδημος, πάροικος, and παροικία.

Displacement and the Stranger in Greco-Roman Culture

The nature of social and national life in the first-century Roman Empire to a large degree stems from the influence of Alexander the Great, who ushered in a new era of worldwide interaction and mutual influence. With the rise of the Roman conquest, no longer could city-states be closed off from the rest of the world, although they retained some degree of independence under local Roman rule.[59] Furthermore, within this historical context, an unprec-

---

56. Ibid., 39.

57. As Andreas Obemann, "Fremd im eigenen Land," 264, points out, the concept of "home" is "foundational" to our existence ("Heimat gehört zu den Grunderfahrungen des Menschen—zu allen Zeiten und Orten konstruierten sich Menschen eine Heimat, erfuhren Heimatgefühle oder thematisierten ihren Lebensort als Heimat").

58. Fagbemi, "Living for Christ in a Hostile World," 12.

59. Philipps, *Kirche in der Gesellschaft*, 11, 13.

edented ability to travel abroad (due to safer and more efficient roads and the near-universal use of Greek) resulted in the further cohesion of various cultures and states that were previously far apart.[60] The Roman Empire, then, forced society into a new era that looked to one great power as the glue that held the world together.

The Roman Empire, naturally enough, viewed itself as superior to the other nations and cultures. Polybius boasted that the Roman army was superior in its infantry because Romans used their own countrymen, not foreigners; consequently, Roman soldiers were brave and willing to gain honor for their own country rather than for themselves or their personal income.[61] Diodorus of Sicily proudly declared that Romans, in contrast to members of other nations, worked whole-heartedly for the common good, putting aside petty rivalries.[62] Thus this superiority was viewed in terms of unity and belonging: the Roman Empire was great because its citizens worked towards the grand ideal of the nation, not their own interests. The worth of an individual, then, consisted of how closely one could identify with the common good and greatness of the Empire.

Within this meta-structure of the Roman empire there generally existed only two main "spheres of life" to which one belonged: "family (in the broadest sense of kinship) and politics (organization and governance of the town)."[63] Religion did not exist separately from these, but was part and parcel of these institutions; religion existed either within the family or within the political sphere or both. Within the latter sphere, religion helped a city retain its individual identity within the greater Roman Empire.[64] Yet conversely, religion also had the effect of emphasizing the unity of the empire. Thus, even within the Asia Minor to which 1 Peter is addressed, Reicke notes, "Since the time of Augustus, several cities of the province competed for the honor of being allowed to construct, with the consent of the senate, a temple of Roma and Augustus."[65] Empire became fused with

---

60. Bernabé Ubieta, "'Neither *Xenoi* nor *paroikoi*,'" 260. Note also Ramsay, *Historical Geography of Asia Minor*, 35, where he demonstrates that a trade route had its roots in the region even during the Persian era and had already gained substantial importance by 300 BC. This, naturally, would have helped lay the foundation for the unity of the Roman Empire.

61. Polybius, *Histories* 6.52.

62. Diodorus Siculus, *Bibliotheca Historica* 31.6.

63. Bernabé Ubieta, "'Neither *Xenoi* nor *paroikoi*,'" 263.

64. Ibid., 263–65.

65. Bo Reicke, *New Testament Era*, 231. Note also Price, *Rituals and Power*, 127, where he notes that "the establishment of a new imperial festival was often drawn to the attention of other cities."

religion. Reinhard Feldmeier aptly states, "The State itself was interpreted religiously; indeed, *it was a sacred institution*."[66] Stephen Mitchell points to the incredibly rapid rise of the "cult of Augustus" within Asia Minor evidenced by, among other things, the widespread influence of the cultic priests throughout those provinces.[67] Consequently, Mitchell is able to state that Cappadocia, for example, clearly "enjoyed organized emperor worship virtually from the moment that it came under Roman rule."[68] Thus, even within an area as diverse as Asia Minor, the Roman imperial cult helped create stability and a unifying order: "Without the imperial cult there might have been little substance to civic life over much of the empire; and the cities themselves, the bed-rock of the empire, could hardly have flourished as they did."[69] In a sense, then, the height of social *and* religious identity was to be identified with the Roman state itself. Lacking that, one could at least take pride in belonging to and being identified with an entity (city-state, local religious organization, etc.) that honored and was acknowledged in return by the Roman state.

Naturally some groups did exist that could care less about Roman rule and yet were nevertheless tolerated by the Romans.[70] Yet this further accentuates how the first-century Mediterranean world consisted of a "group" culture. As Malina notes, "The first century persons would perceive themselves as unique because they were set within other like beings within unique and distinctive groups."[71] Yet even so such groups were "not only internally defined, but also defined externally by their relation to other groups."[72] The natural inclination of the first-century individual, then (with some exceptions), was to desire to be included either in the greater meta-structure of the Roman Empire or in a local group identity of some sort (or perhaps both simultaneously).[73] Those who did not fit within any group identity

---

66. Feldmeier, "Die Außenseiter als avantgarde Gesellschaftliche Ausgrenzung als Missionarische Chance,"165 ("Der Staat selbst wird religiös gedeutet, ja *er ist eine sakrale Institution!*" Emphasis is Feldmeier's). Note also Price, *Rituals and Power*, 248, who points out that "the imperial cult . . . stabilized the religious order of the world."

67. Mitchell, *Celts and the Impact of Roman Rule*, 100.

68. Ibid., 102.

69. Ibid., 117.

70. Philipps, *Kirche in der Gesellschaft*, 13, for example, discusses how under Roman rule unique groups such as the Diaspora Jews could exist.

71. Malina, *New Testament World*, 62. One must be careful not to over generalize, of course, yet Malina's basic point stands.

72. Rohrbaugh, "Social Location of Thought as a Heuristic Construct," 108–9.

73. Lee, in his essay "Social Unrest and Primitive Christianity," 134, does not directly address the issue of foreigners, but regarding "the urban working class," states that "purely in terms of social expectation, the workmen, as well as other disaffected

were truly strangers. For many such people, " . . . there was no hospitality towards resident foreigners (*paroikoi*) who formed a distinct social group in cities. . . . The foreigner was definitively incorporated into city life—with his rights and duties—only when he obtained citizenship for religious or political reasons."[74] By excluding the foreigner, the city fostered unity.[75]

This is not to argue that all people were loyal subjects of the Roman Empire. Nor is this study suggesting that the farmer in the field put an idealized picture of Roman or local solidarity over his or her own immediate concerns for healthy crops. Yet those who rebelled against the Empire did so out of their own group mentality and social identity, while even farmers in the field would have had constant reminders that they were part of something greater than they were, an Empire that demanded taxes, facilitated trade, and allowed her emperor to be called "Savior of the World."[76]

To be a stranger, to be isolated from the social identity stemming from the imperial state and her subject races, was no small matter. The stranger was cut off from the political and religious life of a city and thus had no true social identity. Even if he or she was fortunate enough to find like-minded individuals, as a whole they were still quite often denied basic fellowship with those who "belonged" to the homeland and empire.

What, then, was a "stranger" in the Greco-Roman world? Christian Wolff argues that three things could characterize the identity of a stranger: to be born of another tribe, to possess a different language or set of customs, and to worship a different god.[77] All three elements would be enough to isolate a person at the local level while the last characteristic alone would quite possibly be enough to isolate one at the imperial level (especially if the worship of a strange god excluded the worship of all others, including the emperor). Strangers, ultimately, possessed within themselves the knowledge that they were *different* from those around and that they did not belong.

Within the concept of "stranger," then, resides the implication of displacement, i.e., that the stranger truly has been removed from his or her

---

groups within the urban population, were looking for ways of being *included* in the officially promoted social life of Imperial Rome, not a way of being further excluded as they were certain to be if they joined the Christian sect. These groups, as we have seen, were indeed alienated from the social ideal of Roman civilization, but this alienation did not include a disinterest in social status or privilege as such. Their insistence on full and equal participation in civic life was, in fact, the whole point of their unrest."

74. Bernabé Ubieta, "'Neither *Xenoi* nor *paroikoi*,'" 269.

75. Ibid., 278.

76. "Savior of the Word" was a title applied to Nero. See Burge et al *New Testament in Antiquity*, 92.

77. Wolff, "Christ und Welt," 333.

home. In Greco-Roman literature, this was often viewed as a misfortune that nevertheless could be overcome. Plutarch, for example, in *On Exile* is tasked with comforting a friend who had been displaced from his homeland. Plutarch quotes Polyneices in admitting that losing one's country is truly the greatest misfortune. Plutarch then proceeds to argue that although exile (ἡ φυγή) is truly distasteful, yet just as unpleasant foods can be combined with delicious foods and spices and so rendered agreeable, thus also exile can be made manageable. Indeed, Plutarch argues, it is the man bound to a single city who is truly unfortunate, for the displaced man, rather than being limited to one location, now has the air itself as his sole boundary and is truly free to go where he pleases.[78]

Similarly, Dio Chrysostom, "In Athens, About His Banishment," muses on his own misfortune at being an exile and whether or not the experience might prove to be more fortunate than it would initially seem. Nevertheless, Dio Chrysostom is reminded of Homer, who found that his desire to return to his home trumped even the potential of immortality. Chrysostom is also reminded of the "countless deeds of valour performed and wars waged by exiles seeking thus to be restored to their homes."[79] One does not, then, simply shake off one's place of origin. To be an exile or refugee, of course, is not necessarily the same as being a foreigner or stranger, the terminology used in 1 Peter. Nevertheless, the above discussion illustrates the importance of "home" within the Greco-Roman mind. To be separated from one's home is an unpleasant circumstance that weighs heavily on the mind of the individual and may require comfort. To be homeless is to be a stranger, and to be a stranger meant that one was denied the ability to socially identify with those around.

The Use of Παρεπίδημος, Πάροικος, and Παροικία in the LXX and Extra-Biblical Writings

Having taken a brief look at the general concepts of "displacement," "home," etc. in the Greco-Roman world, we can now turn to a lexical examination of the specific terminology that occurs in 1 Peter: παρεπίδημος, πάροικος, and παροικία.[80]

---

78. Plutarch, *On Exile*, 2–3, 5, 8, 12.

79. Dio Chrysostom, *In Athens, About His Banishment*, 2, 4, 6 (trans. Cohoon).

80. All lexical searches for these three words were done utilizing *Accordance* 8.4 (OakTree Software, 2009) for Josephus, Philo, and the LXX, and the *Thesauras Linguae Graecae* database (The University of California, 2005), online: http://www.tlg.uci.edu, for all other texts. Other variations of these words, including participles of the verb

Παρεπίδημος (1 Pet 1:1) is extremely rare in Koine Greek; in fact, the only first century usage outside of the New Testament (according to the *TLG* database) occurs in Philo. Earlier, however, Polybius uses the term to refer to Greek residents in Rome.[81] At one point in the writings of the pre-Christian Aristophanes of Byzantium (the grammarian, not to be confused with the poet), the term seems to be given a more technical sense regarding the position of a foreigner within a city and his social responsibilities.[82]

Παρεπίδημος occurs twice in the LXX. In Gen 23:4, Abraham declares to the sons of Ket that he is a "πάροικος καὶ παρεπίδημος" in the land among them. Significantly, the sons of Ket respond in the negative, declaring that he is "a king from God" (trans. Brenton) among them and subsequently offering Abraham any burial place among them that he desires. In Psalm 38:13 (12), the author, like Abraham, uses the terms πάροικος and παρεπίδημος to describe his plight, arguing that his status is just like that of all his fathers. The sole occurrence in Philo, *Confusion* 82, is essentially quoting Gen 23:4, although predictably Philo provides his own allegorical spin on the story. Significantly, however, the entire context of *Confusion* 77–80 deals with the concept of displacement and wandering in a realm to which one does not belong. In fact, Philo emphasizes one's affection for the homeland: "For to those who are sent to be the inhabitants of a colony, the country which has

---

forms, do occur. There is one potential usage of παρεπίδημος in Plutarch (first century) the lemma of which is somewhat difficult to determine. In Plutarch, *On the Malice of Herodotus*, 41 [Stephanus 871 F], the text states, ἐν Σπάρτῃ παρεπιδημῶν ἐκ Τεγέας ὄνομα Χείλως . . . ; clearly the reference is to one visiting, in this particular context (and see Lionel Pearson's LCL translation, "a man called Cheileôs was in Sparta on a visit from Tegea"). The word, however, does not appear in the *TLG* database when one asks for an exact lemma search of παρεπίδημος, although it does appear when other variations of a search are performed. The word does, however, look like the masculine plural of παρεπίδημος, the noun form rather than the participle form. If that is the case, the usage here in *On Malice* supports the overall conclusions this study makes regarding the term's meaning. Clearly the concept of displacement is in mind here, although perhaps in a less negative sense as in Pearson's translation "visitor." This writer would be inclined to translate the phrase "In Sparta, one of the strangers out of Tegeas, named Cheilos . . . ." However, the reader should note that a clear distinction seems to exist between παρεπίδημος and ξένοι in the same sentence (although Pearson does not even seem to translate the latter).

81. Polybius, *Histories* 32.6.4; the context involves the history of how the Romans assisted the Greek residents by opposing the tyrant Charops.

82. Aristophanes, *Nomina aetatum (fragmentum Parisinum)* 16. Two other occurrences of this word may be found in Aristophanes. The reader should especially note *Nomina aetatum (fragmentum)* 279, which has what appears to be Aristophanes' definition of ξένος as ὁ ἐξ ἑτέρας πόλεως παρεπίδημος, καὶ ὁ ἐν ἀρχῇ γενόμενος συνηθείας καὶ γνωριμότητος ("The one who is a stranger from another city, and who in the beginning becomes a familiar and an acquaintance"; this writer's translation). The third usage by Aristophanes is in *Fragmenta (Nauck)* 38.

received them is in place of their original mother country; but still the land which has sent them forth remains to them as the house to which they desire to return."[83]

Clearly, then, the term παρεπίδημος is concerned primarily with the concept of displacement or "un-belonging" and is often contrasted with the concept of being a native or one who possesses a sense of belonging in the country of which one is currently dwelling. At the least one can agree with Reinhard Feldmeier that the word family conveys, in general, the fact that such a person does not have his or her home in his or her current location and might not intend to become a permanent resident.[84]

In contrast to παρεπίδημος, the term πάροικος occurs quite frequently in Koine Greek. Naturally, a thorough examination of every usage of the term is beyond the scope of this study (and, unlike the prescient terminology studied in ch. 4, many scholars have already provided us with substantial lexical examinations). In general, however, many of the same observations made for the former can be made regarding the latter. Indeed, the contexts of the occurrences of the two terms are often identical (e.g., Gen 23:4). Interestingly, however, in Gen 15:13, the term is used prophetically of the children of Israel for their lengthy duration in Egypt. In other words, the term refers to a status that can exist even when residing long-term in a particular location.[85] First Chronicles 29:14 indicates that this identification of Israel extended to the united monarchy as well.[86]

In Philo, predictably, the term is used metaphorically quite frequently (e.g., *Cherubim* 120 and 121), although often with roots in a historical situation (e.g., *Confusion* 79). In the three occurrences in Josephus, however, we have a strictly literal usage. In *Ant*. 7.336, David numbers the πάροικοι and sets them to work building the temple. *Ant*. 8.59 specifically refers back to the event in 7.335 and thus retains the same force. Interestingly, in *Ant*. 14.213, Julius Caesar comes to the defense of the Jews and their right to

---

83. Philo, *Confusion* 78b; (trans. C. D. Yonge).

84 Feldmeier, *Die Christen als Fremde*, 11, states, "Allen Stellen gemeinsam ist, daß die Wortfamilie einen (meist Kürzeren) *Aufenthalt von Menschen an einem Ort bezeichnet, an dem sie nicht beheimatet sind und auch nicht dauerhaft ansässig zu werden beabsichtigen*" (emphasis is Feldmeier's). This study will, however, argue that παρεπίδημοι can be *residents* of their current location (in this way the word probably differs from ξένος) who are nevertheless different from other residents in that they are viewed as, and most likely view themselves as, not truly belonging in their current location.

85. This passage, among others, may support Chin's contention in "Heavenly Home for the Homeless," 102, that in the LXX "God's people were consistently known as πάροικοι" (cf. also Chin, "A Heavenly Home for the Homeless," 100). This writer would argue, however, that Chin slightly overextends his argument.

86. Chin, "Heavenly Home for the Homeless," 105.

keep their own religious customs. When addressing the senate, he refers to "the Jews of Delos, and some other Jews that sojourn [τινες τῶν παροίκων' Ἰουδαίων] there in the presence of your ambassadors" (trans. William Whiston). Here the term is not linked to ethnicity as it was in 1 Chron 29:14, for Caesar clearly makes a distinction between two kinds of Jews, those who dwelt in Delos permanently and those who did not.

A few more key occurrences should be noted. In Diodorus of Sicily's *Bibliotheca Historica* 20.84.2, the term occurs twice and is linked with ξένοι and contrasted with the πολῖται. In the context, the Rhodians are preparing to defend the city against invaders but allow both ξένοι and πάροικοι to fight alongside the citizens, if they are willing (and a thousand do end up fighting alongside six thousand citizens).[87] Regarding this particular text, Feldmeier notes the multiple layers of society below citizenship.[88] Such texts may support Feldmeier's contention that πάροικος can be a legal term, although he is careful to note that this can be over-generalized.[89]

In Plutarch's *Lives: Pyrrhus* 10.3, Demetrius has defeated Pyrrhus and cast him out of the region (ῥᾳδίως καὶ ταχὺ τὸν Πύρρον ἐξέβαλε τῆς χώρας), yet Demetrius is worried about leaving Pyrrhus behind as a "difficult stranger and troublemaker" (πάροικον ἐργώδη καὶ χαλεπόν; this writer's translation) for the Macedonians where Pyrrhus might cause some trouble. Here the term is not used necessarily in a technical sense but rather in a general sense—Pyrrhus is an outcast who still possesses the potential to cause trouble; his legal rights are not the issue here.[90] The reader will also note the somewhat more difficult usage in the first-century grammarian Aristonicus' *De signis Iliadis* 234, where the term seems to refer to the displacement and the subsequent reception of a new name for a group of people.[91]

The third Petrine term παροικία (1 Pet 1:17) refers to the social (or metaphorical) state itself rather than the people involved in the state. In other words, παροικία is a non-personal noun that otherwise seems to bear

87. Diodorus Siculus, *Bibliotheca Historica* 20.84.2.

88. Feldmeier, *Die Christen als Fremde*, 12.

89. Ibid., 12–13. Diodorus' usage here also tends to support a distinction between ξένοι and πάροικοι.

90. The LCL translation by Bernadotte Perrin, "neighbor," does not fit the context and is lexically questionable. Also, the reader should note that *Pyrrhus* 10.3 in LCL actually corresponds to 10.5 in the *TLG* database.

91. Aristonicus states, Καὶ γὰρ ὁ συνορίζων τοῖς τόποις ποταμὸς Σελλήεις, ἀφ' οὗ εἰκὸς τοὺς παροίκους Σελλοὺς καλεῖσθαι. The context seems to deal with Aristonicus' attempt to distinguish the "Selloi" (the guardians of Zeus' oracle) from the Greeks. For a definition of the Selloi and a hint at understanding this context, this writer is greatly indebted to Liddell and Scott, *Greek-English Lexicon*, s.v. "Σελλοί" (p. 1590). A translation of Aristonicus has so far proven impossible for this reader to find.

the same lexical range as its counterpart, πάροικος, although it may be lacking the technical sense sometimes present in the latter (note, for example, Acts 13:17; Ps 33:5; Jdt 5:9). A technical sense, however, may be present in such texts as Ezra 8:35; Sir 16:8; etc. Predictably, the sole occurrence in Philo, *Confusion* 80, is metaphorical.⁹²

A few key observations must be made regarding this word group before one can begin to examine 1 Peter. First of all, regardless of whether or not the terms are metaphorical or literal, the sense of "displacement" runs all throughout (and this applies just as easily to texts such as Gen 15:13, where Israel would have still felt a sense of displacement or "un-belonging" despite her long stay). Thus, whether the term is translated "foreigner," "sojourner," "exile," etc., one always has the sense that the person or group is in a place (or, metaphorically, a situation) where they do not feel that they belong.⁹³

Secondly, in light of the cited texts, it is difficult to draw any clear-cut distinction between πάροικος and παρεπίδημος. Feldmeier suggests that a certain tension exists between the two words (although they can be combined in hendiadys in the LXX) while Elliott suggests that when the two terms occur together, the latter "has technical political-legal implications" not present in the former.⁹⁴ Yet in certain citations, the two terms seem to be interchangeable; for example, it is difficult to see any lexical difference between the two when comparing Polybius, *Histories* 32.6.4, with Diodorus *Bibliotheca historica* 20.84.2, cited above (how, indeed, could one be more technical than the other in these contexts?). Chin argues, in light of the interchangeability of the Hebrew terms behind the two words in the LXX, that the distinction cannot be pushed in 1 Peter, asserting, "It is difficult to discern from the MT from which the LXX is translated that such a distinction exists."⁹⁵ Chin has, in this writer's opinion, proven his point. The two terms, then, should be viewed as synonyms in 1 Peter and hypothetical distinctions should not be dogmatically pressed.⁹⁶ In this regard, this study differs from

---

92. A search of the *TLG* database would seem to indicate that the word is extremely rare both before and during the first century AD outside of the LXX and the NT.

93. Cf. Elliott, *Home for the Homeless*, 67, although he does not use the term "displaced." Cf. also Obermann, "Fremd im eigenen Land," where he argues that both words contain the concepts of "homelessness" and "rightslessness" ("Beide Begriffe bezeichnen die real erfahrene Fremdlingsschaft mitsamt der damit einhergehenden Rechts- und Heimatlosigkeit").

94. Feldmeier, *Die Christen als Fremde*, 21; Elliott, *Home for the Homeless*, 30; cf. p. 47 for the glosses Elliott gives all three words. Note also Bernabé Ubieta, "'Neither *Xenoi* nor *paroikoi*,'" 269; and Selwyn, *First Epistle of St. Peter*, 169.

95 Chin, Heavenly Home for the Homeless," 110; cf. 100. Seland, "πάροικος καὶ παρεπίδημος," 252, agrees.

96. Cf. also Michaels, *1 Peter*, 116, where he states, "It is unlikely that Peter is

Elliott, although Elliott's overall thesis hardly hinges on whether or not the two terms are synonymous.

Thirdly, there is no indication at all that the word group refers more broadly to "non-citizenship," contra Steve Bechtler who argues that for πάροικος "what was decisive in those contexts [non-LXX Hellenistic Greek usage] was not whether one was native to an area or not but whether one was a citizen. . . . When either παρεπίδημος or *pregrinus* was used in a *technical* sense in antiquity, what it denoted was *noncitizenship*."[97] To begin with, it is difficult to determine what Bechtler means by *technical* usage, and it is not clear whether or not Bechtler assumes that the usage of πάροικοι outside the LXX is a *technical* usage. For example, Bechtler states, regarding "Hellenistic Greek literature and inscriptions," that "what was decisive in those contexts was not whether one was native to an area or not but whether one was a citizen. The words πάροικοι, κάτοικοι, and *peregrini* could all be used more or less synonymously in this technical, legal sense to denote noncitizens."[98] However, a few lines down, he then states, "These three words were not always used synonymously; nor did they always bear this technical meaning. The important point here is that when either πάροικοι or *peregrinus* was used in a *technical* sense in antiquity, what it denoted was *noncitizenship*."[99] One is not given any clear definition by Bechtler on what exactly constitutes a *technical* definition.[100]

More importantly, Bechtler cites few primary sources to support his statement.[101] Furthermore, an examination of the first-century usage cited

---

making any sharp distinction between πάροικοι and παρεπίδημοι."

97. Bechtler, *Following in His Steps*, 72; emphasis is Bechtler's.

98. Ibid.

99. Ibid. Note also p. 73 where he states, "The important point here is that the terms πάροικοι and *peregrini*—as technical terms—were not simply legal designations for resident aliens but denoted a recognized social stratum *that included both native and nonnative residents* who were not full citizens and so did not possess the rights of citizenship" (emphasis is Bechtler's). Cf. also p. 74 n109: "What I have insisted is that when the παροικ-family was used in a technical sense in the first century, it denoted not literal foreignness but noncitizenship."

100. Also, it is a little difficult to reconcile Bechtler, *Following in His Steps*, 74 n109 ("I have argued neither that a legal, technical use of the παροικ- family was *widespread* in the first century CE nor that, when used in a technical sense, the παροικ- family denoted a specific universally recognized, legally defined social stratum") with his statement on p. 73 that "the terms πάροικοι and *peregrini*—as technical terms—were not simply legal designations for resident aliens but denoted a recognized social stratum *that included both native and nonnative residents* who were not full citizens and so did not possess the rights of citizenship" (emphasis is Bechtler's).

101. See Bechtler, *Following in His Steps*, 73 n106, where he briefly discusses three inscriptions from *Orientis Graeci Inscriptiones Selectae*. This footnote seems to be the

already in this study does not seem to support his contention (e.g., Plutarch, Aristonicus, Josephus, Philo). Whereas non-citizenship is often included, non-citizenship is too broad a term to explain its usage. Indeed, some texts such as Josephus' *Ant.* 14.213 would seem to argue against Bechtler, for in this case Julius Caesar had two specific groups of Jews in mind, only one of which (from his perspective) were πάροικοι yet neither of which constituted citizens. Furthermore, this writer has seen no text where the term would refer to non-citizens (such as women and slaves) *who were not also strangers*. If the term referred to all non-citizens rather than just strangers, one would expect some texts to show evidence that women, slaves, or simply the poor were also in view. Yet so far as this writer can determine, usage of the term can be explained without broadening it to include women, slaves, or other non-citizens. Also, in Diodorus' usage (see above), the πάροικοι seem to be distinct to some degree from the ξένοι even though both πάροικοι and ξένοι are clearly distinct from the citizens. If the word πάροικοι was an all-encompassing, technical term for "non-citizens," then all ξένοι would have naturally been included in the terminology, and it is uncertain why Diodorus would have apparently treated them as two distinct groups. Likewise, in Plutarch, *Pyrrhus* 10.3, citizenship is a moot point; the focus is on the fact that Demetrius is displaced, an exile from his former location who still has the potential to foment trouble. In Josephus, *Ant.* 7.335, it is doubtful that Josephus means "non-citizens," for the concept of "citizen" and "non-citizen" (as understood by Romans) did not seem to exist in Jewish culture at that time outside of the distinction between foreigner, proselyte, and native Jew. Naturally a πάροικος or παρεπίδημος would be a non-citizen (how could it be otherwise?), yet the converse is not necessarily the case. Rather than "non-citizen," the evidence seems to suggest that a sense of displacement, un-belonging, or even "foreigner" predominates.[102]

---

extent of his use of primary sources, outside of the LXX, for the two terms πάροικος and παρεπίδημος (although he does extensively discuss secondary sources and their interaction with primary sources). It is difficult to understand, then, how Bechtler can come to such dogmatic conclusions regarding "Hellenistic Greek literature and inscriptions" (p. 72).

102. Cf. Feldmeier, *Die Christen als Fremde*, 21, and Ortwein, *Status und Statusverzicht*, 313, for an emphasis on the concept of "foreigner" ("Fremde"). Note, however, that Dunning, in *Aliens and Sojourners* 27, argues that "the citizen" was " . . . the 'other' over and against which the alien is defined." There may be some sense in which that is true, and Dunning is certainly correct when he states that the concept of citizenship "functioned as Rome's insider term par excellence during the first centuries of the Empire." Nevertheless in the literature cited above, we never truly see πάροικος used strictly in the sense of "non-citizen" (i.e., referring to a non-citizen who was not a stranger).

Fourthly, in the midst of the "literal" vs. "metaphorical" debate, some scholars place an undue emphasis on Philo's usage when other Koine sources should be taking precedence.¹⁰³ Philo's usage should not be viewed as the norm for any term since Philo's extreme metaphorical interpretation of ordinary biblical narrative is unique among Koine writers; indeed, for Philo even the Patriarchs themselves were sometimes viewed metaphorically and moralistically.¹⁰⁴

In summary, then, both πάροικος and παρεπίδημος refer to one who has been displaced out of his or her own home or country into a new place where he or she lives as a stranger. The distinction between πάροικος and ξένος, then, would be that a ξένος does not necessarily have to be a foreigner *living* in the city/region but could be somebody simply passing through.¹⁰⁵ In contrast, both πάροικος and παρεπίδημος seem to refer to actual residents of the city/region who nonetheless still possess the status of strangers who do not belong. Occasionally the terms may possess a more technical, legal sense, but this does not necessarily have to be the case (and this writer does not see how that could be dogmatically asserted in regards to their usage in 1 Peter). The general sense, then, for both those terms is "a stranger living in a strange land." The impersonal noun παροικία is used similarly to the personal noun and simply denotes the act of staying in a different place than one's homeland. It must be stressed at this point that the definitions above are irrelevant to whether or not the term is used metaphorically. In theory, almost any word can be used metaphorically; context and background will have to decide.

At this point, a few words should be said regarding the verbal cognates παροικέω and παρεπιδημέω. An analysis of every single occurrence of these words is beyond the scope of this study. Nevertheless, both verbs usually seem to indicate a general sense of "wandering in a strange land." For the former, an *Accordance* search yields 65 total occurrences of the word in the LXX, two in Josephus, 16 in Philo, and 2 in the New Testament. In

---

103. This is one area, unfortunately, where Chin's well-written article "Heavenly Home for the Homeless" seems to fall short. After promising the reader that he would be interacting with "the Greco-Roman literature" (98), he barely touches anything other than Philo or the LXX (but see 100 n17 and 108; even in these cases, however, he barely interacts with the sources). Likewise Seland, "πάροικος καὶ παρεπίδημος," places too much emphasis on Philo's usage (256–67; Jobes appropriately critiques him on this point in *1 Peter*, 65, although this writer had come to the same conclusion independently).

104. As Badilita, "Philon d' Alexandrie," 64, notes, "Pour Philon, les personages bibliques sont, pour la plupart, des incarnations de vertus morales."

105. Thus we can agree with Chin, "Heavenly Home for the Homeless," 100, when he suggests that πάροικος "is sometimes contrasted with ξένος, 'a mere passing stranger.'"

Luke 24:18, Cleopas asks the risen Christ whether or not he is a stranger in Jerusalem (reflected by the verb παροικεῖς) because he has not heard of the goings on regarding the crucified Messiah. Interestingly, in this case a shared ethnic identity may have been assumed (presumably Cleopas knew that he was talking to a fellow Jew), yet the verb still indicates one who was a stranger to that region. Hebrews 11:9 describes Abraham's act of "sojourning" in the promised land. The use of the word in the LXX seems to indicate a general sense of traveling or wandering in a place with which one is not familiar or is not welcome (e.g., Gen 12:10, 21:1; Exod 6:4; Ruth 1:1; Jdt 5:8). Some exceptions to this general sense, however, may be seen in Ps 5:5 (LXX 5:4) where the worker of iniquity cannot "sojourn" with God (here, perhaps the idea may be more one of fellowship?) and Ps 31:13 (LXX 30:14), where it is not clear from the context whether or not the sense of "traveling and/or living in a strange land" is meant. Interestingly, both uses in Josephus (*Ant.* 1.21 and 5.86) seem to have almost the opposite sense of "wandering in a strange land," for in the former the verb seems to refer to those residing in a particular country (the "regular" inhabitants), while in the latter the verb refers to a city that lies nearby. Thus one may suggest that this particular verb evidences a broader usage than its noun cognates. By contrast, Philo's two uses of παρεπιδημέω (a verb which does not occur in the NT, LXX, or Josephus), seem to match its noun cognate (see *Agriculture* 65 and *Confusion* 76).

Having examined both the general concept of "stranger/foreigner," as well as some of the specific terminology that could reflect that concept, it would seem that a stranger's social status was marked by the fact that he or she could not identify with those around them. This isolation was, for the most part, an inferior status. As McKnight points out, "Those who occupied these social locations stood firmly on a special rung on Rome's social ladder: below citizens and above slaves and foreigners."[106] A stranger could gain such a status in a number of ways including, perhaps, expulsion from Rome (Jobes' view), voluntarily moving due to reasons of family or commerce, forced relocation after a failed military uprising, etc. The end result was the same: a πάροικος was a stranger living in a place other than home.

---

106. McKnight, "Aliens and Exiles," 381. Note that McKnight is distinguishing παρεπίδημος ("temporary residents in some location") and πάροικος ("non-citizen residents in some location") from simple "foreigner."

THE STRANGER IN 1 PETER: INTERACTING WITH ELLIOTT AND HIS CRITICS

What observations, then, can be made regarding the displacement terminology in 1 Peter? First of all, the terminology naturally possesses negative connotations. Seland objects to this, arguing,

> The use of these terms by the author of 1 Peter suggests that he considers them not as negative terms but as characterizations of honor; the characterization ἐκλεκτοῖς παρεπιδήμοις διασπορᾶς in the introduction of the letter is strange if it was a derogatory characterization; characterizations of recipients in introductory sections are generally made in positive terms.[107]

Yet simply because a word is applied to believers does not mean that it automatically has only positive connotations. The *reference* does not change the *sense*. Indeed, the apostle Paul did not utilize the term δοῦλος in reference to himself and others because it conjured up happy images of carefree days. Granted, the irony is that a δοῦλος of God is superior to a free man or woman of the world, yet the very theological appropriateness of the designation stems from the overall negative sense of the word. A term can, however, still conjure up a negative sense and yet be applied to Christians in general, forcing them to reevaluate how they view life and their status before God.

Furthermore, contra Dryden, it is not at all clear that the displacement terminology in 1 Peter is meant to be viewed as "an identity to be embraced."[108] The use of this terminology differs with other terminology such as ἅγιοι, where the audience is indeed commanded to cling to the concept (1 Pet 1:16). The audience of 1 Peter is never told to become πάροικοι or to start acting as if they were πάροικοι. Rather, the epistle reads as if they were *already* πάροικοι—1 Pet 1:1 ("to the elect foreigners") and 2:11 ("I encourage you as strangers and foreigners"; this author's own translation in both citations). This differs from the author stating, "I exhort you *to become* strangers."[109] Indeed, the imperative in 1 Pet 2:11 is for the readers to do battle with fleshly desires, not to "embrace" their status as strangers. The implication seems to be *not* "become strangers and battle evil temptations" but rather "you are strangers, so battle evil temptations." More importantly, 1 Pet 2 clearly focuses on communal identity, even going so far as to declare the church to be "a holy nation" (1 Pet 2:9, ESV), the exact opposite of the concept of stranger. Thus the sorrow of being a stranger is counteracted

---

107. Seland, "πάροικος καὶ παρεπίδημος," 256.
108. Dryden, *Theology and Ethics in 1 Peter*, 135.
109. Cf. *Home for the Homeless*, 132, for a similar argument by Elliott.

by the new communal social identity within the church. They were "not a people" (i.e., strangers and foreigners) but now have become the people of God (1 Pet 2:10).

Having said that, one must acknowledge that the terminology represents a status that is not meant to be shied away from either. Indeed, the declaration that the audience constitutes a "holy nation" is immediately followed by the declaration that they are "strangers and foreigners." In other words, Peter juxtaposes the two concepts, that of "belonging" and "stranger"; for the time being, the former does not replace the latter. Thus even in their new community, the church, the believers reading this Petrine epistle most likely still faced what Elliott calls "social discrimination because of their being strangers and aliens both socially and religiously, because of their similarity to Israel and in their distinctiveness and conformity, and because of their adherence to an exotic Israelite sect stigmatized as 'Christian.'"[110] Thus on the one hand Christians are not necessarily commanded to pursue a status as strangers (i.e., to pursue discrimination), yet nevertheless they are *reassured* in their status that being a stranger is not a shameful state, but one foreseen by God Himself.

Another major criticism by Dryden is that one cannot have both a literal and a metaphorical sense for the same set of words (πάροικος and παρεπίδημος). Dryden argues, "Once we admit that these terms [πάροικος and παρεπίδημος] are used metaphorically, there is no way to stuff a literal meaning back into them, and no evidence that we ought."[111] He further argues, "If we say that πάροικος and παρεπίδημος describe metaphorically the post-conversion experience of the whole community, then we cannot, at the same time, say that they also describe literally the pre-conversion experience of some of the community. This would mean that these terms have not only dual senses but also dual references."[112] In response to Dryden (and in defense of Elliott), this writer would make the following points: first, Dryden assumes his argument rather than proving it. He offers no evidence of why a word that earlier functions literally cannot also function more broadly in a metaphorical/spiritual sense (e.g., in 1:2 the displacement terminology would function literally while in 2:11, perhaps, it would function both literally and metaphorically). Secondly, and more importantly, Scripture itself offers clear illustrations where a word is used in a social and literal sense in one place, then used in a much broader, spiritual sense *in the very next*

---

110. Elliott, *I Peter*, 103. Notice, then, that Elliott does not deny that conversion produces social pressure and disdain. He is simply arguing, here and elsewhere, that such was there to begin with, and that conversion added on to it.

111. Dryden, *Theology and Ethics*, 128.

112. Ibid., 128, n42.

verse. The reader should note, for example, Eph 6:5 and 6. In v. 5, Paul has in mind literal slaves (δοῦλοι), yet in the very next verse he clearly has a different, spiritual sense of "slaves" in mind (yet with the same referent). Similarly, in Col 4:1, Paul uses the same word in reference to literal slaves (a social status). Yet a few verses down, in Col 4:12, he calls Epaphras a "δοῦλος of Christ." Here, this is simultaneously a totally different sense and a totally different reference than the previous usage.

In this way, Dryden's objections to Elliott's (and this writer's) position fall short, for clearly the very nature of language allows a formerly "literal" word to be used later in a broader, more "spiritual" sense. While I grant Dryden's point that "literal knowledge" of a term is not essential for a metaphor to work, I would nevertheless direct the reader to Karen Jobes' point that an understanding of the literal sense makes the metaphorical sense even more rhetorically powerful.[113] Finally, it must also be pointed out that the "literal" and the "metaphorical" sense at times seem to blend together regarding the concept of "stranger," especially when religious identity comes into play. Thus, would not somebody who had joined a particularly sectarian religious group, for example, feel like and be treated like a "literal" stranger anywhere other than with members of the same group, even if he or she were still in their country of origin? In other words, would not such a person be literally, rather than metaphorically, shunned and spurned?

A more significant criticism of Elliott, stemming from multiple scholars, is that Elliott's view neglects the individual and the nature of individual conversion. Yet this criticism is somewhat overstated. While we can agree with the critics that the epistle concerns itself with individuals, this does not mean that the epistle cannot also focus on the fact that conversion *cures* displacement by giving one an entrance into a greater group, a holy nation. This, indeed, seems to be the point of 1 Pet 2:9–10, esp. v. 10. The recipients of the epistle at one time had been "not a people," i.e., strangers, yet now they had gained both a new nation under God and a new family, namely the church. Elliott aptly states that in 1 Peter, "The strategy of its authors was to *counteract the demoralizing and disintegrating impact which such social tension and suffering had upon the Christian sect* by reassuring its members of their distinctive communal identity."[114] In this way the concept of community plays an immensely important role in the message of the epistle.

Indeed, the point of 1 Peter 2 seems to be not that conversion produces strangers, but rather that *conversion produces nationhood*. In other words, 1 Peter 2 does not say, "You once had a home, but now you are converted

---

113. See Dryden, *Theology and Ethics*, 129 n43; Jobes, *1 Peter*, 25–27.
114. Elliott, *Home for the Homeless*, 148 (emphasis added).

and have become strangers," but rather, "You once were strangers, but now you have a home" (although, as noted above, the concept of "stranger" still lingers). The power of conversion, then, is not that it transforms Christians into strangers, but rather that it makes them citizens and members of a greater family.[115] Thus, contra Poh and Schutter, Elliott's view does indeed seem to capture the spirit of 1 Peter. The audience of 1 Peter consists of

> members of a clearly defined, divinely prescribed community: the elect and holy people of God (1:3—2:10) brought into being by the activity of God the Father, the Holy Spirit and Jesus Christ (1:1-2). To the public they were known as the "Christians" (4:16). Separated from the rest of society through a voluntary termination of, and conversion from, past family, social and religious ties (1:3-5, 10-12, 18-21; 2:4-10; etc.), theirs was a familial-like community or brotherhood (1:22; 2:5, 17; 5:9) defined by a unique faith in Jesus as the Christ, as the agent of the salvation for which they hope (1:2, 3, 6-8, 13, 18-21; 2:3, 4-10).[116]

The actual social background of the recipients, of course, is a key point in the debate. Thus Fagbemi complains that Elliott's view " . . . risks defining the church as consisting of only socially deprived people without the rich and upper class people" and that it further " . . . risks making the church basically that of the 'disinherited' or socially marginalized, which it was not."[117] Furthermore, according to Fagbemi, " . . . to see them as rural non-citizens and resident aliens, as Elliott does, is to undermine their Gentile identity, thereby presupposing them to be all Jewish people."[118]

---

115. Cf. Philippians 3:20. This is not to deny that conversion can (and in many cultures often does) produce a situation where the new Christian becomes displaced, an outcast in regards to his or her own country or even family. The point is, however, that 1 Peter focuses more on the process of being integrated into a new nation than on how a Christian might become displaced.

116. Elliott, *Home for the Homeless*, 75.

117. Fagbemi, *Who Are the Elect?*, 54.

118. Ibid., 143. This writer would argue, however, that this is not a fair representation of Elliott's view. Furthermore, in light of his statement on p. 54 (see above), Fagbemi neglects the fact that not every church, city, or geographical location in the first century *necessarily* had to be characterized by the entire gamut of social positions. Having grown up on a mission field, this writer would argue that in certain countries the gospel may very well be more likely to attract the poor rather than the rich. This hardly means that the gospel is not meant for the rich, but only that the poor and downtrodden may be more likely to be attracted by it (cf. such passages as Mark 10:25, Matt 11:28). Similarly, then, Elliott is not necessarily wrong to assert that the socially displaced may have been *most likely* to be attracted to the gospel.

Fagbemi's first critique suggests that Elliott has over generalized, and this may be a legitimate complaint.[119] However, one could suggest with Pierre Steenberg that " . . . the Christian message might have contained a positive appeal to elements of the lower society at large."[120] John Gager likewise states that "Christian communities of the first two centuries derived their adherents from the lower classes of the Roman Empire—slaves, freedmen, freeborn Roman citizens of low rank, and non-Roman *peregrini* of various nationalities."[121] Thus, while Fagbemi has a valid point, Elliott's view may be closer to reality than Fagbemi is willing to allow.

Fagbemi's second critique, however, simply does not follow. No scholar would suggest that Gentiles could not be "rural non-citizens and resident aliens," least of all Elliott himself, since he clearly argues for a mixed audience in 1 Peter.[122] Elliott most certainly does not assume that all the audience is Jewish, as Fagbemi seems to claim.

Another key critique of Elliott's view focuses on the use of ὡς in 1 Pet 2:11 as an indicator of metaphorical usage, pointing out that ὡς is "regularly used in 1 Peter to identify a metaphorical word or phrase."[123] This statement cannot be denied. However, ὡς can be used to introduce a literal term as well, even in 1 Peter (e.g., 1 Pet 2:12, where the opponents view the Christians as "evildoers"; see also 1 Pet 3:6, where "Sarah" functions literally but analogically). In other words, ὡς is not *necessarily* an indicator of metaphorical usage, even in 1 Peter.

A stronger argument for a metaphorical sense lies in the use of διασπορά at the very beginning of the epistle (1 Pet 1:1). Since διασπορά is metaphorical, some argue, so naturally would be παρεπίδημος.[124] This would make sense if it could be conclusively proved that the term διασπορά was strictly metaphorical. Yet this depends solely on one's view of the recipients. Alfio Corritore, in his recent dissertation, acknowledges that διασπορά could be figurative but argues that the tone of the letter and the fact that specific, literal, geographic locations are mentioned point to a literal, historical term.[125]

119. Cf. Seland, "πάροικος καὶ παρεπίδημος," 257, who wonders how the terminology could possible refer to the literal condition of every single recipient of the letter. Cf. also Poh, "The Social World of 1 Peter," 23.

120. Steenberg, "Reversal of Roles," 108. Note, however, that Steenberg is actually discussing the status of lower class citizens rather than strangers and foreigners per se.

121. Gager, "Religion and Social Class," 99.

122. Elliott, *I Peter*, 95–96.

123. Fagbemi, *Who Are the Elect?*, 70; cf. Achtemeier *1 Peter*, 56.

124. E.g. Chevallier, "Condition et Vocation," 394; Achtemeier, *1 Peter*, 82; Bechtler, *Following in His Steps*, 76–78.

125. Corritore, "Pietro agli eletti della diaspora," 155–56.

For Corritore, interpreters of 1 Peter should work with the assumption of "an actual state of dispersion."[126] Similarly, the significantly older commentary by Pierre-Joseph Picot de Clorivière at least raises the possibility that the letter is addressed to persecuted Jews who were forced to leave their homes and live as strangers in a new place.[127]

Nevertheless, it is difficult to see the entire letter as written strictly to Jewish Christians, and for various reasons this writer would prefer to see a mixed ethnic audience. Furthermore, this writer does not intend to dispute the fact that the New Testament appropriates Jewish terminology for the church in general, both Jew and Gentile.[128] At the very least, however, *some* (perhaps even most) of the recipients of the letter would have had their origins in the literal Jewish διασπορά, so a completely metaphorical view is virtually impossible.

From the very beginning the term διασπορά hearkens back to the OT, and 1 Peter's frequent use of the OT throughout the epistle further drives this point home. Old Testament theology constitutes a major part of 1 Peter and thus legitimately forms the backbone of Chin's extensive counter to Elliott. As noted above, Chin argues against Elliott from the LXX usage of the terminology and from the OT portrayal of exilic Israel as a "sojourning" nation.[129] Chin makes a strong, yet not airtight case. This writer is quite willing to acknowledge that the LXX, more than any other source, should inform one's view on 1 Peter.[130] Clearly, in some cases, such as 1 Chr 29:14–15, the

126. Ibid., 155 ("un effettivo stato di dispersione").

127. De Clorivière, *Explication des Épitres de Saint-Pierre*, 8. The reader should note the similarity between this view and that of Karen Jobes, except that Jobes would replace "Jews" with "Christians" in general and focus specifically on the expulsion from Rome (Jobes, *1 Peter*, 32–33). Interestingly, Clorivière does discuss the presence of Gentiles among the Jews being forced to flee persecution, although he ultimately suggests that Gentile Christians were rare compared to Jewish Christians at this point (see Clorivière, *Explication des Épitres de Saint-Pierre*, 8–9).

128. Deterding, "Exodus Motifs," 61–63. The reader should, however, note Achtemeier's keen analysis in *1 Peter*, 70, that "there is no indication that the Christian community has now taken over the character of chosen people from Israel, or that it is a continuation or fulfillment of the destiny of Israel. The language is simply applied without remainder to this new people of God."

129. Chin, "Heavenly Home for the Homeless," 104.

130. For a discussion of LXX usage in 1 Peter, see Scharfe, *Die Petrinische Strömung*, 70–72, esp. 72. The fourth chapter of Scharfe's work deals with the use of the LXX in 1 Peter. Also, the LXX in 1 Peter has become something of a specialty of Karen Jobes, both in her commentary and in such works as "Got Milk? Septuagint Psalm 33 and the Interpretation of 1 Peter 2:1–3," 1–14. In light of the prominence of the LXX in 1 Peter, it is difficult to understand why Bechtler (*Following in His Steps*, 71) criticizes Elliott for relying too heavily on the LXX usage in determining the meaning of the terminology in 1 Peter. If anything, one would expect the LXX usage, more than any other source,

term is used cosmologically: the Jews are strangers on earth before God. Yet even here the spiritual sense of the term is predicated upon the literal πάροικοι who were their ancestors. Thus, "We are strangers before you and we are living as strangers *just as all our fathers did*" (1 Chron 29:15; this writer's own translation). In other words, Israel's (spiritual) displacement hearkens back to her forefathers' (literal) displacement. The spiritual can only exist because the Jews were taught from childhood about the literal. Chin acknowledges that "... the nature of their forefathers' lives made them realize their status" but also goes on to add that "... life itself made them acknowledge they were πάροικος and παρεπίδημος ἐπὶ γῆς."[131] Chin's point may be granted, yet one is left wondering whether or not this passage should be viewed as the paradigm with which to interpret all of 1 Peter.

Chin also argues that both Psalm 38:13–14 and 118:19 (39:12–13 and 119:19 in the English Bible, respectively) have a clear metaphorical/spiritual sense.[132] Yet for Psalm 38, the terminology is once more dependent upon a prior knowledge of the literal state, for the author declares that he is a παρεπίδημος "just as all my fathers were" (v. 13; author's own translation). In Psalm 118, the expression πάροικος is qualified by the prepositional phrase ἐν τῇ γῇ, which clarifies just how the expression is meant to be taken, a phrase which is lacking in 1 Peter.

Furthermore, the literal use of both πάροικος and παρεπίδημος in the LXX is quite substantial. In fact, every single usage in the Pentateuch with one exception is clearly literal, referring to a particular social status (Gen 15:13; 23:4; Exod 2:22; 12:45; 18:3; Lev 22:10; 25:6; 25:35; 25:40; 25:45; 25:47; Num 35:15; Deut 14:21; 23:7; the sole exception is Lev 25:23). Chin acknowledges that πάροικος in the LXX was used "predominantly in its legal/ secular sense" yet emphasizes that "... the divine covenant with Abraham and the notion of a παροικία are inseparable."[133] Nevertheless, this does not change the fact that Abraham *literally* left his *geographical* home and thus became a *literal* stranger, not just a stranger in the "spiritual" sense. Furthermore, nobody, not even Elliott, would deny that displacement terminology can possess spiritual significance. If the LXX usage teaches us anything, it is that the *literal* experience becomes the background for the *spiritual* application. Thus, with Elliott, one may declare,

---

to be the driving force behind 1 Peter's vocabulary. Bechtler's criticism is even more ironic when one considers that Chin's more extensive critique of Elliott relies heavily on the LXX usage.

131. Chin, "Heavenly Home for the Homeless," 106.

132. Ibid.

133. Ibid., 102. Cf. also Fagbemi, *Who Are the Elect?*, 71 ("Abraham's alien status was necessitated by his theological identity").

Dislocation from home, dispossession of the land of promise, life under the conditions of political, and social religious estrangement were the trying experiences of Israel which shaped the language and symbolism of religious despair and hope. To isolate these formulations of faith from the experience of life whence they derive is unwarranted and unnecessary.[134]

Ultimately, then, good reason exists for viewing the displacement terminology in 1 Peter as possessing at least a *primarily* literal reference (i.e., Peter knew that many of his readers were literal "strangers" and so addressed the whole group as such). As argued above, the concept of πάροικος was no stranger to Greco-Roman thought. Travel, forced displacement, the Jewish διασπορά, etc., all make it likely that many literal strangers and foreigners existed in Asia Minor.[135] It is highly probable that of all the πάροικοι in Asia Minor, some of them were Christians (whether Gentile or Jew). Ultimately, then, one can somewhat concur with McKnight that the need for a metaphorical sense is greatly diminished.[136] In other words, if a literal sense of the terminology does indeed fit with the actual social circumstances of that geographical location, as seems to be the case, then would not the recipients of 1 Peter have naturally assumed a *primarily* literal sense of the terminology? Since the literal sense must, to some degree, be true, then the burden of proof lies on those who would attempt to demonstrate the necessity of a primarily metaphorical sense.

Nevertheless, it is difficult to imagine the terminology literally applying to every single recipient. It is likely, then, that Peter takes the literal reality of *much or most* of his audience and by extension applies it to the rest of his audience. Indeed, metaphorical usage is strongest when the audience is personally familiar with the literal sense and (in this case) the social context of the term. Thus the expression "he hit a grand slam with his argument" would potentially be very difficult for an English-speaking European to comprehend since he or she might lack the proper context for this sports metaphor. Consequently, such a person would not be overly familiar with

---

134. Elliott, *Home for the Homeless*, 29.

135. The reader should also note that Asia Minor was ethnically diverse, yet also included a healthy Jewish presence. As Hemer ("Asia Minor," 1:327) notes, "The country [by the time of the NT] was now a political and ethnic complex with little intrinsic unity . . . Roman rule continued to favor Jewish settlement, despite anti-Semitic outbreaks at Ephesus and elsewhere. The presence of flourishing synagogue communities in many cities attracted Gentiles who sought a purer monotheism, and opened the way for the Christian mission." Cf. also Elliott, *Home for the Homeless*, 67, where he discusses the diversity in Asia Minor.

136. McKnight, "Aliens and Exiles," 383.

what exactly a "grand slam" was to begin with (and, depending upon their exposure to American television commercials, might even confuse the expression with a reference to a certain restaurant's breakfast deal, effectively rendering the metaphor even more puzzling). In the same way, Peter's use of displacement terminology (and related terminology) can be rhetorically effective to the degree that the audience is already intimately familiar with the social concept of displacement (especially given how rare the former word seems to have been in the first century). The use of διασπορά may be explained away, perhaps, by a thorough knowledge of the word in reference to *historical* Israel.[137] Yet παρεπίδημος, πάροικος, and πάροικοι can find an effective metaphorical expression primarily by being based off the current concrete reality of displacement; the same metaphor might not be as effective if Peter was writing to Jerusalem (before AD 70), for example. Thus one can wholeheartedly agree with Elliot when he declares, "Here the metaphor of *paroikia* draws its rhetorical power from the actuality of lived experience."[138] Likewise, Jobes aptly notes, "The nature and extent of the 'foreigner' metaphor in 1 Peter are better explained if it was triggered by a real event or experience instead of just being pulled out of thin air."[139]

In summary, then, many (and possibly most) of the recipients of 1 Peter were literally displaced strangers, far from home. Peter addresses them and uses their literal social status as an opportunity to embark on a discourse on the new community and how the church becomes their new home.

---

137. Thus Mbuvi, in *Temple, Exile and Identity*, 43, is able to state, "The Exodus provides the linguistic framework within which the present situation of the believers can be reinterpreted and actualized." For further discussion see also Elliot, *Home for the Homeless*, 38; Jobes, *1 Peter*, 39–40; and Liebengood "'Don't Be Like Your Fathers,'" 11–13.

138. Elliott, *Home for the Homeless*, xxx. Note that Elliott himself does not argue for *only* a literal sense; see especially *Home for the Homeless*, xxix–xxx.

139. Jobes, *1 Peter*, 39; cf. 25. Yet conversely one must also acknowledge Chin, "Heavenly Home for the Homeless," 111, where he states, "The social status of the readers of 1 Peter needs not to be denied. However, the long theological and literary tradition suggests that something more significant ought to be recognised, *viz.* their cosmological and spiritual journey on earth." Ultimately the difference between Chin and Elliott comes down to a matter of emphasis. This writer, with Elliott, argues that the significance of the spiritual sense can only come to fruition by first acknowledging the truthfulness of the literal/social sense.

One should further note the significant article by Miroslav Volf, "Soft Difference." While Volf does not spend too much time on the debate over the terminology, he does state, "That the members of the Petrine community might have become Christians because many of them were socially marginalized seems an intelligent hypothesis. That they became alienated from their social environment in a new way when they became Christians is what the episode explicitly states" (18).

CONCLUSION: FOREKNOWLEDGE AND HOPE

What, then, does all this have to do with the concept of foreknowledge? It has been noted that 1 Peter deals extensively with the concept of suffering.[140] The very fact that most of 1 Peter's readers knew first hand what it meant to be literally strangers would naturally add to their distress and sense of social isolation. In addition, the epistle indicates early on (1 Pet 1:5) that its recipients were enduring some form of suffering. Significantly, much of the epistle deals with such topics as joy in suffering (1:6–7), being slandered by unbelievers (2:12), slavery under immoral masters (2:18), and undeserved suffering after the manner of Christ (2:21–23). Their circumstances in Asia Minor may have caused them to ask, "Are we not the same isolated and inferior aliens which people claimed us to be prior to our conversion? Are we not as homeless and rootless as ever before?"[141]

Yet, as Achtemier notes, the concept of hope in 1 Peter gives "the necessary antidote" to the suffering experienced by the believers.[142] It is this study's contention that the concept of foreknowledge plays a major part in giving the readers both hope and social identity. Because all their circumstances and the very works of Christ in relation to them were foreknown by God, the readers can rest assured that nothing that happens catches their Father by surprise and that he truly can claim to himself a new people, a holy nation. Their social distress and isolation were already in the mind of God from ages past. If this is the case, then their status as strangers (whether pre-conversion, post-conversion, or both) is no freak accident. Regardless of one's view on literal vs. metaphorical usage of the terminology, then, one can declare with Wolff "that their existence in the *diaspora* is thus no unfortunate accident, one which must be overcome as quickly as possible, but that this, according to God's will, belongs to the way of the Christian."[143] Furthermore, if their social status as strangers was foreknown, then so also their new status as a holy community is foreknown and no less certain than their current social isolation.[144] In this way the concept of foreknowledge

---

140. Achtemeier, *1 Peter*, 64–65; Elliott, *I Peter*, 104.

141. Elliott, *Home for the Homeless*, 105.

142. Achtemeier, *1 Peter*, 65; cf. Marc Kolden, "Are You Serious?," 427. For a more focused study on hope in 1 Peter, see Piper, "Hope as the Motivation of Love," 212–31.

143. Wolff, "Christ und Welt," 334 ("daß ihre Existenz als Fremdlinge in der Zerstreuung kein unglücklicher Zufall ist, den man so schnell wie möglich überwinden müßte, sondern daß dies nach Gottes Willen zum Wesen der Christen gehört").

144. Community, then, truly becomes the antidote for displacement and isolation, even in the midst of suffering. As Jim Butler ("Grace and Suffering," 60) notes, "It is always easier to suffer together than to suffer alone. There is a great strength in the midst of suffering whenever the church can be vividly and practically aware of its unity

acts as a bridge between the social isolation of the παρεπίδημος of 1 Pet 1:1 and the new community, the "holy nation" of 2:9. The following chapters will now attempt to lay the groundwork for a discussion of the relationship between social identity and foreknowledge by conducting a thorough lexical examination of πρόγνωσις and προγινώσκω.

---

and commit itself to maintaining the unity of the Spirit in the bond of peace."

3

The Significance of Semantic Range and Context for Interpretation

"I don't know what you mean by 'glory,'" Alice said.

Humpty Dumpty smiled contemptuously. "Of course you don't—till I tell you. I meant 'there's a nice knock-down argument for you!'"

"But 'glory' doesn't mean 'a nice knock-down argument,'" Alice objected.

"When *I* use a word," Humpty Dumpty said, in rather a scornful tone, "it means just what I chose it to mean—neither more nor less."

"The question is," said Alice, "whether you *can* make words mean so many different things."

"The question is," said Humpty Dumpty, "Which is to be master—that's all."[1]

In Lewis Carroll's classic *Through the Looking Glass*, Humpty Dumpty certainly does not lack for self-confidence in his use of language. Yet Humpty's domineering lexical ideas fly in the face of the *social* nature of language, emphasized roughly around the same time as *Through the Looking Glass* by linguist Ferdinand de Saussure. Saussure spoke of language as both "un produit social" ("a social product") and "un fait social" ("a social occurrence"

---

1. Carroll, *Through the Looking-Glass*, 99.

The Significance of Semantic Range and Context for Interpretation

[or "fact"]).[2] While Saussure's ideas may be critiqued for neglecting the *individual* element in communication, nonetheless much of what he said is, in this writer's opinion, theoretically and practically justified.[3] This is not to say that the "code model" of linguistics is, in of itself, the best method of approaching the problem of communication. Ernst-August Gutt, among others, has convincingly argued that "there are many aspects of human communication for which the code model simply cannot account."[4] Indeed, Dan Sperber and Deirdre Wilson may even be correct when they declare, "The Coded communication process is not autonomous: it is subservient to the inferential process."[5] Furthermore, this chapter will of necessity attempt to take into account some of the contributions that Relevance Theory has made regarding linguistics, communication, and semantic range. The basic point of this chapter, however, is as follows: neglect of a word's usage within society, or the shared socio-linguistic sphere that the speaker or writer is currently participating in, will greatly increase the possibility of miscommunication.

Applied to lexical semantics, a neglect of the social nature of communication results in misunderstanding and failure to communicate. In other words, there is no guarantee that communication will occur if a speaker discards what others think a word means. Indeed, Humpty's failure to communicate with Alice (via his peculiar usage of a certain word) demonstrates this significant linguistic problem. If the speaker or writer utilizes his or her own personal semantic range for a particular word, uninformed by the usage of those in the same environment, that speaker has demonstrated his or her "mastery" only at the expense of any form of meaningful dialogue. G. B. Caird, after commenting on the above section from Carroll's work, points out, "The purpose of speech is communication; and when user's meaning and hearer's meaning do not coincide, this is nothing more or less than a failure of understanding, a breakdown of communication."[6]

---

2. De Saussure, *Troisième cours de linguistique générale*, 9 and 97; translation by Komatsu and Harris.

3. Saussure may, for example, be critiqued both for failing to account for ". . . the reality of variation in human speech communities" (Blackburn, *Code Model of Communication*, 89) and for neglecting the concept of "negotiated meaning" between individuals (I am indebted to my friend Mike Rudolph for this second point and the term "negotiated meaning," as well as for pointing me to Blackburn's work). I believe, however, that Saussure's basic emphasis on the social nature of communication is generally accurate, though it may certainly be overemphasized.

4. Gutt, *Relevance Theory*, 11

5. Sperber and Wilson, *Relevance*, 176.

6. Caird, *Language and Imagery of the Bible*, 40. This does not mean that a hearer or reader may not learn words from their context, for this is indeed a basic part of

Consequently, Humpty's initial failure to communicate what he meant by "glory" illustrates the problem with neglecting the semantic range of key words, especially rare words, when interpreting a biblical passage. Unfortunately, this is precisely what characterizes the work of many in examining πρόγνωσις and προγινώσκω in 1 Peter. Thus this chapter will make a case for the need to examine the semantic range of these two words in conjunction with their specific biblical contexts. The subsequent chapter will then examine every first century AD occurrence of πρόγνωσις and προγινώσκω in the published Greek literature of that time. As will be demonstrated, the literature uses those two words mostly (but not exclusively) in the sense of simple foreknowledge. If, then, the sense of "knowing something ahead of time" is the prevailing usage, this should affect one's interpretation of the key passages in 1 Peter in the absence of clear, contextual indicators to the contrary.[7] This is not to deny that a particular speaker and/or writer, e.g., the Petrine author, may modify a particular word's relationship to a particular concept. This is simply to say that such an author, if he or she wishes to increase the probability of clear communication, does not generally create new meanings for words *ex nihilo*.

The wide field of linguistics, not to mention lexical semantics, precludes doing justice to all the various theories, models, paradigms, and key studies of the past centuries, except for some interaction with Relevance

---

learning a language (see Bloom, *How Children Learn*, 191–92). Yet if a hearer/listener already has his or her own sense of meaning for a word, and if that sense differs from the speaker's or writer's, then communication might not occur.

7. This chapter, then, holds to the basic assumption that secular linguistics (e.g., the field of lexical semantics) and biblical hermeneutics (the attempt to discern an author's meaning) can work hand-in-hand, contra Thomas, "Modern Linguistics Versus Traditional Hermeneutics," 23–45. In this writer's view, linguistics in its most basic form is (to borrow from Noam Chomsky's terminology) simply the study of a language's "[internalized] system of rules that relate sound and meaning in a particular way" (Chomsky, *Language and Mind*, 23). The modern linguist, like the modern biblical hermeneutic, has a very pragmatic question in mind—namely, how does communication work? Thus secular linguist Dummett, "What is a Theory of Meaning?," 99, states simply, "Our interest in meaning, as a general concept, is, thus, an interest in how language works . . ." In the same way that archaeological or historical findings can illuminate scriptural passages (when methodological presuppositions are taken into account), so also secular linguistics may assist the biblical hermeneutic. Thus Taber, "Exegesis and Linguistics," 152, has appropriately argued that "inguistics provides a rational and replicable basis for the intuitive findings of the best, most sensitive exegetes and lexicographers." For another helpful discussion on the interaction of hermeneutics and linguistics, see Verhaar, "Language and Theological Method," 3–29 (esp. 17–18 and his critique on Rudolf Bultmann and "continental hermeneutics" which neglected linguistics and proper exegesis; this is somewhat ironic in light of Thomas' various assertions that the *inclusion* of secular linguistics essentially corrupts proper exegesis [see esp. Thomas, "Modern Linguistics Versus Traditional Hermeneutics," 27–28]).

Theory, especially its discussion of "concept" (see below).[8] Nevertheless, I would like to offer two simple ways in which this chapter's argument could be falsified without necessarily bringing in any particular linguistic theory or model. First of all, the argument of this chapter and the following chapter (and, perhaps, the argument of much of this study) could be falsified if one could demonstrate that the broad concepts of either "choosing/foreordaining/taking determinative action" or "love/relationship" were frequently reflected by the terms πρόγνωσις and προγινώσκω in first-century Greek at any level. Secondly, in the absence of evidence for the former, one could refute the main argument of these chapters by convincingly demonstrating that the recipients of 1 Peter would still have understood such terminology that way due to certain linguistic, sociological, or spiritual factors (short of the audience possessing a modern systematic theology that conveniently defined "foreknowledge" for them in terms that certain modern scholars prefer). In the absence of those arguments, this writer would suggest that an examination of πρόγνωσις and προγινώσκω in extra-biblical Koine remains important for understanding their use in the NT.

---

8. For an introduction to Relevance Theory, see especially Sperber and Wilson, *Relevance*; Carston, *Thoughts and Utterances*; Smith, "Bible Translation and Relevance Theory," esp. 35–37. Relevance Theory emphasizes, among other things, the inferential process that occurs on the side of the listener or reader. In the communication process, "Humans instinctively try to keep the amount of effort they have to expend on something to a minimum. Therefore, the less effort it requires to process a stimulus, the more relevant people will deem it. This factor is referred to as *processing effort*" (Smith, "Bible Translation and Relevance Theory," 37). It is this writer's opinion that Relevance Theory does not necessarily contradict this chapter's thesis. Many of those writing on Relevance Theory seem to acknowledge the importance of investigating how a listener or reader would understand a particular word. Smith, for example, writes, "Naturally, it is the speaker's responsibility to anticipate what contextual assumptions the audience has access to and to produce an utterance that will be unambiguous in that context" (36 n36). Carston provides an example on p. 19 of *Thoughts and Utterances* that clearly demonstrates the miscommunication that occurs when semantic range (as described by this writer) is not taken into consideration. Furthermore, as Sperber and Wilson explicitly state, the code model of communication can coexist with Relevance Theory. Indeed, "The code model and the inferential model are not incompatible; they can be combined in various ways" (Sperber and Wilson, *Relevance*, 3; see also 27). Finally Gutt, in *Relevance Theory*, states, "So Relevance Theory does not claim that communication necessarily works without coding" (11). In other words, both encoding and inference can work hand-in-hand; one issue under debate, however, is which of those is primary in communication. Sadly, it is beyond the scope of this study to investigate that question.

KEY ASPECTS OF LINGUISTICS PRESUPPOSED BY THIS STUDY

The field of linguistics, even lexical semantics applied specifically to the New Testament, spans too broad a spectrum for one study to do it justice.[9] Nevertheless, before narrowing in on semantic range and context in lexical semantics, a few broader topics must be dealt with so as to avoid misunderstanding.

First of all, this study presupposes that the Greek of the NT is generally Koine Greek rather than a special "biblical language." While it may be acknowledged that the *theological* subject matter of 1 Peter (and every other book in the NT) demands particular uses of words as well as particular expressions and idioms, this would hold true for any topic and does not constitute a "special" type of Greek (any more than a discussion of football would constitute a distinct dialect or "special" type of English, despite certain technical terminology and distinctive meanings for some words).

Consequently, one must acknowledge that the Greek of the NT represents the Greek of the day, at least in a general sense. Thus, as James Moulton aptly points out when praising the work of Adolf Deissmann,

> It is needless to describe how these lexical researches in the papyri and the later inscriptions proved that hundreds of words, hitherto assumed to be "Biblical,"—technical words, as it were, called into existence or minted afresh by the language of Jewish religion,—were in reality normal first-century spoken Greek, excluded from literature by the nice canons of Atticising taste.[10]

While it must be stressed that the language of the NT is genuine Koine, this does not mean that it is an unimaginatively uniform dialect spoken the same way across the empire. Rather, it is the "standard variety of language of the empire," the great enabler of interracial and international communication across the Caesar's land.[11] With David Alan Black, then, one must acknowledge that

> The New Testament writers do on occasion rise to the literary heights of the Atticists, but on the whole the language of the New Testament parallels so closely the language of the papyri

---

9. At the most basic level, Green, "Lexical Pragmatics and the Lexicon," 317, is certainly correct when he states, "*Lexical Semantics* explores how words encode concepts" (emphasis is Green's). Any further definition or description of lexical semantics is beyond the scope of this paper.

10. Moulton, *Prolegomena*, 4.

11. Reed, "Language of Change and the Changing of Language," 125.

that there can be no doubt that it was written in the same vernacular Koine Greek.[12]

Yet on the one hand, the *Jewishness* of the Greek of the NT cannot be denied, and we may acknowledge to a certain degree George Winer's point regarding ". . . the predominant Hebrew-Aramaic complexion of the style of the N. T. writers, who were not, like Philo and Josephus, acquainted with Greek literature, and did not aim at writing correct Greek."[13] On the other hand, the NT, especially 1 Peter, was written to Hellenistic Jews and Gentiles, and surely even the Hellenists in Asia Minor would have been influenced by the use of Koine they heard around them in the market place and various forums.

One must, of course, acknowledge that along with the ethnic varieties of Koine, there existed also various degrees of "literary" and "vulgar" Koine.[14] Whether 1 Peter belongs to the former or the latter may be difficult to determine. Deismann, for one, made a clear distinction between casual "letters" and more formal, literary "epistles," placing 1 Peter squarely in the latter category (while Paul was in the former).[15] Resolving this question is beyond the scope of this study, though one wonders why 1 Peter (or any other NT book) could not be both epistle *and* letter (i.e., a letter sent to a community that was later expected to be passed around to others, as in Col 4:16).[16] Admittedly, the language of 1 Peter may differ stylistically from

---

12. Black, *Linguistics for Students of New Testament Greek*," 161.

13. Winer, *Grammar of the Idiom of the New Testament*, 33. This writer does believe that Winer somewhat overstates his point. It cannot be completely ruled out that Paul, for example, was familiar with Greco-Roman literature or, at least, popular literary phrases (e.g., Titus 1:12). Significantly, however, Winer does state on the next page (34), "Still, it is an exaggeration to assert, . . . that the authors of the N. T. in composition did all their thinking in Hebrew or Aramaic . . . Men who, though not regularly trained in the study of language, were constantly hearing Greek spoken and very frequently, yes ordinarily, speaking it themselves, must soon have acquired such a command of its words and phrases and such skill in expression, that in composition the Greek would present itself directly, and not solely through the medium of Hebrew or Syro-Chaldaic words and phrases."

14. Radermacher, *Koine*, 47. Cf. also Robertson, *Grammar of the Greek New Testament*, 57–60, for a discussion of "literary" Koine.

15. Deissmann, *Licht vom Osten*, 117–18, 198, 206–7; on 198 Deissmann declares, "Die Paulusbriefe sind nicht literarisch; sie sind wirkliche Briefe, keine Episteln" ("The Pauline letters are not literature; they are truly letters, not epistles"). In contrast, on 206–7, he clearly labels 1 Peter as an "epistle." Yet for a brief critique of Deissmann on this very point, see Smith, "Development of Style," 24–25.

16. One must also grapple with the question as to when even the "personal" elements of the New Testament might have been bound together in a final edition to be published (thus exhibiting an awareness on the part of the author himself that these

other letters or epistles, but any differences must not be pressed too far for linguistic analysis. The language is the same, and it is hard to imagine that the author's range of vocabulary or lexical usage would differentiate too widely from similar literature (to the extent of being another dialect, for example).[17]

Thus the overall point of this discussion is simply that the Greek literature of the first century AD should be considered admissible evidence for the advancement of this writer's thesis. Scripture was not written in a vacuum, and Moulton is certainly correct when he declares, "The Holy Ghost spoke absolutely in the language of the people, as we might surely have expected He would . . . The very grammar and dictionary cry out against men who would allow the Scriptures to appear in any other form than that 'understanded of the people.'"[18] While one may debate what level of Greek 1 Peter corresponds too, this chapter will proceed under the assumption that any Greek of the first century AD, in addition to that of the Septuagint of previous centuries, can potentially shed *some* light on New Testament usage.

Secondly, it must be emphasized that the following chapter will examine evidence from the first century AD instead of other centuries (with the exception of the LXX). Practically, it would be impossible to examine every single use of πρόγνωσις and προγινώσκω throughout Greek literature. More importantly, however, it is the *contemporary usage* of a word that can best point to the meaning of a word in a particular context. Moisés Silva aptly notes,

> We must accept the obvious fact that the speakers of a language simply know next to nothing about its development; and this certainly was the case with the writers and immediate readers of Scripture two millennia ago. More than likely, even a knowledge of that development is not bound to affect the speaker's daily conversation: the English professor who knows that *nice* comes

---

"letters" can and should be read by more than the original recipients). For a treatment of the New Testament as a published edition, see Trobisch, *First Edition of the New Testament*.

17. Ultimately, then, the "style" of 1 Peter is irrelevant to this chapter. Indeed, this writer would even follow Smith, "Development of Style," 23–39, in cautioning against over-generalizing on matters of style in relationship to the NT (e.g., that a book would necessarily only consist of one "style" of writing). In a similar vein, one would do well to remember Robertson's words in *Grammar of the Greek New Testament*, 84, that "It would indeed have been strange if men like Paul, Luke and the author of Hebrews had shown no literary affinities at all."

18. Moulton, *Prolegomena*, 4–5.

from Latin *nescius*, "ignorant," does not for that reason refrain from using the term in a complimentary way.[19]

Similarly, Peter Cotterell and Max Turner argue, "We no more need to know the *history* of a language, or of its lexical stock, to understand the sense of utterances today, than we need to know precisely what moves have been made in a game of chess in order to understand the state of the game and its potentialities now."[20] This is not to say that diachronic studies of a language have no place in biblical studies.[21] It is simply to assert, with Silva, that "the priority of synchrony, the *dominant* function of usage, must be maintained."[22]

This naturally leads to a discussion of etymology. Once again, it is not the purpose of this chapter to completely discredit any benefits etymological studies might have.[23] Nevertheless, as James Barr asserts, "Etymology is not, and does not profess to be, a guide to the semantic value of words in

---

19. Silva, *Biblical Words and Their Meaning*, 38. This is contra Thomas, "Modern Linguistics Versus Traditional Hermeneutics," 32, who seems to argue that etymology was somehow "subconsciously available for an ancient culture and therefore an implied element in his usage of a given word." Consequently, "This is the only way modern man has to 'get into the minds' of the ancients and so better understand their intentions in the choice of words." Of course, it is impossible to disprove (or prove) Thomas' idea that etymology was "subconsciously" in the minds of ancient writers and hearers; yet personally I would strongly object to Thomas' suggestion simply on the basis of what I am writing right now. None of the words I am using in this particular paragraph were picked on the basis of any "subconscious" knowledge of what they meant centuries ago (at least as far as Thomas or I can prove).

20. Cotterell and Turner, *Linguistics and Biblical Interpretation*, 132.

21. For an argument for a more "holistic" approach to the Greek language that incorporates diachronic studies, see Caragounis, *Development of Greek and the New Testament*, 2–4.

22. Silva, *Biblical Words and Their Meanings*, 51. Cf. also John Lyons, *Language and Linguistics*, 54, where he states (following Saussure), "But each of the successive states of a language can, and should be, described on its own terms without reference to what it has developed from or what it is likely to develop into."

23. Thus Black, *Linguistics for Students of New Testament Greek*, 122, appropriately states, "Hence the etymology of a word may help to determine its meaning, but only if it can be demonstrated that the speaker was aware of that etymology." One may also grant the point made by Hill, *Greek Words and Hebrew Meanings*, 8, when he argues that key theological terms "came to the biblical authors with their own particular content and associations, and as semantic markers of a concept: therefore the investigation of their historical and traditional usage is a necessary preliminary to discovering the extent of indebtedness of uniqueness in their use by a writer within a specific context." Yet this would seem to mostly apply to LXX usage (and Hill himself later proceeds to argue in 15–17 for the importance of the LXX in lexical research). It is hard to imagine, for example, the Apostles caring what a word meant four hundred years prior in classical Greek.

their current usage, and such value has to be determined from the current usage and not from the derivation."[24] John Sawyer, drawing from the work of Barr, rightly rebukes the notion that "because a word has a particular meaning in one context, it automatically has the same meaning in another quite different context a couple of thousand years earlier."[25] One may close with the simple yet poignant words of nineteenth-century French linguist Michael Bréal—"The one who holds onto etymology without taking care of the deterioration of meaning [over time] may bring about strange errors."[26]

Related to the etymological fallacy is the idea that compound words (e.g., προγινώσκω as πρό + γινώσκω) automatically equal the sum total of their parts (i.e., their semantic range is equal to the sum of the semantic range of the two words making up the compound word). In some cases a compound word might function in that manner, but language holds no guarantee that it will do so. Thus in English, for example, the word "playground" has a much narrower semantic range than the combination of "play" and "ground." The word "play" may be used to refer to a theatrical production whereas "playground" would (currently) never be used of an outdoor theater (despite this being a "logical" possibility from the combination of "play" + "ground"). In the same way, the word for "train" in Japanese is *densha*. When written out, it is a combination of the two *kanji* (Chinese characters, used in Japanese writing) where the first is the character for "electricity" (or "lightning") and the second is "carriage" (roughly speaking). Yet the semantic range of the combination of those two characters is significantly narrower than what would be expected; this compound word cannot, for example, mean "electric car" (even though the second *kanji* by

---

24. Barr, *Semantics of Biblical Language*, 107. It is worth pointing out that almost all of chapter six of Barr's book deals with the etymological fallacy. For one of the best definition of the etymological fallacy, however, see Lyons, *Language and Linguistics*, 55, where he defines it as "the assumption that the original form or meaning of a word is, necessarily and by virtue of that very fact, its correct form or meaning." The problem with such an assumption, according to Lyons (55), is that "The argument is fallacious, because the tacit assumption of an originally true or appropriate correspondence between form and meaning, upon which the argument rests, cannot be substantiated."

25. Sawyer, *Semantics in Biblical Research*, 9.

26. Bréal, *Essai de sémantique*, 103–4 ("Celui qui s'en tient à l'étymologie sans prendre garde à l'affaiblissement des sens peut être amené à d'étranges erreurs"). One more related point may be made regarding etymology. Oftentimes an appeal to the etymology of the word assumes a certain "key" meaning that has transcended the ages. Yet as Silva, *Biblical Words and Their Meaning*, 105, states, "To speak of the 'basic' or 'proper' meaning of a word invites confusion." Black, *Linguistics*, 122, similarly writes, "it is not legitimate to say that the 'original' meaning of a word is its 'real' meaning, *unless* that meaning coincides with the usage of the word under consideration" (emphasis is Black's).

itself can refer to "car"). Thus Turner and Cotterell are absolutely correct when they state, "We should not, however, be beguiled . . . into thinking that compound lexemes always, or even usually, bear a meaning that is little more than a summation of the separate meanings of the elements of which the word is composed."[27]

Consequently, the combination of πρό and γινώσκω is, for all practical purposes, irrelevant to this study. Both πρόγνωσις and προγινώσκω will be treated as unique words in their own right. This also means that arguments based on the Hebrew *yada* as the background to the γνῶσις and γινώσκω in πρόγνωσις and προγινώσκω remain unconvincing (especially since *yada* is never the basis for the use of πρόγνωσις or προγινώσκω in the LXX).[28]

Next, the subsequent chapter will be focusing on what πρόγνωσις and προγινώσκω can *mean* rather than what they can *refer* to. Ultimately, the reference of a word is the narrow, specific application of that word. In the expression "I am going to the store," the word "store" may have as its reference a particular company such as "Walmart," but the word itself does not *mean* "Walmart" unless such a company were to put all others out of business and consequently gift "store" with a highly technical sense.[29] Likewise, as Turner and Cottrell point out, the Ethiopian eunuch in Acts 8:34 is not interested in the "sense" of Isaiah 53, but the "reference" (i.e., he did not need to know what it meant, but *who* it *referred* to).[30] In the same way, πρόγνωσις in a certain context may (or may not) *refer* to something like "God's exhaustive foreknowledge of future events which by theological necessity corresponds to all he foreordains," but the word itself does not necessarily possess the meaning "what God foreordains."[31]

---

27. Cotterell and Turner, *Linguistics and Biblical Interpretation*, 130.

28. For arguments on the meaning of πρόγνωσις and προγινώσκω based on the Hebrew *yada*, see, for example, Moo, *Epistle to the Romans*, 532 n140; Schreiner, *Romans*, 452; Baugh, "The Meaning of Foreknowledge," 192–94.

29. For further discussion on the difference between "meaning" and "significance," see Cotterell and Turner, *Linguistics and Biblical Interpretation*, 87; and Barr, *Semantics of Biblical Language*, 217–18, 222.

30. Cotterell and Turner, *Linguistics and Biblical Interpretation*, 87.

31. One must also caution against developing a theological concept which is then read back into the semantic range of a word. This is exactly what Barr, *Semantics of Biblical Language*, 188–90, warned against. Indeed, elsewhere Barr bluntly states, "authors have allowed philosophical-theological and linguistic judgments to mingle confusedly" (196). If one develops the theological concept that all that God foreknows he necessarily foreordains (a concept which may or may not be correct; *it is irrelevant to this discussion*), then it is a small step to forcing Greek terminology that means "knowing something ahead of time" to *necessarily* mean "foreordain," even if the biblical author simply wished to focus on God's prescient knowledge.

Next, this writer in no way wishes to unduly minimize the role of sentences and larger discourse units in providing meaning. Sentences and their relationship to each other do play a key role; nevertheless, just as individual bricks are laid before walls can be built, so also individual words may be examined within specific sentences. This must not, however, minimize the fact that individual bricks are, by themselves, little use to a builder unless combined with others. Thus Benjamin Baxter is generally correct in stating, "it is only when words are examined within the sentences of the biblical text that their meaning can be discerned."[32] In addition, the meaning of a sentence is not simply the combination of all the words constituting a sentence.[33] Meaning depends on much more, including the construction of the sentence as well as other aspects of language (including even the omission of certain words).[34] Consequently, in chapters 5 and 6 this study will deal with the larger discourse structures of 1 Peter. For now, since it is the semantic range of πρόγνωσις and προγινώσκω that has been misunderstood, this chapter will focus mostly on words.

Finally, a brief mention must be made of the complexities of the meaning of "meaning" itself. To extensively examine this notoriously difficult topic would send this chapter in a totally different direction.[35] Eugene Nida and Johannes Louw point to this difficulty when they state, "there is no consensus about the meaning of *meaning*."[36]

Yet for a study that deals with the meaning of two particular words, some discussion must be provided regarding "meaning." To begin with, it must be acknowledged, "Meaning is not another word" (i.e., meaning does not consist of simply a dictionary gloss).[37] Rather, "Meaning is a set of semantic features, or for that matter a set of semantic components" and can be described in terms of what it "contributes" to a sentence.[38] At the broadest level (i.e., how a word functions in the entirety of a language), meaning

---

32. Baxter, "The Meaning of Biblical Words," 89.

33. Louw, *Semantics of New Testament Greek*, 67.

34. Ibid., 68; Nida and Louw, *Lexical Semantics of the Greek New Testament*, 10; Louw, "How Do Words Mean," 125 ("Perhaps the most notorious misconception is that language is primarily a matter of words and what they mean").

35. The curious reader, however, may wish to consult the following sources for a discussion on this topic: Donald Davidson, "Truth and Meaning," 304–23; Dummett, "What is a Theory of Meaning?"; and Grice, "Meaning," 377–88.

36. Nida and Louw, *Lexical Semantics of the Greek New Testament*, 1 (emphasis original). The reader should also note that chapter 8 of Louw's own *Semantics of New Testament Greek* offers a helpful discussion on the various "types" of meaning, as does chapter 3 of Cotterell and Turner's *Linguistics & Biblical Interpretation*.

37. Louw, "How Do Words Mean?" 139; cf. also 138.

38. Ibid., 139.

could be defined as "the sum total of its senses."³⁹ This could, perhaps, be described as the "dictionary meaning." Yet at the narrower level of the sentence, the "meaning" of a word will be defined in this paper as "the concept or grammatical relationship it brings to bear upon the reader's mind at that particular moment."⁴⁰ This, of course, begs the question of how exactly a "concept" differs from a "word"; that particular issue is dealt with below.

WORDS, CONCEPTS, AND MULTIPLE MEANINGS: UNDERSTANDING THE SEMANTIC RANGE OF A WORD

The distinction between the *concepts* of "knowing something ahead of time" or "foreordaining something" and the specific *words* πρόγνωσις and προγινώσκω is absolutely essential to this study. It cannot be stressed enough that "words" and "concepts" are not necessarily the same thing, though there is certainly a degree of overlap. If this distinction is properly understood, then the way will be paved for a discussion of the role of semantic range and context in determining meaning.

Jerrold Katz states bluntly, "Concepts . . . are abstract entities."⁴¹ While not a completely satisfactory definition (and, to be fair, this is not necessarily what the author intended), nonetheless Katz provides us with a decent starting point. A concept, by its very nature, may not be tied down to a single word, for words change meaning over time, and a word itself is rarely sufficient enough to describe an entire concept. This can be simply illustrated by considering any teacher (especially of younger children) who is introducing a new concept to his or her students for the first time. Multiple words, sometimes multiple sentences, are used to explain a new concept, and for pedagogical purposes, simpler words and concepts are used to explain more complex ones.

Naturally, the relationships between words and concepts themselves are not as clear as one would hope. The Japanese, for example, have borrowed the English term "juice" (transliterated) to refer to a different concept than the term represents in America (the Japanese, at least those which this writer grew up with, use the term to refer to soft drinks in general). On the

---

39. Katz, *Semantic Theory*, 450.

40. I am using "narrow" here in a different sense than Katz, *Semantic Theory*, 450. Of course, the reader may wish for a more concise definition of "meaning," in which case we may turn to Louw, "What Do Words Mean," 130, where he concisely defines "meaning" as "the content of what people inted [sic] to communicate."

41. Katz, *Semantic Theory*, 38. Cf. Church, "The Need for Abstract Entities," 62 ("The abstract entities which serve as senses of names let us call *concepts*" [emphasis original]).

other hand, different regions of America may use "pop" or "soda" to refer to the same concept (namely, soft drinks/carbonated beverages). Thus Nida and Louw are correct when they state, "The boundaries of meanings are indeterminate in the sense that they can be vague and have fuzzy edges. For example, it is impossible to tell how thick a string has to be before it should be called a cord, or how thick a cord must be before it should be called a rope."[42]

When discussing the communication of concepts, special attention must be given to Relevance Theory. As noted above, Relevance theorists stress the inadequacy of the code model of linguistics to account for all communication. A significant amount of inference is necessary on the part of the hearer/reader to truly understand what is being said, for "the meaning encoded in the linguistic expressions used, the relatively stable meanings in a linguistic system, meanings which are widely shared across a community of users of the system, underdetermines the proposition expressed (what is said)."[43] However, this is offset by the fact that the user can develop an "*ad hoc* concept," by which is meant a concept that is "constructed pragmatically by a hearer in the process of utterance comprehension."[44] In Gene Green's words, "In utterance interpretation certain meanings of words are not merely 'called up' in discourse but are rather modified and constructed in discourse."[45] This, according to Relevance Theory, involves a "broadening" or a "loosening" of a concept by the reader to create a new sense.[46] One example, provided by Carston, would be the expression "Ken's a (real) *bachelor*," referring to a certain type of behavior or lifestyle even when Ken is actually married. In this case the term "bachelor" is broadened beyond the normal usage, and this may represent an ad hoc concept.[47]

Consequently, Green declares, "Words uttered in a particular context provide access to concept schemas but, in any and every particular utterance, the concepts themselves shift and morph . . . ."[48] In Green's argument, a speaker may declare "Sue is a rock" and mean "firm resolve" (concept #1) but elsewhere mean "frustrating obstinacy" (concept #2) by the same phrase.[49] Nevertheless, this writer would suggest that concepts are still not

---

42. Nida and Louw, *Lexical Semantics of the Greek New Testament*, 17.
43. Carston, *Thoughts and Utterances*, 19–20.
44. Ibid., 322.
45. Green, "Lexical Pragmatics and Biblical Interpretation," 811.
46. Carston, *Thoughts and Utterances*, esp. 228–334.
47. Ibid., 328–30.
48. Green, "Lexical Pragmatics and the Lexicon," 321.
49. Ibid., 322.

being created *ex nihilo* for each individual at a particular point in time. Even Carston suggests that when an "*ad hoc* concept" usurps the "lexically encoded concept," it is still "pragmatically derived from the lexical one.s"[50] Furthermore, the ad hoc concept "resembles the encoded one in that it shares elements of its logical and encyclopaedic entries, and that hearers can pragmatically infer the intended concept on the basis of the encoded one."[51]

Consequently, if one truly wishes to communicate, there are practical limits to how one can express a concept.[52] If, in Green's example above, the speaker had said "Sue is a banana" to try to express the concept "frustrating obstinacy," the result would most likely have been confusion instead of communication. The use of "rock" to describe Sue as obstinate seems appropriate because rocks are "hard" and often "unmovable."[53] Thus a concept may be expressed with a variety of different words but, if communication is desired, only from a limited selection.[54]

Nevertheless, this writer's own definition of "concept" probably differs somewhat from those scholars cited above.[55] For the sake of this section, a concept will be defined as "an entity, either abstract or with a concrete coun-

---

50. Carston, *Thoughts and Utterances*, 27-28

51. Ibid., 322

52. Cruse, "The Lexicon," 263, speaks of a "mental lexicon" that everybody possesses: "Each of us has in our cognitive system some kind of inventory of all the words that we know, together with all the information—semantic, grammatical and phonetic/graphic—necessary for their correct use." Nevertheless, "Every person's mental lexicon is different from everyone else's, yet by and large we manage to understand each other; this presumably indicates an adequate degree of overlap between individual lexicons."

53. Nevertheless, see Carston, *Thoughts and Utterances*, 350–54, for the extreme difficulty involved in the use of metaphors, including the concept of "metaphors within metaphors." I acknowledge that my treatment here is simplistic and does not account for the complexity of language; to go further would be to delve into areas not strictly relevant to this study (and even Carston does not attempt to solve all the problems in her magisterial work!). Nevertheless, I believe my basic point holds: one generally does not create new meanings for words *ex nihilo*, even in metaphorical usage. The good communicator is sensitive to how his or her audience will perceive his choice of vocabulary.

54. It is worth noting that a new concept may actually be learned through the use of words. Bloom, *How Children Learn*, 254, gives a helpful example of this by demonstrating how somebody new to the game of ice hockey may learn the *concept* of a "hat trick" by having somebody explain it to them through non-technical words.

55. In reference to both Green's and Carston's argument, this writer would tentatively suggest that their examples are not so much ad hoc concepts, per se, but rather the *ad hoc* representation of certain concepts by a new set of words (that, nevertheless, makes sense in light of normal usage). In other words, it is not necessarily concepts that differ between speakers, but the phrases or words used to refer to the same concept (this especially becomes apparent when comparing two different languages).

terpart in the physical world, which can be expressed and defined through the use of words." Yet at no point may a concept be necessarily tied down to a single word or phrase. Thus, for example, the three distinct concepts of "knowing something ahead of time," "determining something ahead of time," and "loving somebody ahead of time" may or may not be expressed by the words πρόγνωσις and προγινώσκω. They will not, however, be tied explicitly to those words as if they could *only* be expressed by those words or as if those words could express no other concepts.

A particular concept, then, may be expressed by different words or combinations of words (i.e., "synonymy").[56] Thus the concept of "knowing something ahead of time" may be expressed by the following: προγινώσκω, προβλέπω (LXX Ps 36:13), προοράω (LXX Ps 138:3; Josephus, *Jewish Antiquities* 17.211), θεσπίζω (various uses in Philo), and even προεπίστομαι (Josephus, *The Life*, 106). All of these words may be synonymous in certain contexts (i.e., reflect the same concept), yet in other contexts may be used in such a way that their degree of overlap is considerably lessened. Furthermore, the concept of "knowing something ahead of time" may not even require any of those words. Thus, as will be argued in chapter 5, 1 Pet 1:10–12 deals with the concept of "knowing something ahead of time" without using any particular word that by itself corresponds to the concept (the word "προφητεύω" is probably too technical to match up directly). Consequently, the concept of "knowing something ahead of time" cannot be limited solely to a discussion of πρόγνωσις and προγινώσκω. Indeed, well did David Black warn: "a theological concept cannot be discussed in an article about a single word."[57]

Yet just as a single concept (such as "knowing something ahead of time") may be expressed by various words, so also a single word can express multiple concepts (though generally not at the same time).[58] Thus, *in theory*, πρόγνωσις and/or προγινώσκω may easily mean "knowing something ahead of time," "determining something ahead of time," or even "loving somebody ahead of time" in different contexts if semantic range and context allow for this to be the case. Lyons may be correct when he states, "Lexemes do not have a determinate number of distinct meanings . . . It is of the essence

56. For a comprehensive discussion of synonymy, see Lyons, *Introduction to Theoretical Linguistics*, 428–50.

57. Black, *Linguistics*, 123.

58. Nida and Louw, *Lexical Semantics of the Greek New Testament*, 11, state, "If the context does not suggest two or more meanings of a word, one should assume that in any one context a lexeme has a single meaning." Cf. also Black, *Linguistics*, 129 ("Generally speaking, only *one* meaning of the word will be intended in any given passage"), and Cotterell and Turner, *Linguistics and Biblical Interpretation*, 175.

of natural languages that lexical meanings shade into one another and are indefinitely extensible."⁵⁹ Nevertheless, each word does not have an infinite supply of concepts (which I am using synonymously with "meanings") that it can refer to; rather, this will be limited by semantic range (as argued in the next section). In the end, however, this idea of polysemy is what causes linguistic context to be so important in understanding meaning. As Black articulates, "Because most words are polysemous, the context is usually necessary to *disambiguate* (clarify) the meaning of the polysemous word by indicating which of the several possible meanings is intended in that particular occurrence of the word."⁶⁰

Here, then, is the point that must be made: the *English* theological term "foreknowledge" as defined by certain theologians might refer to either the concept of "determining something ahead of time" or the concept of "loving/having a relationship with somebody ahead of time" in addition to "knowledge of future events," but this is not necessarily what is going to be reflected by Peter's use of the *Greek* words πρόγνωσις and προγινώσκω.⁶¹ The recipients of 1 Peter did not possess a systematic theology to explain to them how the word "πρόγνωσις" necessarily includes (according to some scholars) the theological concepts of "foreordaining something" and/or "loving somebody ahead of time." Thus words and concepts must be kept thoroughly separated, despite a degree of overlap.⁶²

---

59. Lyons, *Language and Linguistics*, 148.

60. Black, *Linguistics*, 129 (emphasis original). See Bréal, *Essai de sémantique*, 156–57, for a helpful discussion of how words can have multiple meanings without causing confusion.

61. In other words, I am suggesting that scholars have potentially allowed theological presuppositions to cloud their judgment regarding the possible meanings of πρόγνωσις and/or προγινώσκω. I believe my concerns are similar to Barr's linguistic concerns about half a century ago (e.g., Barr, *Semantics of Biblical Language*, 196, where he states, "authors have allowed philosophical-theological and linguistic judgments to mingle confusedly"; cf. also 222).

62. Much of Barr's critique of the *Theological Dictionary of the New Testament* stems from his belief that they confused "concepts" with "words" (see esp. *Semantics of Biblical Language*, 210). In critique of Barr, Boman, Review of *The Semantics of Biblical Language* and *Biblical Words for Time*," 320, states, "Barr entertains the astonishing idea that words cannot express concepts (209f, 263, *et passim*)." Yet in defense of Barr, Tånberg, "Linguistics and Theology," 305, states, "What Barr means, however, is that the majority of words have vague meaning or more than one meaning so that they can only express thoughts or concepts in syntactical contexts that resolve ambiguity." My own reading of Barr agrees more with Tånberg. Finally, it is also worth noting Caird's words in *Language and Imagery of the Bible*, 42, where he states, "words and concepts only rarely coincide" (referring to exact correspondence). I believe that Barr, Tånberg, and Caird are all essentially correct in their discussion here.

In conclusion, the interrelationship of concepts and words presupposed by this study can be illustrated by the following figure:

Figure 1—An Example of the Interrelation between Concepts and Words

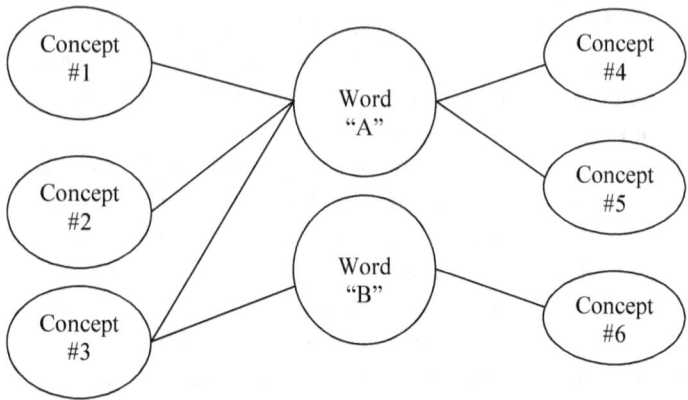

This next section, then, will examine the interplay of context and semantic range that determines what particular concept a word is pointing to (i.e., what meaning a word possesses in a specific context).

THE INTERPLAY OF CONTEXT AND SEMANTIC RANGE

"Context is king!"[63] So rings the mantra, and to a certain degree this is true. Yet if context is king, then semantic range is most certainly "parliament," for it places limits on context just as context limits the potential meaning(s). In other words, both context and semantic range interact with each other to produce meaning; neither functions alone.

The inadequacy of taking words out of context has already been touched on above with the discussion of polysemy. Yet the inadequacy of context without consideration of semantic range may be demonstrated in the following factual anecdote: a missionary to Japan, with whom this writer is very close, once engaged a Japanese lady in conversation in hopes of giving her a Gospel tract. In the process, he noticed that her very young son was hiding behind his mother, fearful of the *gaijin* (foreigner). Wishing to make light of the young boy's nervousness, the missionary attempted to say,

---

63. For a definition of context, this writer is content to follow Green, "Lexical Pragmatics and the Lexicon," 327, where he states, "'Context' is all the information relevant for the interpretation of an utterance."

"He does not seem to like me, does he?" In the process, however, he made a very significant and unfortunate semantic error. Grasping for the appropriate word, he combined "*ya*," a simple particle which expresses dislike (a favorite exclamation of young Japanese children when served a food they dislike!) with the adjectival suffix "-*rashii*" which means "seems to be" (e.g., *so-rashii* = "that seems to be the case"). Unfortunately, when combined, *ya-rashi* possesses an entirely different semantic range (had the missionary said, "*kirai-rashii*," though slightly awkward, he would have at least communicated his intended meaning). The lady suddenly expressed outrage, grabbed her little boy, and stalked off. Later, searching in his dictionary, the missionary realized to his horror that when he said, "*Ya-rashii, desu ne?*," instead of saying "He seems to dislike [me], doesn't he?," the missionary had actually said, "He seems to be morally repugnant, doesn't he?"

Consider that in the above (factual) example, the missionary had context on his side (i.e., the little boy was obviously uncomfortable in the presence of a foreigner, yet there was nothing in the context of the conversation that should have led the lady to take offense at the missionary's statement). Furthermore, one could even argue that he had etymology on his side (since, had the lady stopped to consider, she might have understood the combination of *ya* and *rashii* that the missionary was attempting to express). Yet the fact that context *should* have clarified what the missionary meant did not prevent miscommunication, for the semantic range of *ya-rashii* simply did not include "seems to not like me" as an option in contemporary Japanese. Since language and communication are social entities, one person's "mastery" of a word does not guarantee communication, contra Humpty Dumpty.[64]

Although context remains extremely important in determining meaning, it does not by itself create meaning *ex nihilo*. E. D. Hirsch aptly clarifies this point when he states,

---

64. In Nida and Louw, *Lexical Semantics of the New Testament*, 36, they describe part of the communication process in the following manner: "As a person listens to a discourse in his or her mother tongue and hears a word or phrase which is entirely new or is known but not in a sense which fits the context, the hearer immediately begins to interact with the context in trying to determine precisely what is meant. This usually means checking first with other words in the immediate context in order to narrow down the meaning of any obscure or ambivalent expression. If this doesn't prove satisfactory, a hearer is likely to do a 'retake' of the pronunciation to see if there was a possible mistake in speaking or hearing." I would suggest that Nida and Louw's description fits *some* of the time, but other times there will simply be a misunderstanding without further attempt to determine the author's meaning (as in the example above). Also, Alice's reaction to Humpty Dumpty at the very beginning of this chapter must be kept in mind: simple confusion with a request for clarification (a request that cannot be made in the case of written texts).

It is sometimes said that "meaning is determined by context," but this is a very loose way of speaking. It is true that the surrounding text or the situation in which a problematic word sequence is found tends to narrow the meaning probabilities for that particular word sequence; otherwise, interpretation would be hopeless. And it is a measure of stylistic excellence in an author that he should have managed to formulate a decisive context for any particular word sequence within a text. But this is certainly not to say that context determines verbal meaning. *At best a context determines the guess of an interpreter (though his construction of the context may be wrong, and his guess correspondingly so). To speak of context as a determinant is to confuse an exigency of interpretation with an author's determining act. An author's verbal meaning is limited by linguistic possibilities but is determined by his actualizing and specifying some of those possibilities.*[65]

Put simply, writers and speakers are limited in what they can do with a word. They may, of course, make up their own meanings on the spot (as Humpty Dumpty did), but the result would probably fail to communicate.[66] Practically speaking, then, a writer possesses knowledge of a particular word's semantic range and utilizes that knowledge when he or she writes. Leon Morris aptly states, "Yet it is unreasonable to expect that Paul would use a word without a thought of its meaning in ordinary usage. Surely the right procedure is to find out what the word meant to his contemporaries, then to examine Paul's writing to see whether he used it in the same way, or whether he attached a new meaning to it."[67] Cotterell and Turner put it best: "The significance of the words cannot be changed by the individual if his signals are to be correctly perceived by others."[68]

Ultimately, then, if a writer desires communication, he or she must realize the *social* nature of language. As Paul Bloom explains,

---

65. Hirsch, *Validity in Interpretation*, 47–48 (emphasis added).

66. There is a sense, then, in which we are examining the communication of a text or speech rather than authorial intent *per se*. Regarding this topic, see Gibson, *Biblical Semantic Logic*, 90.

67. Morris, *Apostolic Preaching of the Cross*, 15 n1. This is not to deny that Paul or Peter could use a word in a completely new way or with a new meaning. To do so without miscommunicating, however, they would need clear contextual clues.

68. Cotterell and Turner, *Linguistics & Biblical Interpretation*, 18; cf. p. 55, where they state, "meaning is society's usage." Silva, *Biblical Words and Their Meaning*, 67, similarly states, "One need hardly document the fact that to a very large extent lexical use is a matter of the writer's *choice*, a key concept in linguistic stylistics . . . On the other hand, that choice is limited by the lexical structure of the writer's language."

The Significance of Semantic Range and Context for Interpretation 93

Learning a word is a social act. When children learn that rabbits eat carrots, they are learning something about the external world, *but when they learn that rabbits refers to rabbits, they are learning an arbitrary convention shared by a community of speakers, an implicitly agreed-upon way of communicating.* When children learn the meaning of a word, they are—whether they know it or not—learning something about the thoughts of other people.[69]

What, then, is the proper role of context in relation to the determination of meaning? Practically, context narrows down the reader's options and so points the reader (unconsciously) to the speaker's meaning. Thus, with Nida and Louw, one may state, "The correct meaning of a word within any context is the meaning which fits the context best."[70] Richard Whitaker further observes,

> The dictum, "context determines meaning," is not true in the sense that you can substitute any word into a context without changing the meaning of the context. The meaning of the context is determined by words. But it is true that single words are rarely used without a context, even though that context may not always be a context of words. Word contexts have meanings that are not just the sum of the meanings of the particular words, and in that sense "context determines meaning."[71]

In other words, the very structure of the larger and smaller discourse units will contribute to the understanding of a particular word.[72] Thus there is an interdependence within the words in a context.[73] While ambiguity may occur (else no need would exist for exegesis), the interrelation of the words and grammar and structures of a particular extended discourse help dissolve that ambiguity. Thus, for the sake of this study, the interrelationship

---

69. Bloom, *How Children Learn*, 55 (emphasis added).

70. Nida and Louw, *Lexical Semantics of the Greek New Testament*, 12. It must be acknowledged that the term "context" can refer to much more than the sentences surrounding an utterance; it can, for example, refer to shared social norms, circumstances of a speech, or events occurring at that moment (see Lyons, *Introduction to Theoretical Linguistics*, 413). For the most part, however, this chapter is dealing with the literary context.

71. Whitaker, "Concordances and the Greek New Testament," 94–95.

72. At the theological level, Barr, *Semantics of Biblical Language*, 269, is certainly correct when he states, "the linguistic bearer of the theological statement is usually the sentence and the still larger literary complex and not the word . . ."

73. Gibson, *Biblical Semantic Logic*, 102; Kempson, "Pragmatics," 413–14.

between context and semantic range can be visualized in the following chart:

Figure 2—Context, Semantic Range, and Meaning

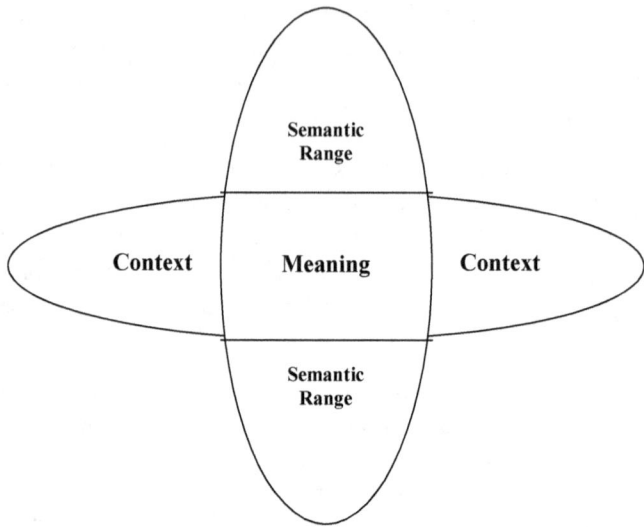

In other words, both context and semantic range limit each other and consequently give meaning to a word.

Yet here the linguist runs into a problem. On the one hand, to say that context determines the meaning of a word runs the risk of circularity, for context itself consists of words. On the other hand, to say that semantic range determines meaning also runs the same risk, for how can one determine the semantic range of meaning for a word in a particular context when, in principle, the entire same process would need to be repeated when examining other texts (as this study proposes to do)? In other words, what right does this writer have to look at extrabiblical usage to shed light on New Testament meaning rather than vice versa? This problem is aptly stated by Nida and Louw:

> In trying to arrive at a satisfactory analysis of the meaning of any one sign, it is essential to consider the meanings of all the other signs within the same semantic domain. And in setting up the limits of any domain, it is necessary to consider the semantic ranges of other contiguous domains. This ultimately means that one cannot really know the meaning of any one sign without determining the meaning of all other signs, since the verbal signs

of any language constitute a complex but remarkable integrated system.[74]

Indeed, this is what Lyons calls "the inevitable 'circularity' of semantics," for "there is no point in the vocabulary from which you can start and from which you can derive the meaning of the rest."[75]

It is, perhaps, in realization of this fact that John Piper, when dialoging with N. T.Wright, objects against the latter's emphasis on word studies in Second Temple literature. Piper writes,

> The problem with that emphasis is that it obscures the facts (1) that "the author's use of the word" is *the* most crucial evidence concerning its meaning and (2) that all other uses of the word are themselves other instances that are as vulnerable to misunderstanding as is the biblical use. There is no access to "how words were used in that world" other than particular uses like the one right there in the Bible.[76]

Yet while Piper is correct in noting that each individual usage stands on its own, he misses the fact that, practically speaking, one can still work from the *simpler* to the *more complex* in discovering the meaning of words. When learning English for the first time, for example, a non-native speaker would hardly be expected to understand the meaning(s) of the word "car" in a complex treatise on mechanical combustion where every other word is totally new to him or her. That student is more likely to learn the meaning(s) of "car" in simple sentences, such as when a friend points to a Ferrari and states, "That is a nice car." Just as in algebra where "solving for x" remains considerably easier in some problems than in others, so also "solving" for πρόγνωσις and προγινώσκω (i.e., determining their overall semantic range so meaning can be understood within a particular context) will be helped along by examining easier (and non-controversial) texts, as well as texts from the broad range of Koine Greek, not just a handful of NT texts. As argued from the anecdote about the missionary, individual usage is open to miscommunication if it does not conform to society's usage.

Furthermore, when approaching theological texts, interpreters generally have their own theological biases that may or may not color their perception of the NT data. In such cases, it would be helpful to examine non-controversial texts first (whether within or without the NT) and then come back to the theologically controversial texts. Thus, regardless about

---

74. Nida and Louw, *Lexical Semantics of the Greek New Testament*, 19.
75. Lyons, *Introduction to Theoretical Linguistics*, 410.
76. Piper, *The Future of Justification*, 36 n5.

who is "correct" in the debate about justification, N. T. Wright's following rejoinder to Piper is well worth noting:

> When we meet a word or term which is used in a consistent way across a range of literature of a particular period, and when we then meet the same word or term in an author we are studying, the natural presumption is that the word or term means there what it meant elsewhere.[77]

Here, then, are two principles by which semantic range may be established. First, one should work from the simple to the complex. In other words, usage of the word in simpler contexts (e.g., "the plane flew over the city") may help shed light on usage in more complex or controversial contexts (e.g., "the plane committed itself to a strafing run over the base while dodging SAMs"). Furthermore, alongside of the "simple" texts, one should also give priority to those texts that may be relatively complex but would contain a non-controversial usage of πρόγνωσις or προγινώσκω (i.e., the meaning in that context is not debated). In some cases, of course, the text may be too difficult (or the usage of the word too ambiguous) to arrive at a consensus as to how the word is being used. Care will be taken, then, not to force such texts to fit this study's thesis.

Secondly, one should work from concurrent usage. In other words, the usage of a word in its broader first-century AD environment sheds light on a particular author's usage, for it influences his or her audience's expectations regarding meaning. Communication does not occur in a vacuum. We repeat, then, Caird's apt point: "The purpose of a speech is communication; and when user's meaning and hearer's meaning do not coincide, this is nothing more or less than a failure of understanding, a breakdown of communication."[78] Thus we see that contemporary usage is extremely important in determining a word's meaning in a particular context.

---

77. Wright, *Justification*, 49.

78. Caird, *Language and Imagery of the Bible*, 40. There is also, however, a sense in which we work from the immediate past to the present; i.e., one wishing to communicate draws from his or her knowledge of how a word or phrase has been used in the immediate past up until that point (see Saussure, *Troisième cours de linguistique générale*, 97). This is neither an over-emphasis on diachronics nor a denial that language changes (indeed, Saussure, *Troisième cours de linguistique générale*, 98–103, spends much time discussing how language does, in fact, change; for a contemporary example of the flexibility of language, see Grubel, "Australian 'Misogyny' Speech Prompts Change to Dictionary," n.p. This is, however, a recognition of the fact that, generally speaking, a communicator is indebted to how a word was commonly used the day before, the week before, and even throughout the past year.

The Significance of Semantic Range and Context for Interpretation 97

One more point must be made before examining πρόγνωσις and προγινώσκω in first-century Greek. Many scholars ignore the "non-theological" usage of these terms. Yet it is difficult to understand why "secular" usage should not shed light on theological usage. A concept such as "the act of governing justly and fairly" does not necessarily undergo a radical change simple because it is used to describe God rather than a man or woman (the *significance* of it may change, of course; i.e., God's governing may be more trustworthy, for example, and may point to his perfect character). If a concept does not radically change, it is difficult to see why the words used to express a particular concept should undergo a radical semantic change when applied to God. In another example, the concept of "showing kindness to somebody" does not radically change whether it is applied to God, man, woman, or nation (for example, a good deed does not cease to be a good deed simply because it is describing God's action). Thus this writer would strongly contend that the concept of "knowing things ahead of time" remains essentially the same whether describing God or human, although the *extent* or *significance* of it may change. Many theologians, for example, would argue that God knows substantially, if not infinitely, more than humanity. Others would argue that God necessarily foreordains all that he foreknows. Regardless, conceptually "knowing something ahead of time" is not the same as "determining something ahead of time."

In other words, whether or not God "ordains/chooses ahead of time" all that he "knows ahead of time" is completely irrelevant to this discussion, because *those are two completely separate concepts, regardless of whether or not they apply to a human or a deity*. Thus one may still discuss the concept of "knowing something ahead of time" separately from "choosing something ahead of time," and this does not change from secular to theological usage, unless one wishes to argue that it does not even make conceptual sense for God to know *anything* ahead of time. Consequently, there is no compelling reason why πρόγνωσις and προγινώσκω should *necessarily* come to mean "foreordain" simply because they are applied to the divine. Had the Biblical authors wished to discuss "the act of predetermining something or choosing someone," they had many words at their disposal, including τάσσω (Acts 13:48) and προορίζω (Rom 8:29–30; Eph 1:5). The possibility does exist that either πρόγνωσις or προγινώσκω could mean "foreordain," yet this must be established from the lexical evidence, not from theology.

CONCLUSION

Context may be the "king" of linguistics, but most kings cannot rule without certain limitations imposed upon them. In linguistics, the semantic range of a particular word at a particular time limits what it can or cannot say in a particular context (at least without risking miscommunication), and the context itself narrows the semantic range into a single meaning. Both context and semantic range, then, are essential to understanding what a word means in a particular passage. With this in mind, the following chapter will examine every single occurrence of πρόγνωσις and προγινώσκω in the literature of AD 1–100 and in the Septuagint.

4

The Semantic Range of Πρόγνωσις and Προγινώσκω in First-Century Writings and the Septuagint

This study now turns to every occurrence of πρόγνωσις and προγινώσκω in literary Greek from AD 1 to 100 as well as in the Septuagint. Ideally, such an investigation would also include the extant papyri, yet an examination of Adolf Deissmann's *Light from the Ancient East* as well as the later *New Documents Illustrating Early Christianity* yielded no sign of either term.[1] In order to examine all occurrences of πρόγνωσις and προγινώσκω in AD 1–100, this writer utilized the search engine within the *Thesaurus Linguae Graecae* database.[2] For Philo, the New Testament, Clement of Alexandria, and the Septuagint, this writer consulted both *TLG* and the texts available in *Accordance* 8.4.[3] For Josephus, this writer consulted *TLG*, *Accordance*, and the Loeb texts (LCL). For Plutarch, this writer relied on both *TLG* and the LCL editions of his work.

In one case, *TLG* included an author who may have lived in part of the first century but would have written in the previous or next century. This author is Appianus, and his works were not included in this examination.[4]

---

1. This writer examined the indices of Deissmann, *Light from the Ancient East*; and volumes 1–10 of *New Documents Illustrating Early Christianity*, variously edited by Horsley, Llewelyn, and Harrison.
2. *Thesaurus Linguae Graecae* (University of California, 2009).
3. *Accordance Bible Software* 8.4 (OakTree Software, 2009).
4. For information on Appianus, see his listing in *DGRBM* 1:247 (note: normally this source lists the author of an entry, but for this particular entry no author was listed).

In two cases, *TLG* listed a particular set of writings as belonging to the first century, when they probably did not. These include the pseudo-Clementine literature and the *Cyranides* (for which this writer could not find any consensus as to when they might been written). As with the works of Appianus, both of these groups of texts have been omitted from the data.

For three particular writings, the dating is rather controversial. *TLG* lists the astrologer Antiochus of Athens, for example, as belonging to both the first centuries of BC and AD, but there appears to be some debate as to when he actually wrote. James Holden suggests that he "apparently flourished in the latter half of the 2nd century" (though Holden does not specify in that paragraph whether he means BC or AD, an examination of the previous entries in the chapter seems to indicate AD).[5]

Secondly, the date at which Clement of Rome wrote his epistle to the Corinthians is also highly controversial.[6] For both Clement (the genuine material) and Antiochus, however, this writer will treat them as belonging to the first century AD. Finally, the philosopher and rhetorician Longinus (full name Longinus Dionysius Cassius), author of *De sublimitate*, is listed by *TLG* as belonging to "A.D. 1?" (i.e., he probably wrote in the first century, but *TLG* is unsure). Leonhard Schmitz, however, places Longinus in the third century AD and describes his life fairly thoroughly.[7] In contrast, F. A. Wright suggests that there is good evidence he wrote in the first century.[8] Nevertheless, this writer has tentatively included his work in the data below.

Finally, in the case of the physician Rufus of Ephesus, *TLG* lists him as belonging to the first century AD when in fact he wrote during the reign of Trajan and would have written in the last few years of the first century AD and the first two decades of the next.[9] In this writer's opinion, this is "close enough," and thus Rufus has been included in the data.

Although the Septuagint was written well before this time period, its significance for early Christianity and the formation of the New Testament, especially 1 Peter, demands its inclusion.[10] Thus its data will be considered

---

5. Holden, *History of Horoscopic Astrology*, 64.

6. For a comprehensive survey that defends a relatively early authorship, see Stover, "The Dating of First Clement," 2012.

7. Schmitz, "Longinus Dionysius Cassius," 2:803–5.

8. Wright, *History of Later Greek Literature*, 187.

9. See Smith, *New Dictionary of Greek and Roman Biography, Mythology, and Geography*, 759.

10. For a discussion on the value of the LXX for NT lexical studies, see Hill, *Greek Words and Hebrew Meanings*, 15–17. It may be possible, however, to overstate the relationship between style and vocabulary when comparing the NT and the LXX (see the discussion in Robertson, *Grammar of the Greek New Testament*, 96–100).

The Semantic Range of Πρόγνωσις and Προγινώσκω 101

of equal value to, if not greater than, the data from the rest of the sources cited.

With those qualifications, a *TLG* search yielded a total of 70 occurrences of πρόγνωσις and προγινώσκω in the first century AD and in the Septuagint—25 occurrences of the noun and 45 occurrences of the verb (excluding 1 Peter). Difficult usage (i.e., where the meaning is not quite so obvious) will be noted and discussed.[11] Finally, all translations are this writer's own unless otherwise noted.

PART 1: ΠΡΟΓΝΩΣΙΣ IN THE FIRST CENTURY AND THE SEPTUAGINT

The Septuagint

Only two occurrences of the noun πρόγνωσις occur in the LXX, and both of these are in Judith (9:6 and 11:19). In Judith 9, the titular heroine pours out her heart to God, imploring him to destroy the Assyrians. As a prelude to this request, she recounts her Lord's accomplishments in wrecking vengeance upon Israel's past enemies. In light of his works in times past, Judith then declares in 9:6, ". . . and those things that you desired stood and said, 'Behold, we are present!' For all your ways are prepared, and your judgment is in [*or* 'with'] προγνώσει" (καὶ παρέστησαν ἃ ἐβουλεύσω καὶ εἶπαν 'Ἰδοὺ πάρεσμεν· πᾶσαι γὰρ αἱ ὁδοί σου ἕτοιμοι, καὶ ἡ κρίσις σου ἐν προγνώσει).

This particular usage is significant, because it is clearly connected to divine determination (i.e., all that the Lord wishes to do regarding his enemies comes to pass). Thus a case could be made that divine foreordination is in view (resulting in the following translation: "for all your ways are

---

11. For this study, this writer has not consulted lexicons regarding the meaning of πρόγνωσις and προγινώσκω. This is not to dispute the practical value of such sources, nor to deny the hard work that has gone into building them. Yet this study is an attempt to examine πρόγνωσις and προγινώσκω "from the ground up," as it were. Lexicons, by their very nature, do not provide the sort of discussion of primary sources that this writer needs. In fact, they often rely too much on each other for their conclusions. I am here drawing upon the analysis of Lee, *History of New Testament Lexicography*, 177, who states, "Yet New Testament lexicography has failed to deliver the results one might expect from such long-sustained attention. Instead of a commodity that provides accurately described meanings and a reliable summation of the relevant data, we have haphazard coverage of the latter and a considerably flawed treatment of the former. The reasons for this outcome have been identified in the foregoing chapters: undue reliance on predecessors, an unsatisfactory method of indicating meaning, interference from translations, and inadequate means of gathering evidence and opinion."

102   Foreknowledge and Social Identity in 1 Peter

prepared, and your judgment is with foreordination"), and this passage is occasionally cited as an example of how πρόγνωσις can indeed possess that meaning.[12] Nevertheless, it would equally make sense (especially in light of v. 5) that Judith is simply saying that the Lord acts with perfect knowledge of the future (i.e., his judgments are always perfectly informed by what will happen). At the very least, however, foreknowledge and foreordination are very closely linked within the immediate context.[13] The evidence here could go either way.

In Judith 10-11, the heroine puts her plan into action to deceive the story's villain, Holofernes (Ολοφέρνης). Speaking with him in chapter 11, she essentially promises Holofernes all of Jerusalem, declaring that she can speak authoritatively on such issues "because these things were spoken to me according to my πρόγνωσίν" (11:19; ὅτι ταῦτα ἐλαλήθη μοι κατὰ πρόγνωσίν μου"). Here determination or foreordination is not in view, for Judith is simply explaining that she knows ahead of time that Holofernes will dominate Jerusalem (a deliberate lie on her part).

Josephus

Flavius Josephus, of course, needs no introduction. His usefulness for this study consists of the fact that he was a Jewish author who wrote in Greek during the first century. Thus his style and vocabulary give the reader an unparalleled look into a Jewish-Hellenistic writer that is concerned with history, especially biblical history.

Josephus uses the noun πρόγνωσις a total of seven times. In the context of *Jewish Antiquities* 8.234, Josephus has been narrating how Jeroboam builds an altar in Bethel in order to sacrifice but is confronted by a prophet (προφητής; Josephus actually identifies him by name as Ἰάδων in 8.231). This prophet speaks of the coming of Josiah and the destruction of the altar

12. E.g., Michaels, *1 Peter*, 10.

13. Moore, in *Judith*, 192, translates the last clause in the verse as "you judge with foreknowledge," though he does not expand much on the theological significance of this expression. Regarding the previous verse, however, he states the following: "Although the Greek of v. 5 is rather clumsy, the author is giving clear enough expression to an idea frequently found in Deutero-Isaiah, namely, the foreknowledge of God (cf. Isa 41:22-23; 42:9; 43:9; 44:7; 46:9f)." The reader should note, however, that Olson, "Lexical Study of Foreknowledge and Predestination," 3-4, argues much more dogmatically that πρόγνωσις in Jdt 9:6 cannot mean "to choose beforehand." While this writer's thesis is in basic agreement with Olson's presentation, this writer is not as willing to treat this usage as dogmatically as Olson. The term *may* mean "foreknowledge," but then again, it may not. For now, this occurrence will be treated as too difficult to determine either way.

(this section of *Jewish Antiquities* roughly corresponds to 1 Kings 12-13, though naturally Josephus adds some detail). Unwisely attempting to seize the prophet, Jeroboam consequently loses the use of his hand. At this point, Josephus states that Jeroboam, "Learning that he was a truthful man and one who had divine πρόγνωσις, urged him to beg God to fix his right hand" (Μαθὼν δὲ ἀληθῆ τὸν ἄνθρωπον καὶ θείαν ἔχοντα πρόγνωσιν παρεκάλεσεν αὐτὸν δεηθῆναι τοῦ θεοῦ ἀναζωπυρῆσαι τὴν δεξιὰν αὐτῷ). Here πρόγνωσις is clearly connected to a knowledge of the future rather than determination of the future, and thus it possesses a prescient sense.

In *Ant.* 8.418, Josephus has just finished narrating the death of Ahab as foretold by two prophets (Micah and, apparently, Elijah; see *Ant.* 8.406-407). Josephus briefly switches to sermonizing mode, discussing how Ahab's death demonstrates how one should give glory to God and think highly of the true gift of prophecies (plural in the Greek; see the subsequent pronoun) and the πρόγνωσις that comes through such prophecies (καὶ τῆς διὰ τῶν τοιούτων προγνώσεως). Here πρόγνωσις is closely tied to prophecy (i.e., the knowledge of future events). To be fair, a hint of foreordination may be implied, since in *Ant.* 8.419 Josephus suggests that ultimately even a knowledge of future events may not be enough for one to avoid them (Josephus here even speaks of "the power of fate" [τὴν τοῦ χρεὼν ἰσχύν; trans. Whiston]).[14] Nevertheless, even if there is a connection to divine determination, the particular term πρόγνωσις still refers to the matter of knowing events ahead of time.

Antiquities 13.300 deals with the post-OT era and the role of Hyrcanus and his reign in Judea. Josephus says, "For the Divinity (τὸ θεῖον) was present with him and granted to him πρόγνωσιν of those things about to take place and [the ability] to know and to foretell (προλέγειν) in this manner ..." Once again, the term πρόγνωσις is clearly linked to prophecy in a simple, mantic sense. Similarly, when discussing Herod's relationship with the Essenes in *Antiquities* 15, Josephus mentions a particular Essene in 15.373 who "had from God πρόγνωσιν of things about to occur" (*Ant.* 15.373). Again, in *Ant.* 17.43, a group of Pharisees foretell (προύλεγον, from προλέγω) the end of Herod's reign since they were "believed to have received πρόγνωσιν through divine visitation."

In *Ant.* 18.195-201, the unfortunate Agrippa is languishing in captivity. Upon seeing a certain bird land on a tree next to Agrippa, a fellow prisoner, a German, comes before Agrippa and predicts (or prophecies) that Agrippa will soon be released. In this speech, Josephus has the German

---

14. This is how William Whiston translates it. A more technical sense of "fate" makes sense here and seems to appear elsewhere in Josephus' writings, e.g., *J.W.* 6.49 and 6.314. In fact, in the latter passage Josephus bluntly states, "But men are not able to flee χρεὼν" (my translation here, not Whiston's).

prisoner using the term πρόγνωσις (in the dative case) to describe his own predictions in *Ant*. 18.201 (predictions which are linked back to the knowledge of his own pagan gods—"προαγόρευσιν τῶν θεῶν" [*Ant*. 18.199]).

Finally, in *Against Apion* 1.232, Josephus is in the process of defending the authenticity of Jewish history by referring to ancient authors. In 1.228, he begins to critically interact with Manetho and his history of Egypt. He then quotes Manetho at length, including a reference to an Egyptian named Amenophis, who supposedly possessed "wisdom and πρόγνωσιν of future [events]" (1.232).

Thus we see that in every single occurrence of the noun πρόγνωσις in Josephus, the sense of "simple knowledge of the future" seems to fit best (though connection to divine determination may be seen in *Ant*. 8.418–419).

Clement of Rome

Of all the writings of the church fathers, few would occur before A.D 100 outside of the Apostles themselves. *First Clement* ("The Epistle to the Corinthians"), however, may very well fit within the last decade of the first century AD. Consequently, for the sake of this study, it will be treated as part of the evidence. Only one occurrence of the noun πρόγνωσις occurs in *1 Clement*, however (though a surprisingly large number occur in the pseudo-Clementine writings).

In *1 Clement* 42, the author begins discussing the appointment of overseers and deacons by the Apostles. In *1 Clement* 43–44, he compares the discord over Aaron's appointment as high priest in Israel to the potential debate over the title of overseer (περὶ τοῦ ὀνόματος τῆς ἐπισκοπῆς [44.1]) in the early church. Moses knew ahead of time (πρόοιδα, in *1 Clem*. 43.6) that only Aaron's rod would bud, yet nevertheless established this test to prevent problems arising over the issue of leadership. In the same way, Clement argues, so also the apostles, having been given perfect (τελείαν) πρόγνωσιν, of their own accord appointed overseers and deacons in order to avoid the potential conflict arising over the office of the overseer.

Thus we see that in Clement, the term πρόγνωσις refers to accurately predicting what a group of people would do in the future. One could argue, of course, that a supernatural component is involved here, as indicated by the adjective τελείαν (i.e., this could be divinely appointed foreknowledge). Regardless, the term is used to indicate the state of knowing (or predicting) something ahead of time. The Apostles, like Moses, simply knew something ahead of time.

Plutarch

The noun πρόγνωσις occurs nine times in the works of Plutarch. In *The 'E' at Delphi* (*De E apud Delphos*), Plutarch is narrating a discussion between various figures, including Nicander, Ammonios, and Theon. In response to some statements by Nicander, Theon expounds on the relationship between logical discourse (διαλεκτικός) and deity (386.D; alternative numbering 6).[15] In this discussion, Theon clearly connects the role of the deity to an innate ability to prophecy (ὁ θεὸς μαντικὴ; 387.A). In the following sentence, he then uses the term πρόγνωσις in reference to the nature of prophecy: "For there is no such thing as a causeless origin or a reasonless foreknowledge; . . ." (ὐδενὸς γὰρ οὔτ᾽ ἀναίτιος ἡ γένεσις οὔτ᾽ἄλογος ἡ πρόγνωσις· . . .). From there, Theon discusses the inter-connections between all events (past, present, and future) and how it is possible, then, to understand the future. One must acknowledge that the *significance* of πρόγνωσις here goes beyond mere knowledge of the future; nevertheless, the *meaning* is still mantic, not determinative.

In *The Oracles at Delphi no Longer Given in Verse* (*De Pythiae oraculis*), the speaker Boëthus has suggested that prophets who would tell the future merely get lucky occasionally; furthermore, their words are not true prophecy, for one cannot truly predict (προεῖπον, a popular word for this particular speaker) that which does not exist (i.e., future events do not truly exist). In response, Sarapion in 339.D (alternative numbering 11) argues that Boëthius' observations are very true for general statements by diviners, but that their specific statements can indeed indicate true knowledge of the future. As evidence, Sarapion cites an oracle that he argues points to the following specific events: 1. Roman victory over Hannibal, 2. Roman defeat of Philip, and 3. the (apparent) formation of a new island. Regarding these three events being so closely linked in the prophecy, Sarapion states, "There is nobody who could say that these all came together and coincided according to chance and accident, but [their] arrangement reveals the πρόγνωσιν" (οὐκ ἂν εἴποι τις ὡς ἀπήντησεν ἅμα πάντα καὶ σθνέπεσε κατὰ τύχην <καὶ> αὐτομάτως, ἀλλ᾽ ἡ τάξις ἐμφαίνει τὴν πρόγνωσιν). The point seems to be that the fact that these three particular events all happened validates the oracle's predictive power. Thus, since Sarapion is defending the validity of prophecy, a mantic and prescient sense of the term seems implied.

In *Whether Land or Sea Animals are Cleverer* (*De sollertia animalium*; also known as *On the Intelligence of Animals*), Plutarch spends much of his time discussing the unique qualities of various animals. In the process,

---

15. Babbit, in LCL, translates διαλεκτικός as "logical reason" here.

he attributes the quality of πρόγνωσις to an animal three different times. In *Whether Land or Sea Animals are Cleverer* 979.A (or 28), he mentions only in passing how the hedgehog (ἐχίνου ... χερσαίου, apparently to clarify that this is a land creature) possesses πρόγνωσιν ... πνευμάτων. Though there are not enough contextual clues to be certain (since Plutarch mentions the creature only in passing), a sense of "foreordination" does not seem to work here. The hedgehog possesses knowledge of the winds, and this knowledge is apparently foreknowledge.[16] Later within the same work, we see a similar statement regarding a particular fish, the θύννος (the tuna). In 979.E (29), Plutarch begins by describing this fish's knowledge of seasons; midway through the section, he refers to "its mathematical πρόγνωσιν of the changes of the sun ..." (τὴν μαθηματικὴν αὐτῶν τῆς τοῦ ἡλίου μεταβολῆς ... πρόγνωσιν, ...). Due to this use's similarity to the previous citation, no doubt the same conclusion may be drawn. Likewise, in 982.C (34), Plutarch is discussing the crocodile (κροκόδειλος) and mentions how it can uncannily predict the growth of the Nile so that it knows where it can lay its eggs. As a result, "they say that the πρόγνωσιν of this creature is not so much a matter of logical reasoning but rather of supernatural prophecy; ..." (φασι λογικὴν ἀλλὰ μαντικὴν εἶναι τὴν ἐπὶ τούτου τοῦ θηρίου πρόγνωσιν· ...).[17] Interestingly, one may note that the term πρόγνωσις does not, in of itself, necessarily possess supernatural significance, for here Plutarch must needs distinguish between knowledge of the future that comes from the use of logic and knowledge of the future that seems to be more supernatural (which some ascribe to the crocodile). Nevertheless, it is clearly a simple knowledge of the future that is in view here.

The term πρόγνωσις occurs four times in Plutarch's *Fragmenta*. Oddly enough, however, these four occurrences appear only in the main title and subtitles of the fragment of a work entitled ΕΙ Η ΤΩΝ ΜΕΛΛΟΝΤΩΝ ΠΡΟΓΝΩΣΙΣ ΩΦΕΛΙΜΟΣ (*Whether or Not Πρόγνωσις of the Future Is Profitable*).[18] On the one hand, it is impossible to completely analyze the

---

16. It should be noted that the LCL translation by Cherniss and Helmbold reads "the hedgehog's foreknowledge of the winds." The reader should also note that Plutarch refers to Aristotimus as the source for this tidbit of information.

17. There is a textual variant here between the LCL text and the *TLG* text (ἐπί vs. παρά); in this case, I have gone with the LCL text.

18. This occurs at the very beginning of the series of fragments edited by F. H. Sandbach (both in LCL and *TLG*). The following three occurrences of πρόγνωσις in the subtitles are almost all the same: Πλουτάρχου ἐκ τοῦ εἰ ἡ τῶν μελλόντων πρόγνωσις ὠφέλιμος (21), Ἐκ τοῦ Πλουτάρχου εἰ ἡ τῶν μελλόντων πρόγνωσις ὠφέλιμος (22), and Ἐκ τοῦ Πλουτάρχου εἰ ἡ τῶν μελλόντων πρόγνωσις ὠφέλιμος (23). The reader should note that the *TLG* text here corresponds to 96–102 of the LCL edition of *Moralia*, vol. 15 (1969).

usage of a term in a series of fragments. On the other hand, a few tentative conclusions may be drawn. First of all, the term definitely deals with knowledge of the future (the genitive τῶν μελλόντων makes this abundantly clear). Secondly, however, a sense of foreordination does seem to be present, especially in fragment 21 where Plutarch seems to suggest that what will occur in the future is unavoidable. No doubt this is what necessitates that Plutarch answer the question of the title, i.e., whether or not knowledge of the future is useful in the first place if all is unavoidable. This he does in the next two sections (22 and 23) where he argues that the *method* by which events come about is also important and that knowledge of the future (not necessarily supernatural knowledge) gives one the ability to determine how to best deal with future matters. Thus, although Plutarch suggests that what is foreknown is predetermined, the focus nonetheless is on a prescient sense of the term πρόγνωσις (i.e., simple knowledge of the future).

Other Texts

Predictably, the use of the noun πρόγνωσις in the works of the astrologer Antiochus (three total occurrences) concerns foretelling the future via the use of the Zodiac and the positioning of celestial bodies such as the moon. Thus, in Antiochus' *Fragmenta (e cod. Napolitano 19)*, 4.154, we have the preface, Περὶ <τῆς> τοῦ Κυνὸς ἐπιτολῆς καὶ τῆς προγνώσεως τῶν ἐξ αὐτοῦ συμβαινόντων, Ἀντιόχου, or "Concerning the rising of the dog [star] and the προγνώσεως of those things coming together out of it, by Antiochus," followed by a discussion of the observation on the "rising dog star" on the 20th of the month in conjunction with the moon, etc. After this we have a series of statements concerning predictions based on the positions of the Zodiac in relation to the moon (e.g., *Fragmenta [e cod. Napolitano 19]* 4.155, Ἐν Λέοντι οὔσης τῆς Σελήνης, ἐὰν ἀνατολὴ γένηται τοῦ Κυνός, σίτου φορὰ πολλὴ καὶ ἐλαίου καὶ οἴνου ἔσται καὶ τῶν ἄλλων πάντων εὐωνία· . . . ["When Leo exists (*i.e.*, appears) with the moon, if the dog (star) rises, there will be much corn and oil and wine and good stuff of all other kinds"]).

Naturally, the usage of πρόγνωσις within an astrological context does not in of itself mean that the term cannot refer to foreordination. Yet because πρόγνωσις is connected closely to a human, Antiochus, and because any reference to fate or divine control in the immediate context seems to be absent, it seems safest to see this as a strictly prescient term here (especially since astrology is, after all, about prediction).

Secondly, in Antiochus' *Fragmenta (e cod. Paris)* 8.3.108, we have the following statement (in a series of numbered statements concerning the positions of constellations): Περὶ τῶν τικτομένων ἀπὸ τοῦ πολεύοντος καὶ διέποντος πρόγνωσις. While the lack of a finite verb and the placement of the nominative πρόγνωσις at the very back are rather odd, the text may be roughly translated as follows: "The πρόγνωσις [derived] from that which wanders about and traverses [i.e., planets, etc.], concerning those giving birth." Once again, a primarily mantic sense seems logical, especially since the context (the other numbered statements) deal with the positioning of the moon, sun, constellations, planets, etc. This writer could find no mention of fate or divine decree in the immediate context.

Thirdly, in the same text, *Fragmenta (e cod. Paris.)* 8.3.119, there is a highly technical discussion of the various astrological positions of the zodiac followed by the phrase λαμβάνεσθαι πρόγνωσιν. The text of the difficult last sentence of this paragraph reads,

> Ποικιλοῖ γοῦν τοὺς σχηματισμοὺς τούτων πρός τε τὰ κέντρα καὶ πρὸς τὰ ἀποκλίματα καὶ πρὸς τὰς ἐπαναφορὰς τῶν ζῳδίων, ἔτι δὲ καὶ πρὸς τοὺς ἄλλους ἀστέρας, ὅσοι τοῦ κυριεύειν καὶ οἰκοδεσποτεῖν κατ' ἐκεῖνον καιρὸν οὐ μετέσχον, κἀκ τούτων φησὶν τὴν τῶν ἐσομένων λαμβάνεσθαι πρόγνωσιν.

A completely satisfactory translation is beyond the ability of this writer, especially given the complete absence of a finite verb in the entire sentence. Clearly the sentence deals with the various positions of stars, constellations, and their interpretation (note the reference to the "cardinal point of the Zodiac" [τὰ κέντρα . . . τὰς ἐπαναφορὰς τῶν ζῳδίων]).[19] Most likely here πρόγνωσις does not mean "foreordination" because one does not "receive" foreordination," whereas one definitely can receive "foreknowledge" (i.e., knowledge of things yet to come). One could, of course, receive "divine personal relationship," but this would be the least likely meaning in astrological contexts such as this.

Next, in a fragment of his extant work on Hippocrates (*Fragmenta* 33.27), Erotianus describes how that ancient physician disdained superstition: Οἵ τε τὴν δεισιδαιμονίαν οἰόμενοι εἰρῆσθαι σφόδρα εἰσὶν εὐήθεις. Οὐ γὰρ ἔμελεν Ἱπποκράτει περὶ προγνώσεως γράφοντι μεμνῆσθαι τῶν διὰ τὰς τροφὰς νοσούντων, ἀλλ'οὐδὲ τὴν μανίαν οὐδὲ τὸ ἐνθουσιαστικὸν πάθος ("And those supposing to find a supernatural cause are very stupid. For Hippocrates did not care to call to mind [anything] by [such] writers about the πρόγνωσις of those who had diseases through the food but not madness or divine misfortune)." Clearly, then, πρόγνωσις here is tied to superstition, and Hippocrates

---

19. I am highly indebted to Liddell and Scott's *Greek-English Lexicon* for assistance with difficult terminology, especially astrological terminology. They supply many technical meanings not often covered in other sources.

The Semantic Range of Πρόγνωσις and Προγινώσκω   109

was opposed to such when determining the cause of disease. Once again, the Greek term seems to possess a mantic sense, though a technical, medical sense cannot be ruled out.[20]

Finally, the astrologer Balbillus in *Fragmenta* 8.104.20 connects πρόγνωσιν with the "horoscope" (ὡροσκόπου) in a context that seems to deal with the astrological art of knowing ahead of time the mortality, the social status, etc., of particular human beings. Once again a mantic sense seems to fit πρόγνωσις (due to the very small nature of this particular fragment, I have opted not to reproduce the paragraph in its entirety).[21]

The New Testament

There is only one other occurrence of the noun πρόγνωσις in the NT outside of 1 Pet 1:2. In Acts 2:23 we read that Christ was handed over . . . τῇ ὡρισμένῃ βουλῇ καὶ προγνώσει τοῦ θεοῦ . . . Here divine foreknowledge clearly works hand in hand with divine foreordination (τῇ ὡρισμένῃ βουλῇ certainly possesses a strong determinative sense).[22] Indeed, the fact that a single article governs both nouns implies a closeness (though not necessarily conceptual identity).[23]

---

20. For information on Erotianus, see William Alexander Greenhill, "Erotianus," 2:51.

21. For information on Balbillus, see Holden, *History of Horoscopic Astrology*, 29–32.

22. Pervo, *Acts*, 81, calls this "That compressed expression of Luke's view of divine providence . . ."

23. The reader will note that although Granville Sharp, in his *Remarks on the Uses of the Definitive Article in the Greek New Testament*, 3, under "Rule 1," argued for identity of personhood in a TSKS construction (article + noun+ καί + noun) when both are singular and neither are proper names, he was not applying his rule to abstract nouns (or non-personal nouns of any kind). The fact that he specifically refers to "persons" in his discussion seems to rule out the application of his rule to abstract nouns. For further discussion, see Wallace, *Granville Sharp's Canon and Its Kin: Semantics and Significance*, 63–177. Note that Wallace concludes, in *Granville Sharp's Canon and Its Kin*, 177, that ". . . the evidence—both within the NT and outside—overwhelmingly points in one direction: impersonal constructions do *not*, as a rule, imply an identical referent." Wallace provides, in this writer's opinion, original research all throughout his book that supports his conclusion. If the TSKS construction in Acts 2:23 is meant to represent identity between two abstract nouns, then it is one of the few places (if not the only place) in the New Testament where this is conclusively so. At the very least, one cannot appeal to Granville Sharp's rule to argue this, for Sharp himself did not apply the rule this way (see above), and there would be too many exceptions in the NT alone to make this any sort of a "rule." Nevertheless Baugh, "Meaning of Foreknowledge," 190, is certainly correct by describing a "close interconnection" between the two words here in Acts 2:23.

Nevertheless, David G. Peterson, among others, argues that the term πρόγνωσις here refers to "more than his [God's] ability to anticipate the future. It is another way of talking about his determination of events in advance, . . ."[24] Yet Peterson offers no lexical considerations as to why this should be so. Indeed, it is hard to understand why two separate (although interrelated) concepts could not be in view here. Certainly the concept of "knowing something ahead of time" can exist separately from "determining something ahead of time" while still being a part of the overall description of God's character. Edgar C. James claims, "Certainly foreknowledge *knows*, but it does not *perform an act* like the delivering of Jesus to His enemies" (since the noun is in the instrumental case).[25] While James has a point, his argument is only valid if the dative here necessitates "performing an act" rather than (for example) an attribute that supplements a particular action (i.e., God foreordaines [*act A*] informed by his foreknowledge [*of events B*]). At the least other possibilities must be considered regarding how the dative here functions.

PART 2: ΠΡΟΓΙΝΩΣΚΩ IN THE FIRST CENTURY AND THE SEPTUAGINT

The Septuagint

The verb προγινώσκω occurs three times in the Septuagint, but only in the apocryphal Wisdom of Solomon. In Wis 6.9–22, the author is extolling the glory of Wisdom and her graciousness in making herself known to those who desire her. In Wis 6.13, Wisdom φθάνει τοὺς ἐπιθυμοῦντας προγνωσθῆναι ("Wisdom is reaching out to the ones desiring her, to be προγνωσθῆναι [by them]"). In other words, "The sense is that Wisdom is ever anxious to make herself known to men: she cannot enter into them without being solicited, but she always endeavors to dispose them to welcome her."[26] This is a rather odd usage that seems to almost combine a prescient sense with a sense of relationship. It is not Lady Wisdom that is doing the "foreknowing" (whatever that might entail), but rather Wisdom

---

24. Peterson, *Acts of the Apostles*, 146.

25. James, "Is Foreknowledge Equivalent to Foreordination?," 217. Nevertheless, a more balanced perspective is given by Baugh, "Meaning of Foreknowledge," 189, who mainly interprets this verse as signifying that "Christ's death did not take God by surprise."

26. Reider, *Book of Wisdom*, 103.

The Semantic Range of Πρόγνωσις and Προγινώσκω   111

who wishes to be foreknown by humans. Thus a relationship is implied (especially in light of the personification of Wisdom), yet a simple knowledge of the future also seems to be a part of the meaning. Nevertheless, it seems safest to classify this usage as possessing at least the strong implication of "intimate relationship."

In Wis 8.8 and the surrounding context, we see what instruction and virtues Wisdom can provide for those who seek her. In this particular verse, Wisdom σημεῖα καὶ τέρατα προγινώσκει; thus Wisdom provides knowledge of future spectacular events.[27] A prescient sense seems to be most likely here.

Finally, in Wisdom 18, the author is discussing how the Exodus generation escapes while the Egyptians are punished. In Wis 18.6, the night on which the Egyptian firstborn are slain is made known ahead of time to the heads of the households (Ἐκείνη ἡ νὺξ προεγνώσθη πατράσιν ἡμῶν, . . . ["That night it was προεγνώσθη to our fathers, . . ."]).[28] As in the previous occurrence, simple foreknowledge is in view.

Josephus

The verb προγινώσκω occurs twenty times in the works of Josephus. In *Jewish Antiquities* 1.311, Josephus narrates Jacob's interaction with Laban and how the former was preparing to leave the latter. In this text, Jacob takes half the cattle, while Λαβάνου μὴ προεγνωκότος, an expression which seems to simply point to Laban's ignorance of what Jacob had planned.

In *Ant.* 2.86, Joseph is in the process of explaining the meaning of two dreams to the Egyptian king. Joseph explains to the Pharaoh that God's purpose in such dreams is not to cause humans to despair (οὐκ ἐπὶ τῷ λυπεῖν), but rather that, knowing ahead of time what is to come, they might make appropriate preparation. The perfect participle προυγνωκότες is used to describe the knowledge humans receive from God via dreams (the implied subject is the dative τοῖς ἀνθρώποις from the previous line, not θεὸς).

In *Ant.* 4.121, Balaam is responding to King Balak concerning why he has blessed the people of Israel instead of cursing them. As part of his defense, Balaam declares that "those who attempt προγινώσκειν from their own power are completely incapable (παντελῶς ἀσθενεῖς) of doing so . . ." Since prophecy is in view, at first glance a simple mantic meaning may work. Yet something a bit more complicated may be at play here. Balaam

---

27. Reider, ibid., 121, interprets this as a reference to "having a foreknowledge of natural phenomena, such as eclipses, storms, earthquakes, etc."

28. For further discussion, see Winston, *Wisdom of Solomon*, 315; Reider, *Book of Wisdom*, 207.

was to place a "curse" (the dative κατάρᾳ in *Ant.* 4:118) on Israel; thus, perhaps, "determinatively foreknow" would be a possibility, in the sense that Balaam was to actually bring upon the Israelites what he was foreknowing about them (it is worth noting, however, that the content of Balaam's blessing in 4.122 seems to be simple knowledge rather than anything proactive on the part of Balaam). A better sense, perhaps, is indicated by William Whiston's translation "foretell" (i.e., "to declare something ahead of time"). Whiston's version reads as follows: "for those that take upon them to foretell the affairs of mankind, as from their own abilities, are entirely unable to do it, . . ."[29]

In *Ant.* 5.358–359, Eli receives tidings of the fate of both the Jewish army and the Ark of the Covenant. Josephus contrasts Eli's reaction to both of those events; the latter event causes him grief or shock to the point of death, whereas the relating of the fall of the army had caused no such reaction, for ὡς ἃ προεγνωκὼς παρὰ τοῦ θεοῦ τὸ συμβησόμενον . . . ("since he προεγνωκὼς from God that which had taken place . . .").[30] The meaning "to know ahead of time" seems to work here.

In *Ant.* 6.54, Samuel is explaining to Saul how Saul would be soon proclaimed king. To alleviate his doubts, Samuel promises Saul, δὲ ἔσται σοι σημεῖον ὅ σε βούλομαι προγινώσκειν· . . . ("but there will be a sign for you which I want you προγινώσκειν; . . .). Clearly Samuel wishes Saul to be aware of something ahead of time. One may conclude, then, that the sense points to simple foreknowledge.

In *Ant.* 6.344–350, Josephus embarks upon a philosophical dialogue about the manner of Saul's death and how he chose, despite knowing of his imminent death from Samuel's prophecy via the witch of Endor, to enter battle rather than flee. Josephus remarks rather positively on men who face death without cowardice despite knowing their fate ahead of time. In *Ant.* 6.348, Josephus uses the participle προγινωσκόμενον to describe such men who know that their fate is to die. Clearly in this case a simple prescient sense fits best.

In *Ant.* 7.57, David is at Hebron, and the various tribes come to him to acknowledge his leadership. Among those coming to him are the men of Issachar, numbering twenty thousand, who apparently possess some knowledge or insight into the future (οἱ προγινώσκοντες τὰ μέλλοντα).

---

29. Whiston's translation is taken from the text in *Accordance*.

30. Though technically an active participle with Eli as the subject, this "foreknowledge" nevertheless comes from God. In this case, something along the lines of "made aware ahead of time by God" might be an appropriate translation.

The Semantic Range of Πρόγνωσις and Προγινώσκω   113

In *Ant.* 8.418, Josephus is discussing how Ahab's prophesied death comes to pass, and he uses the noun πρόγνωσις parallel with προφητεία to describe two things which, through God's mercy, are συμφορώτερον ("beneficial"; see the discussion of this text in the previous section). Yet ironically, in the very next verse (8.419), Josephus declares that, as evidenced by what happened to King Ahab, one cannot truly escape what is foreknown (ὅτι μηδὲ προγινωσκόμενον αὐτὸ διαφυγεῖν ἔστιν). Here foreknowledge is indeed tied with divine foreordination (or, perhaps, "fate"), yet nevertheless the word is used in a mantic sense to simply describe what the king knew ahead of time via prophecy.

Next, in *Ant.* 13.175, Josephus has been narrating how the armies of Demetrius march to oppose the Jewish Jonathan. In the process of defending Judea, the latter receives information that the enemy is preparing to attack him and consequently makes appropriate preparations. Regarding Jonathan's reception of this key information, Josephus uses the participle προγνούς, apparently meaning simple foreknowledge.

In *Ant.* 16.214, Josephus has been discussing a quarrel between King Herod, Pheroras, and Salome. Herod has accused Pheroras of spreading slander, an accusation which causes Pheroras (out of fear) to blame Salome. Salome naturally objects, claiming that Pheroras' accusations are typical of those who wish to remove Salome from the king's side because she cares about the king and has always προγινώσκουσα τοὺς κινδύνους ("προγινώσκουσα the perils [which threatened you]"). Simple foreknowledge seems to make sense here.[31]

Next, in *Ant.* 18.218, Tiberius, who was apparently quite obsessed with all sorts of soothsaying and divination (see 18.217), is distressed that he must now die while possessing full knowledge (the participle προεγνωκὼς) of the future calamity that would befall those close to him (i.e., dying in ignorance of future events would have been preferable). Simple foreknowledge seems to be the natural meaning here.

Josephus' *The Jewish War* contains six total occurrences of the verb. The first occurrence, in *J.W.* 1.55, is a simple description of a youth knowing ahead of time the plot to kill John Hyrcanus and hurrying to inform the city—Προγνοὺς δὲ τὴν ἔφοδον ὁ νεανίσκος παραγενέσθαι εἰς τὴν πόλιν

31. After this particular text, the *TLG* search engine next lists *Antiquities* 18.201. This, however, is the dative noun προγνώσει which has already been covered in this study. *TLG*'s search engine has made a mistake (perhaps assuming it was the present active indicative third singular verb), and the *Accordance* search engine does not list this text as containing the verb προγινώσκω. This writers' examination of the text confirms that the verb does not exist in this verse (occasionally *TLG* seems to confuse a noun form with a verb form; another example of this in *TLG* is the listing of Acts 2:23 among the texts which contain the verb προγινώσκω).

ἠπείγετο, . . . ("But the young man, προγνοὺς the approach [of the enemy], hurried to come into the city, . . ."). Simple knowledge of a future event seems the most likely meaning here.

Next, in *J.W.* 1.608, Herod is anticipating the return of Antipater (his enemy, but also son) from Rome but fears lest Antipater προγνοὺς what is in store for him. Consequently, Herod proceeds with his plotting against Antipater. Here knowledge of potential future circumstances seems to be in view; Herod is worried that Antipater might foresee his plans against him.

In *J.W.* 2.159, Josephus is describing the Essenes and discusses how some among them, through various methods, seek τὰ μέλλοντα προγινώσκειν; this would appear to be a strictly mantic sense concerning the foreknowledge of future events.

In *J.W.* 3.484, Roman general Titus is orating an inspirational speech to rally his men to fight the Jews. In the process, he declares, καὶ προγινώσκετε σαφῶς, ὅτι τῆς ἔξω μάχης πλέον τι κατορθώσομεν." H. J. Thackery, on the one hand, renders it in the following manner in his LCL translation: "and be assured that, beyond mere victory in this battle outside the walls, we shall achieve some further success" (LCL). On the other hand, William Whiston renders it thus: "Know this also before we begin, that we shall now have better success than we should have, if we were to fight at a distance" (*Accordance*). This writer's own translation would read as follows: ". . . and plainly know ahead of time that we shall accomplish a certain great deed outside of the main battle."[32] Regardless, the sense of simple foreknowledge fits best.

In *J.W.* 4.220-236, John has manipulated the Zealot leaders Eleazar and Simon into enlisting the help of the Idumeans against Ananus. In *J.W.* 4.236, with the Idumean army approaching Jerusalem, Ananus (despite his ignorance of the messages sent out to the Idumeans) is able to get the gates closed in time due to his knowledge of their coming (προγνοὺς γὰρ ἀπέκλειέ τε τὰς πύλας αὐτοῖς). Here simple foreknowledge is clearly in view.

In *J.W.* 6, Josephus has begun describing the desolation of Jerusalem as the Roman assault nears its final hours. In lamenting the horrible destruction of the city, he declares that nobody who had seen the city in its previous glory would have been able to recognize it now. Oddly enough, at this point Josephus seems to use προγινώσκω (as a perfect participle) to describe the act of having previously known something that has now changed.

---

32. The verb κατορθόω is used elsewhere by Josephus to mean "perform a great deed/achieve success," as in *Ant.* 6.81 and 12.312; the noun μάχη would be in reference to the coming main battle, since Titus here was only embarking on a relatively minor skirmish with a small cavalry force (albeit against a larger force; see earlier in *J.W.* 3.470).

Hence, he states in 6.8, καὶ οὐκ ἄν τις ἐξαπίνης ἐπιστὰς τῶν προεγνωκότων ἐγνώρισε τὸν τόπον" ("and there is nobody who, having προεγνωκότων it and now suddenly happening upon it, would know the place"). While simple knowledge is in view, it is not truly "foreknowledge" as understood in English, but rather the concept of "knowledge in a previous time of something that has changed in the present." Thus the verb (as a perfect participle) could be translated as "having known" rather than "having foreknown."

In *Against Apion* 1.200–204, Josephus narrates the rather amusing tale of a Jewish archer in Alexander the Great's army. When confronted with a seer who told them that the actions of the army should depend upon whether a certain bird stood in place, flew forward, or flew in the opposite direction, the Jewish archer promptly shoots the bird, killing it. When faced with the wrath of the seer and others, the Jew objects that it would be foolish to rely on such a bird for information on what the army should do when the bird itself was incapable of knowing its own future. Indeed, εἰ γὰρ ἠδύνατο προγιγνώσκειν τὸ μέλλον, εἰς τὸν τόπον τοῦτον οὐκ ἂν ἦλθε φοβούμενος" ("for if it [the bird] were able προγιγνώσκειν what was about to happen, it would not have come to this place, being afraid"). A sense of simple knowledge of future events makes the most sense in this text.

Later, in *Ag. Ap.* 1.256, Josephus discusses a supposedly wise prophet (σοφὸς ἦν ὁ μάντις) whom a particular Egyptian king had hoped to utilize in a quest to behold the gods. Regarding this prophet, Josephus asks, Καὶ πῶς οὐ προέγνω τὸ ἀδύνατον αὐτοῦ τῆς ἐπιθυμίας; ("And [if he was so wise] how did he not προέγνω the impossibility of his [the king's] desire?"). Clearly simple knowledge (or lack thereof) is in view here.

Finally, in *The Life* 103–106, Josephus describes his interactions with the city of Sepphoris during his time as a Jewish military leader. In 105, he describes how the inhabitants hired out a certain man to ambush Josephus and his band of men. In 106, Josephus states that his band was ἀνετοίμοις καὶ μηδὲν προγινώσκουσιν" ("[they were] unprepared, and προγινώσκουσιν nothing"), clearly indicating that he and his men were clueless as to the villain's intentions.[33] A prescient sense for προγινώσκω seems to be warranted.

Philo

A single occurrence of προγινώσκω can be found in Philo, *On Dreams* 1.2. Here Philo is discussing those particular types of dreams which, under divine

---

33. In light of the context, it is difficult to understand why Josephus uses the third plural form προγινώσκουσιν instead of the first plural form.

influence, render the individual capable προλαμβάνειν καὶ προγινώσκειν τι τῶν μελλόντων ("to receive and προγινώσκειν what is about to happen"). Clearly Philo has a mantic sense in mind, especially since in the very next verse Philo describes how God revealed the future to Isaac via the famous dream of the ladder.

Plutarch

The verb προγινώσκω occurs eleven times in Plutarch's writings (five times in his *Lives*, four times in *Moralia*, and twice in the fragments). First, in his *Comparison of Pericles and Fabius Maximus* 2.3, Plutarch is discussing how an effective general is able to accurately predict the future (as far as issues of strategy are concerned). He states that Pericles προέγνω how the Athenian war would end. The verb here is parallel to Plutarch's broad statement regarding generals a few lines up, namely that they are able τεκμαίρεσθαι περὶ τοῦ μέλλοντος ὀρθῶς τὸν ἀγαθὸν στρατηγόν" or "to correctly judge a good strategy concerning the things that will come to pass." A good general, then, possesses a certain degree of predictive power regarding military events.

Next, in *Alcibiades* 24.4, the Spartans and Agis have conspired against Alcibiades to kill him. Alcibiades, however, gets wind of their plot and thus is able to avoid what is in store for him. Plutarch uses ἡσυχῇ προγνοὺς to indicate that the protagonist quietly finds out the plot against him. Although the word refers to finding out about somebody's intents, it still means "knowing about something ahead of time" (since, technically, it is the enemies' plans for the protagonist's future that are being discussed).

In *Sulla* 37.1, Plutarch states simply, Ὁ δὲ Σύλλας οὐ μόνον προέγνω τὴν ἑαυτοῦ τελευτήν, ἀλλὰ τρόπον τινὰ καὶ γέγραφε περὶ αὐτῆς ("But Sulla not only [προέγνω] his own death, but in a certain manner he had also written about it"). Clearly, then, prescient knowledge of Sulla's (own) death is in view.

Next, Plutarch uses the verb twice in *Dion* 21.8. Here Dionysius' sister Theste is being rebuked by Dionysius for not telling him about her husband Polyxenus' escape (Polyxenus had become Dionysius' enemy). Theste, however, stands up to her brother and tells him that had she known ahead of time (προγνοῦσα) about her husband's escape, she would have joined her husband. Nevertheless, she claims, she had no such indication of his escape (ἀλλ᾽οὐ προέγνων'). The word seems to mean simple knowledge of future events in both cases.

The Semantic Range of Πρόγνωσις and Προγινώσκω 117

In *Bravery of Women* 255.C (alternative numbering 18), Plutarch tells us how Lampsace, the daughter of king Mandron, rescues some Greek colonists who had benefited from her father's generosity but had instigated jealousy among the surrounding people. Lampsace had learned that her people, in the absence of her father, were planning on harming the Greeks. Showing compassion, she warns them of their danger. Plutarch uses the expression τὴν ἐπιβουλὴν προέγνω to describe how the girl gains knowledge of the plot (note the similarity in usage to *Alcibiades* 24.4).

Next, in *The Obsolescence of Oracles* 431.E (39), Lamprius is dialoging with Ammonius regarding the nature and relationship of disembodied souls, foreknowledge, and "daemons" (οἱ δαίμονες, not to be confused with the Christian concept of "demons," though the Greek word is the same). Here Ammonius seems to describe daemons as possessing the ability to foreknow future events, for he states, ᾗ τὰ μέλλοντα καὶ προγιγνώσκειν πεφύκασι καὶ προδηλοῦν οἱ δαίμονες; . . ." ("by which also have not the daemons naturally developed [the ability] προγιγνώσκειν beforehand the future [τὰ μέλλοντα]?").[34]

In *On Being a Busybody* 519.F (10), Plutarch provides his audience with the optimal way to appropriately deal with a "busybody." He states, Διὸ καὶ χρήσιμον ὡς ἔνι μάλιστα πρὸς τὴν ἀποτροπὴν τοῖς πολυπράγμοσιν ἡ τῶν προεγνωσμένων ἀνάμνησις ("Therefore, what is especially profitable for the discouragement of the busybody is the [busybody's] remembrance τῶν προεγνωσμένων"). The usage here is somewhat difficult; in what way does one "remember what was foreknown"? The context, especially the following paragraphs, seems to indicate that what is in view here is the fact that busybodies, through their own obsessive inquisitiveness, manage to compile a record of the vices of others. Were they to give heed to what they have learned through their inquiring into matters (more or less the meaning of προγινώσκω here), they would understand enough to staunch the tide of their vice, "busybody-ness." Thus while knowledge and comprehension is in view here, it is not so much *prescient* knowledge as remembrance of what one has learned.

Plutarch's *On the Delays of the Divine Vengeance* is essentially an apologetic of sorts for the perceived slowness of divine justice. In a surprising parallel to Dante's *Inferno*, much of Plutarch's *Divine Vengeance* deals with the journey of a certain Thespesius (complete with a guide) to view the punishments of the wicked. In 567.D (31), the reader is given a description of the

---

34. The word translated "beforehand" is προδηλοῦν; this word could potentially be translated as "clearly" instead of "beforehand" in this context (thus avoiding a possible redundancy).

punishment of certain souls who, even when they try to flee (φεύγειν) their punishment, are brought back for more and consequently ὀλοφυρομένας τῷ προγινώσκειν τὴν τιμωρίαν ("were bewailing τῷ προγινώσκειν the vengeance [awaiting them]." Here the articular infinitive of προγινώσκω points to their knowledge of future torment.

Finally, we have two occurrences of the verb προγινώσκω in Plutarch's *Fragments* (in LCL, this is the section entitled *Other Fragments*). *Fragments* 216c consists of a difficult paragraph discussing the "nature" (τὸ πεφυκέναι, perfect infinitive of φύω) of things. This writer is incapable of improving on F. H. Sandbach's translation here, so Sandbach's rendering will be reproduced in full. It reads,

> That to say "that's its nature [πεφυκέναι]" is a clumsy amateurish phrase, which will serve as a reply to anything. It does not avoid the necessity of inquiring what sort of a thing this "nature" [τὸ πεφυκέναι] is. The nature of one thing differs from that of another; thus the nature of the rational soul is to recognize what is before it [τὰ παρόντα] from what was previously known [τῶν προεγνωσμένων].

The similarity between *Fragments* 216c and *Busybody* 519.F is striking. In both cases προγινώσκω has only a slight resemblance to the common prescient usage and seems to signify the act of having found out or known something in the past..

The final occurrence in *Fragments* 217a is also similar to 216c and *Busybody* 519.F. Plutarch is describing a Platonic argument (τὸ ἐπιχείρημα Πλατωνικόν) regarding the nature of learning. This particular argument is simply that the act of distinguishing one thing from another (Εἰ ἀφ'ἑτέρου ἕτερον ἐννοοῦμεν) is only possible if something had already been previously known (Οὐκ ἂν εἰ μὴ προέγνωστο; one could probably translate this as "If it had not been discovered previously"). For the third time in Plutarch one can see the use of προγινώσκω to refer to the act (in the past) of uncovering knowledge about something.

Other Texts

In *De signis Iliadis* (*The Book of Iliad*) 23.857, Aristonicus of Alexandria (a literary critic of Homer) states, "Ὅς δέ κε μηρίνθοιο τύχῃ ὄρνιθος ἁμαρτών: ἡ διπλῆ ὅτι βέλτιον ἦν τοῦτο μὴ προλέγεσθαι ὑπὸ Ἀχιλλέως, ὥσπερ προγινώσκοντος τὸ ἀπὸ τύχης συμβησόμενον.[35] The second half of this cita-

---

35. For more information on Aristonicus of Alexandria, see Schmitz, "Aristonicus," 1:312.

tion, following ἡ διπλῆ (a grammarian's notation, possibly textual), may be translated as follows: "It was a noble thing for Achilles not to speak of this ahead of time [*literally*, "not to be spoken ahead of time by Achilles"], even as [he] προγινώσκοντος that which would come about by chance." Clearly this passage refers to simple foreknowledge, since the expression ἀπὸ τύχης would make no sense if describing what Achilles "foreordained" (or "loved beforehand"). The astrologer Dorotheus' *Fragmenta Graeca*, like other astrological texts, discusses the moon (σελήνη), the stars (plural ἀστέρες), and other astrologically significant bodies, entities, and concepts (and, in this immediate context, the origin of diseases: καταρχόμεναι νόσοι).[36] In *Fragmenta* 424.6, he declares, Ταῦτα οὖν σκοπῶν οὐ μόνον τὴν ἡμέραν τῆς εὐφορίας ἢ δυσφορίας προγνώσῃ, ἀλλὰ καὶ τὴν ὥραν ("Therefore these observers προγνώσῃ not only the day of goodness or misery but also the hour"). As with other astrological texts, the use of προγνώσῃ seems fairly straightforward. A mantic sense seems reasonable within the context of astrology and astrological prophecy (the possibility of "fate" playing a role cannot be totally discarded, however; nonetheless, this writer could not find that in the context).

Next, we find the verb προγινώσκω in *Vocum Hippocraticarum collectio* 109 of the grammarian Erotianus. Unlike the previously examined usage of the noun form in Erotianus, however, this occurrence of the verb seems to occur in a list of Hippocratic words and definitions. Unfortunately, the verb occurs in the section defining the word rather than as the word actually being defined. Thus we have Erotianus defining the word προβουλεύοντες as προγιγνώσκοντες καὶ προφυλαττόμενοι. For the word being defined, Erotianus gives us the participle (nominative plural) form of the verb προβολλεύω (alternative spelling: προβολεύω). In Liddell and Scott's *Greek-English Lexicon*, this word occurs underneath προβουλεία and is defined as "[to] *contrive* or *concert measures before*" or "*debate, consider first*"; similarly, they define πρόβουλος as "*deliberating beforehand*" or, in the plural, a "*standing committee to examine measures* before they were formally proposed to the people."[37] Erotianus, then, defines this with the following two combined nominative plural participles: προγιγνώσκοντες (a perfect participle) linked with προφυλαττόμενοι (a present participle). The exact form of the latter term (lexical προφυλάσσω) occurs in Philo, *Spec. Laws* 3.103, where it seems

---

36. For more information on Dorotheus, see Holden, *History of Horoscopic Astrology*, 33–34.

37. See Liddell and Scott, "προβολλεύω" and "πρόβουλος," *Greek-English Lexicon*, 1472 (emphasis original).

to mean something along the lines of "being careful [to do or not to do something]," or, perhaps, "the act of preparing beforehand."[38]

Quite possibly, then, in this usage by Erotianus, the verb προγινώσκω refers to somebody or thing taking action and not just simply knowing beforehand, though it is difficult to determine for sure. Indeed, προβολεύω, in Liddell and Scott's definition, does refer to the act of planning out something. With a deity as subject, the verb might refer to divine foreordination. Thus a verb that could very well mean "foreordain" is being defined in terms of προγινώσκω and another verb that seems to mean "planning ahead of time" or "taking heed (to do or not to do something)." One could potentially translate Erotianus' definition in the following manner: "προβουλεύοντες—the act of taking council and planning ahead of time." On the other hand, it would also make sense for the same word to be defined as "the act of knowing ahead of time and (consequently) making plans." Several other options would be as follows: 1. "προβουλεύοντες—the act of foreknowing and foreplanning," 2. "προβουλεύοντες—the act of deliberating and planning ahead of time," or 3. "προβουλεύοντες—the act of debating and planning ahead." In some of these cases the verb προγινώσκω would clearly go beyond a mere prescient meaning. Ultimately, coming to a lexical decision on προβολεύω is beyond the scope of this study, but at the least this writer will acknowledge that here is an example where προγινώσκω *may* mean "foreplanning" rather than simply "foreknowing."

In Longinus' work of literary criticism, *De sublimitate* 9.12, in a context dealing with a comparison of the Iliad and the Odyssey, he writes the following sentence:

> Δῆλος γὰρ ἐκ πολλῶν τε ἄλλων συντεθεικὼς ταύτην δευτέραν τὴν ὑπόθεσιν, ἀτὰρ δὴ κὰκ τοῦ λείψανα τῶν Ἰλιακῶν παθημάτων διὰ τῆς Ὀδυσσείας ὡς ἐπεισόδιά τινα [τοῦ Τρωικοῦ πολέμου] προσεπεισφέρειν, καὶ νὴ Δί' ἐκ τοῦ τὰς ὀλοφύρσεις καὶ τοὺς οἴκτους ὡς πάλαι που προεγνωσμένοις τοῖς ἥρωσιν ἐνταῦθα προσαποδιδόναι.

A rough translation is as follows:

> For it is evident from many parts that he [Homer] had put together this narrative secondly [i.e., as a sequel to the *Iliad*], especially [demonstrated by] the contribution of the remnants of the suffering of Troy ["Iliakos"] throughout the Odyssey as episodes

---

38. In this occurrence in Philo, the term is used to describe how one naturally guards against any harm that can befall from snakes. C. D. Yonge translates the term here as "taking care" within the expression "taking care not to expose ourselves to any injury from them . . ."

of the Trojan War, and yes, by Zeus, [as demonstrated by] the homage of sorrow and pity paid to the heroes, as προεγνωσμένοις at that ancient time.³⁹

Interestingly, both H. L. Havell and W. Rhys Roberts, in their own translations, render this participle of προγινώσκω in a more determinative sense ("in fulfillment of some previous design" and "as though he were carrying out a long-cherished purpose," respectively).⁴⁰ Yet both Havell and Roberts seem to be assuming that προεγνωσμένοις refers to Homer, which would be odd indeed since the participle is plural, not singular (and even if it did refer to Homer, it is not at all clear that a determinative sense would be the best fit). Contra Havell and Roberts, the most logical subject for the participle is the dative "heroes" (τοῖς ἥρωσιν). The most likely *reference* of προεγνωσμένοις, in this writer's opinion, would be the sorrow and suffering the heroes faced, that which they had to look forward to. In other words, Longinus is speaking of the heroes experiencing ("knowing," in a sense) suffering and anguish. At the very least, a determinative sense seems unlikely, though the fact that two separate translators take it as such should at least be taken into account. For now, this usage in Longinus will be classified as "unsure."

Next, the Stoic Epictetus, in *Dissertationes ab Arriano digestae* 2.10.6, declares, Νῦν δ' ὅτι οὐ προγιγνώσκομεν, καθήκει τῶν πρὸς ἐκλογὴν εὐφυεστέρων ἔχεσθαι, ὅτι καὶ πρὸς τοῦτο γεγόναμεν ("But now that we have not προγιγνώσκομεν, it is proper to make well-formed [*i.e.*, "clever"] choices, because we were made for this purpose").⁴¹ The context deals with the duty of a citizen (πολίτου—see the preceding sentence) and the need to make wise choices. Indeed, the verb προγιγνώσκομεν here seems to be used synonymously, or at least parallel to, the verb προῄδει a few lines back. Epictetus' overall point, in proper Stoic fashion, is that a citizen should hold the state and the "whole" (ὅλον) as more important than the "parts" (μέρους; i.e., the individuals), and that if one did happen to know the future (προῄδει), he or she should still cooperate with whatever fate had decreed, even to his or her own death (see 2.10.5–6). Since humans do not possess foreknowledge, however, one must simply make the best choices that one can. Here the

---

39. As noted above, it is not completely clear when Longinus wrote this.

40. Their respective translations can be found at http://www.gutenberg.org/files/17957/17957-h/17957-h.htm; and http://classicpersuasion.org/pw/longinus/desub002.htm.

41. For more information on Epictetus, see Christian A. Brandis, "Epictetus," 2:31–33. Although the above translation is this writer's own, an alternative translation is available at Epictetus, "*The Discourses*," n.p. Online: http://classics.mit.edu/Epictetus/discourses.2.two.html (translator unknown).

verb προγιγνώσκομεν clearly refers to simple foreknowledge with no sense of foreordination.

Finally, we have two difficult occurrences in the Greek physician Rufus of Ephesus' *Quaestiones medicinales* (as mentioned earlier, Rufus probably wrote during the very last years of the first century AD and the first two decades of the second). In 20-21, we have the following statement:

> Καὶ τὰ συνήθη πάντα ἀμείνω καὶ τῷ νοσοῦντι καὶ ὑγιαίνοντι. Καὶ προγνωσθείη δ' ἄν τι ἀκριβέστερον ἐκ τῶν ἐθισμῶν περί τε κρίσιν [καὶ κλίσιν] τοῦ ἀνθρώπου καὶ διάλεξιν καὶ ῥαθυμίαν καὶ ἡντιναοῦν ἄλλην ἐνέργειαν· τὰ γὰρ ὑγιαίν <οντι> ὄντα δι' ἔθους οὐδὲν ἐν ταῖς νόσοις ἐπίσημον δηλοῖ.

This paragraph uses some technical medical terminology (e.g., περί τε κρίσιν = "concerning the turning point" [i.e., a "sudden change" in the state of the illness or the condition of the sick person]).[42] A few lines down, in *Quaestiones medicinales* 21, we have the statement, ἀρκεῖν γὰρ καὶ τὰ ἐφ' ἑκάστῳ σημεῖα τό τε πάθος σημῆναι καὶ τὴν αἰτίαν αὐτοῦ, ἐξ ὧν καὶ προγινώσκεσθαι πάντα καὶ θεραπεύεσθαι ἄμεινον ("For the symptoms for each [are] also to be sufficient, and the suffering and its cause to be pointed out, from which also everything [is] to be προγινώσκεσθαι and to be better healed"). In both uses by Rufus, it is quite possible that προγινώσκω has taken on a technical sense of "diagnosis," a sense that most likely would not appear anywhere else. The sense of "foreordained" or "loved ahead of time" would not make much sense, but neither would simple foreknowledge. It is perhaps significant that by the second century AD, προγινώσκω is used quite frequently by the physician Galenus.

The New Testament

Finally, the verb προγινώσκω occurs four times in the NT outside of 1 Peter 1:20. Two of those occurrences are technically "non-theological." Sadly, these are often neglected by contemporary discussions of the term, yet this writer has already argued that they are relevant to understanding how the verb is used.

First, in Acts 26:5, the Apostle Paul is in the process of making his defense towards Agrippa. In this text he claims that the Jews προγινώσκοντές με ἄνωθεν, ἐὰν θέλωσι μαρτυρεῖν, ὅτι κατὰ τὴν ἀκριβεστάτην αἵρεσιν τῆς ἡμετέρας θρησκείας ἔζησα Φαρισαῖος ("[who] προγινώσκοντές me before, if they so desire to testify, that I lived [as] a Pharisee according to the strict

---

42. See Liddell and Scott, "Κρίσις," 997.

sect of our religion"; this writer's translation). Clearly simple knowledge is in view, yet the verb is not being used in the normal sense of prescience. Rather, its usage is similar to Plutarch's *On Being a Busybody* 519.F in that the focus is on past knowledge in reference to something in the present (which would be future to when the subject(s) had acquired that knowledge). Regardless, the point is that the Jews now currently know something about Paul from the past, namely that he lived as a Pharisee.

The significance of this usage lies not in its meaning, however, but in the accusative με that follows. Some writers argue that when foreknowledge points to people (as opposed to events), a prescient sense would be nonsensical, for one does not foreknow "people" (see below for this argument). Yet here is a clear case where a *person* is the direct object of προγινώσκω, yet nevertheless *knowledge*, not foreordination or relationship, is meant. Context then extrapolates what exactly is foreknown in the expression "[who] are foreknowing me." The point is this: the verb προγινώσκω can clearly have one or more persons as its direct object and still refer to knowledge instead of foreordination or relationship. The burden of proof, then, is on those who would attempt to posit anything other than simple prescient knowledge for this word.

With that in mind, one may proceed to the two theologically charged texts in Romans. First of all, in Rom 8:28–30, we have Paul's famous description of divine love. All things work towards good for those who love God and are called; these are the ones that God has προέγνω, προώρισεν, ἐκάλεσεν, etc. On the one hand, a divine relationship with believers is certainly implied by the context, and foreordination of some kind is demanded by the second verb. Many then claim one or the other as the meaning of προγινώσκω here.[43] Nevertheless, it is unnecessary to claim that a prescient meaning is impossible for προγινώσκω in this context.

Some scholars, however, argue that since people are the object of προγινώσκω here, a mantic sense is unlikely. Douglas Moo, for example, states,

> That the verb here contains this peculiarly biblical sense of "know" [i.e., "enter into relationship with before" or "choose or

---

43. For the latter, see Wilckens, *Der Brief an die Römer*, 163. Moo, *Epistle to the Romans*, 533, seems to argue for both senses ("the difference between 'know or love beforehand' and 'choose beforehand' virtually ceases to exist"). Morris, *Epistle to the Romans*, 332, wisely suggests that scholars "must also remember that Paul's next verb is *predestined* and we must be on our guard against making the two say the same thing." Morris, however, still suggests a sense of "chose beforehand" (332). Olson, "Lexical Study," 4, makes a similar observation as Morris regarding the odd redundancy of making προγινώσκω synonymous with προορίζω.

determine before"] is suggested by the fact that it has a simple personal object. Paul does not say that God knew anything *about* us but that he knew *us*, and this is reminiscent of the OT sense of "know."[44]

Yet as we have just seen in Acts 26:5, it is entirely possible for προγινώσκω to have a person (or people) as its object without losing its sense of "knowing something (about someone) ahead of time." Furthermore, taking the verb in such a way would in no way lessen the overall sense of both divine determination and intimate relationship prevalent in the text; these concepts hardly need the verb προγινώσκω to be made obvious to the reader.

The theological *reference* (as opposed to the lexical sense) of προγινώσκω in this context is beyond the scope of this paper to discuss thoroughly, though possibilities might include God's foreseen purpose for his people (thus denying neither the prescient sense nor the emphasis on divine appointment in the context) or the Arminian view of foreseen faith (certainly a controversial view, and one that this study will neither attempt to prove nor disprove). Regardless, there are many ways in which the meaning "knowing ahead of time" would make sense in the context.[45]

Next, in Rom 11:2 we have the declaration that God has not cast aside his people whom he προέγνω. Thomas Schreiner argues that the participle "functions as the antonym to ἀπώσατο."[46] Yet simply because two words are contrasted does not automatically make them antonyms.[47] In this text, the verb could just as easily be pointing out that God has not rejected his people *despite* knowing ahead of time all their flaws.[48] This would fit well with the context, which focuses on Israel's multiple failures. Indeed, even Schreiner notes that the OT context of Paul's discussion (e.g., 1 Samuel 12 and Psalm 94) points to the fact that God will not reject his people *despite* their sin.[49] In other words, God fully knows of Israel's failings (such as idolatry, v. 3), yet nevertheless refuses to reject them. In this way the sense of simple foreknowledge fits well with the context of

---

44. Moo, *Epistle to the Romans*, 532–33.

45. For an Arminian perspective on this and other passages, see McCall and Stanglin, "S. M. Baugh and the Meaning of Foreknowledge: Another Look," 30–31. Significantly, though, McCall and Stanglin do not take issue with Baugh's word study, only with the theological significance of the terminology (see p. 22).

46. Schreiner, *Romans*, 452, 580.

47. One could, for example, contrast baseball with football, yet nobody would argue that those words are antonyms.

48. Olson, "Lexical Study," 4, argues this same point, though I arrived at this conclusion independently.

49. Schreiner, *Romans*, 579–80; see Rom 11:3 regarding Israel's sin.

Romans 11. James argues, "Certainly if this means only a mere prevision here, then in view of their unfaithfulness this would be reason for God to discontinue His promises—not to continue them."[50] *Yet this is precisely the point*! God had every reason to forsake Israel due to his foreknowledge of their consistent sin, yet mercifully he does not. Despite their continued sin, God still reserves a remnant (Rom 11:3–15).

Finally, we have another non-theological usage in 2 Pet 3:17. Here the author urges his audience that, προγινώσκοντες [the content of the previous verses], they should now be wary lest they be led astray. Clearly προγινώσκω entails prescient knowledge, yet it is knowledge that is meant to give those who possess it a spiritual advantage.

ANALYSIS OF THE EVIDENCE

The usage of πρόγνωσις and προγινώσκω from AD 1–100 and in the LXX breaks down as follows:

Table 4.1: Occurrences of the Noun

Text (πρόγνωσις)	Proposed Meaning
LXX Jdt 9:6	Unsure: *either* "knowledge of the future" *or* "determination of the future"
Jdt 11:19	"knowledge of future events (or an event)"
Josephus *Ant.* 8.234	"knowledge of future events (or an event)"
Ant. 8.418	"knowledge of future events (or an event)"
Ant. 13.300	"knowledge of future events (or an event)"
Ant. 15.373	"knowledge of future events (or an event)"
Ant. 17.43	"knowledge of future events (or an event)"
Ant. 18.201	"knowledge of future events (or an event)"
Ag. Ap. 1.256	"knowledge of future events (or an event)"

---

50. James, "Is Foreknowledge Equivalent to Foreordination?" 219.

Text (πρόγνωσις)	Proposed Meaning
Clement 1 Clem. 44.2	"knowledge of future events (or an event)"
Plutarch The 'E' at Delphi 386.D	"knowledge of future events (or an event)"
The Oracles at Delphi 339.D	"knowledge of future events (or an event)"
Animals 979.A	"knowledge of the future (meteorological patterns)"
Animals 979.E	"knowledge of the future (phases of the sun)"
Animals 982.C	"knowledge of the future (patterns of the Nile)"
Fragments (Title)	"knowledge of future events (or an event)"
Fragments 21 (subtitle)	"knowledge of future events (or an event)"
Fragments 22 (subtitle)	"knowledge of future events (or an event)"
Fragments 23 (subtitle)	"knowledge of future events (or an event)"
Antiochus Fragmenta (e cod. Napolitano) 4.154	"knowledge of future events (or an event)"
Fragmenta (e cod. Paris) 8.3.108	"knowledge of future events (or an event)"
Fragmenta (e cod. Paris) 8.3.119	unsure, but possibly "knowledge of future events (or an event)"
Erotianus Fragmenta 33	unsure, but possibly "knowledge of the future events" or a more technical, medical sense
Balbillus Fragmenta 8.104	"knowledge of future events (or an event)"
NT Acts 2:23	"knowledge of future events (or an event)"

As seen above, a total of 22 occurrences of the noun clearly point to simple knowledge of the future. One usage (Jdt 9:6) is ambiguous with at least two meanings that would fit. Finally, two occurrences (one of Antiochus' fragments and Erotianus' *Fragmenta* 33) are too difficult to determine conclusively (though they seem to indicate some sort of knowledge of future

The Semantic Range of Πρόγνωσις and Προγινώσκω

events). Thus the breakdown is as follows: twenty-two occurrences clearly refer to knowledge of future events (88 percent), one occurrence could be either prescient or determinative (4 percent), and two occurrences are too difficult to determine conclusively (8 percent). Clearly the overwhelming use of the noun points to simple foreknowledge (and it is quite possible that 100 percent of the occurrences actually do so). While this does not *require* such a meaning in 1 Pet 1:2, it makes it more likely (in the absence of clear contextual clues indicating otherwise).

Table 4.2: Occurrences of the Verb

Text (προγινώσκω)	Proposed Meaning
LXX Wis 6:13	"to intimately know somebody in the future"
Wis 8:8	"to know future events (or an event)"
Wis 18.6	"to know future events (or an event)"
Josephus *Ant.* 1.311	"to know future events (or an event)"
Ant. 2.86	"to know future events (or an event)"
Ant. 4.121	"to foretell future events as blessing or curse"
Ant. 5.358	"to know future events (or an event)"
Ant. 6.54	"to know future events (or an event)"
Ant. 6.348	"to know future events (or an event)"
Ant. 7.57	"to know future events (or an event)"
Ant. 8.418	"to know future events (or an event)"
Ant. 13.175	"to know future events (or an event)"
Ant. 16.214	"to know future events (or an event)"
Ant. 18.218	"to know future events (or an event)"
J.W. 1.55	"to know future events (or an event)"
J.W. 1.608	"to know future events (or an event)"
J.W. 2.159	"to know future events (or an event)"
J.W. 3.484	"to know future events (or an event)"
J.W. 4.236	"to know future events (or an event)"
J.W. 6.8	"to have known in a previous time something that has changed in the present"

Text (προγινώσκω)	Proposed Meaning
Ag. Ap. 1.204	"to know future events (or an event)"
Ag. Ap. 1.256	"to know future events (or an event)"
Life 106	"to know future events (or an event)"
Philo Dreams 1.2	"to know future events (or an event)"
Plutarch Comparison of Pericles and Fabius Maximus 2.3	"to know future events (or an event)"
Alcibiades 24.4	"to know somebody's plans for the future"
Sulla 37.1	"to know future events (or an event)"
Dion 21.8	"to know future events (or an event)"
Bravery of Women 255.C	"to know somebody's plans for the future"
Obsolescence 431.E	"to know future events (or an event)"
Busybody 519.F	"to have previously discovered knowledge (regarding patterns of human conduct)"
Divine Vengeance 567.D	"to know future events (or an event)"
Fragments 216c	"to have previously discovered something"
Fragments 217a	"to have previously discovered something"
Aristonicus Iliadis 23.857	"to know future events (or an event)"
Dorotheus Fragmenta Graeca 424.6	"to know future events (or an event)"
Erotianus Vocum Hippocraticarum collectio 109	unsure, but possibly either "to plan ahead of time" or "to take council about future events"
Longinus De sublimitate 9.12	"to experience"
Epictetus Dissertationes ab Arriano digestae 2.10.6	"to know future events (or an event)"
Rufus Quaestiones medicinales 20	unsure, possibly used in a technical, medical sense ("to diagnose")
Quaestiones medicinales 21	unsure, possibly used in a technical, medical sense ("to diagnose")
NT Acts 26:5	"to have previously discovered knowledge (regarding a particular person's conduct)"

Text (προγινώσκω)	Proposed Meaning
Rom 8:28	unsure: *either* "to know future events or an event" *or* "to choose ahead of time"
Rom 11:2	unsure: *either* "to know future events or an event," *or* "to choose ahead of time," *or* "to possess an intimate relationship with"
2 Pet 3:17	"to know future events or an event"

The use of the verb προγινώσκω is much more varied than its noun cognate. Once again, however, knowledge of future events is the predominant sense. Of forty-five total occurrences, thirty clearly refer to simple knowledge of the future. This accounts for 66.7 percent of the data. We also see, however, a grouping of occurrences (five) that seems to mean something along the lines of "knowledge in the past that is somehow applicable to the present" (J.W. 6.8; *Moralia: Busybody* 519.F; Plutarch's *Fragments* 216c and 217a; and Acts 26:5). This accounts for 11.1 percent of the data. Romans 8:28 and 11:2, the single occurrence in Erotianus' *Vocum Hippocraticarum collectio*, the occurrence in Longinus' *De sublimitate*, and the two occurrences in Rufus' medical work will all be classified as "unsure" since either there is controversy involved or various meanings would equally make sense (13.3 percent). Two occurrences in Plutarch (*Alcibiades* and *Sulla*) seem to mean "to know somebody's plans for the future," which must be distinguished from the normal usage since here it is *potential* events of the future that are in view (4.4 percent). Josephus' use in *Ant.* 4.121 seems to be unique in that it involves "foretelling" as part of a blessing or curse (2.2 percent). Finally, one occurrence in the LXX (Wis 6:13) does indeed seem to indicate a personal relationship with somebody (2.2 percent).

Three key observations may be drawn from this data. First, in neither group of texts do we see any *clear* instance of πρόγνωσις or προγινώσκω ever meaning "foreordination," "choosing ahead of time," or anything related to this broad concept, though in a few instances it *may* mean that (Longinus' *De sublimitate* being the most likely candidate). This, then, raises the question of whether or not a biblical author would have invented a new meaning for either word. Had he done so, would this not have confused his readers, especially if another meaning would have made sense in the context? In other words, how likely would the reader have been to have caught the writer's intended sense, if "foreordination" were meant?

Secondly, one occurrence does seem to refer to "having a relationship with" somebody (in this case, Lady Wisdom). No other meaning seems to make sense within that context, and the fact that Wisdom is personified all throughout Wisdom of Solomon allows the context to point to "having personal relationship with Wisdom" as the likely meaning. Most likely, then, the reader would not have been confused with this particular usage. It is worth pointing out, however, that this is a solitary, perhaps idiosyncratic, usage in Wisdom of Solomon that does not even parallel the other two occurrences of the verb in this book. Thus it is doubtful whether or not this particular meaning "of having a relationship with" would have occurred to the readers of the New Testament. The possibility, however, must be acknowledged, especially if other possible meanings do not make sense in a particular biblical context.

Finally, this study has demonstrated that the overwhelming use of both the noun and the verb is that of simple knowledge of future events, often (but not necessarily) tied to prophecy. This, then, should shed light on the usage in 1 Pet 1:2 and 1:20. In light of the discussion in the last chapter, it is difficult to imagine the author deliberately intending an obscure meaning when most of his audience would expect a prescient sense to the words, especially if such a "normal" usage fits well with the context. Had Peter meant "foreordination" or "having a relationship with," he most likely would have left more contextual clues than one finds in these passages (or have used different words altogether).

Having established the semantic range of πρόγνωσις and προγινώσκω in Koine Greek roughly around the time of 1 Peter, this study will now examine how the concept of "knowing something ahead of time" (which includes both of the above words) functions in three key passages in 1 Peter.

5

The Concept of Foreknowledge in Three Key Texts in First Peter (1:2; 1:10–12; and 1:20)

In the previous chapter I demonstrated that the most common, though not exclusive, sense of πρόγνωσις and προγινώσκω in this era was simple foreknowledge (prescience). Each word appears once in 1 Peter (1:2 and 1:20, respectively), but the concept of "foreknowledge" (i.e., "knowing something ahead of time") also occurs in 1:10–12. This chapter will examine those three texts and begin to demonstrate how foreknowledge functions as a word of comfort to the "elect strangers" of 1 Peter.

1 PETER 1:1-2

In its otherwise formulaic greeting, 1 Peter's introduction of the recipients as "the elect strangers of the Diaspora" is without parallel among other NT documents (though James comes the closest, addressing his letter "to the twelve tribes among the Diaspora").[1] As argued in chapter 2, this study (mostly) follows John Elliott in seeing the reference to "strangers" as a literal depiction of the situation the readers found themselves in, a description that also functions as a broader spiritual paradigm.[2] In other words, a significant

---

1. All translations of Greek and other foreign languages are this writer's own, unless otherwise noted. For a brief discussion of the similarities between 1 Peter and James in their mention of the Diaspora, see Hillyer, *1 and 2 Peter, Jude*, 26; Hort, *First Epistle of St. Peter I.1–II. 17*, 15.

2. Elliott, *I Peter*, 313–14.

131

portion of Peter's audience were literal strangers living as outsiders in Asia Minor.

Yet the reference to "the Diaspora/dispersion" is difficult to interpret. Some, by postulating a primarily Jewish audience, take the expression as mostly literal: ethnic Jews living outside their homeland.[3] Most, however, see the terms more-or-less merging both literal and metaphorical usage, referring to Christians "'scattered' among other peoples, Jewish and Gentile."[4] J. Ramsey Michaels, for example, writes,

> The genitive διασπορᾶς implies not that his readers belonged to the Jewish diaspora or were living as strangers among the dispersed Jews, but that they themselves constituted a diaspora, the only diaspora, in fact, that Peter gives evidence of knowing. He sees them not in relation to the Jews (not even as displacing the Jews in the plan of God) but (like the Jewish diaspora itself) always in relation to "the Gentiles" (cf. 2:12; 4:3).[5]

Somewhat similarly (though with a stronger emphasis on the literal sense of the term), Elliott argues that

> the term *Diaspora* here has a customary literal (geographical) rather than figurative force . . . [It] expresses simply the physically dispersed situation of the addressees in *regions beyond the traditional Israelite "Land of inheritance"* . . . *and the historical continuity of the elect strangers with the frequent condition of Israel as a vulnerable minority in foreign and hostile regions.*[6]

Regardless of whether or not the recipients of the letter are mostly Jews or a mix of Gentiles and Jews (as this writer would tentatively suggest), one can nonetheless posit a mostly literal sense where believers are truly dispersed strangers living among unbelievers in Asia Minor.[7]

Yet a more important aspect of this opening phrase must be stressed. The epistle provides, from the very beginning, a special focus on the social-spiritual status of the recipients. Indeed, the letter uses the following curious

---

3. Witherington, *Socio-Rhetorical Commentary on 1-2 Peter*, 65–66, 70; Liebengood, "'Don't Be Like Your Fathers.'"

4. Hillyer, *1 and 2 Peter, Jude*, 26.

5. Michaels, *1 Peter*, 8; cf. Kelly, *Commentary on the Epistles of Peter and of Jude*, 40.

6. Elliott, *I Peter*, 314; emphasis is Elliott's.

7. This is not to deny any type of spiritual significance. Rather, even while realizing their literal, dispersed status, the readers (to borrow Wayne Grudem's words) ". . . would conclude that Peter thought of them as having a privileged status before God at least equal to that enjoyed by the chosen people whom God protected, preserved and blessed in the Old Testament (*cf.* 1 Pet. 2:4–10)" (Grudem, *1 Peter*, 48).

The Concept of Foreknowledge in Three Key Texts in First Peter 133

expression: "elect strangers." Consequently, the letter posits a "paradox" due to the fact that the author "... places side-by-side two competing descriptions of his audience: chosen and exile (1:1).... In the intimate alignment of these two terms we find the apparent contradiction that Peter addresses throughout the letter: chosen by God, rejected by humans."[8] Thus we have what Reinhard Feldmeier argues is "the central theme of the letter," namely, "Christian existence between the election by God on the one hand and exclusion by society on the other."[9] Without a doubt, then, both the spiritual and the social status and identity of the church/community is in view, and this creates one of the major motifs of the epistle.[10] Wayne Grudem appropriately notes, "The phrase 'chosen sojourners' thus becomes a two-word sermon to Peter's readers..."[11] Yet it is to the negative aspect of their identity, their status as persecuted strangers, that the concept of foreknowledge speaks in 1 Peter.

In order to understand the role of foreknowledge in 1 Pet 1:1–2, however, the following questions must be asked and answered: first, what exactly do the prepositional phrases in 1:2 modify? Second, what is the meaning of κατὰ πρόγνωσις in verse 2? Finally, what is the broader role and significance of the three prepositional phrases within this context?

What Do the Three Prepositional Phrases Modify?

Before one can discuss the broader role of the prepositional phrases within 1 Peter's introduction, it is necessary to first determine which particular word or words they modify. So far as this writer could determine, three main positions exist: 1. they modify "apostle," 2. they modify "elect," or 3. they modify multiple words within the first verse (two variations of this latter view exist). In addition, one should also consider the possibility that they modify either "strangers" or "Diaspora" (though these possibilities

---

8. Green, "Living as Exiles," 317. Cf. Joseph, *Narratological Reading of 1 Peter*, 75–76 ("The term 'ἐκλεκτοῖς παρεπιδήμοις' creates an obvious paradox that permeates the epistle"); cf. also Elliott, *I Peter*, 315.

9. Feldmeier, *Der erste Brief des Petrus*, 34 ("... christliche Existenz zwischen Aussonderung durch Gott und Ausgrenzung durch die gesellschaft"). All translations are by this writer unless otherwise noted.

10. Indeed, Schröger, in *Gemeinde im 1. Petrusbrief*, 12, states that "a fundamental dogma for 1 Peter" is how the existence of the community/church is grounded in the initiative of God himself ("Daher ist es für den 1. Petrusbrief grundlegendes Dogma: Gottes vorauslaufende Initiative begründet die Existenz der Gemeinde"). Cf. also Michaels, *1 Peter*, 6.

11. Grudem, *1 Peter*, 48–49. Cf. Donelson, *I & II Peter and Jude*, 26.

are almost never discussed). In the end, this writer will agree with Wayne Grudem that the prepositional phrases of v. 2 modify the entire situation of the readers.

The first view, that the prepositional phrases modify "apostle," is generally considered passé by modern scholarship. Indeed, this writer could not find any scholar within the past one hundred years who argues that the prepositions modify *only* "apostle" (though a few argue that they point to both "apostle" and some other word or words).

Nearly two hundred years ago, Wilhelm Steiger listed a number of scholars who, in his words, "mistakenly held" to this position, yet Steiger himself held to the conventional view that the words modify "elect."[12] In a modern response to the idea that they modify "apostle," J. N. D. Kelly points to the distance between the two terms, the focus on the reader's "vocation," and the fact that "Peter's authority did not need propping up regardless of whether he or somebody else was the author."[13] Michaels convincingly argues that if the prepositional phrases were meant to modify "apostle of Jesus Christ," then "they would have been placed between that designation and the destination of the addressees."[14] Furthermore, "The identity of the recipients is a more central concern to the author than his own identity."[15] This view, then, can be safely dispensed with.

The vast majority of scholars view the prepositional phrases as modifying "elect." While a survey has already been given in chapter 1, a few scholars will be highlighted here. Karl Schelkle, though initially appearing to suggest that the prepositional phrases modify ἐκλεκτοῖς παρεπιδήμοις, is rather typical of those who focus on "elect" as the key word. He states, "The election is grounded in the council of God, mediated through the work of the Spirit, and has as its aim the community with Christ."[16] Paul Achtemeier argues that the three prepositional phrases modify "elect" because "the reality of divine election for estranged and persecuted Christians goes to the heart of the problem this epistle is addressing."[17] Karen Jobes, in opposition to Wayne Grudem's view (which will be discussed

---

12. Steiger, *Der erste Brief Petri*, 36–37. It is quite possible that very few scholars past 1832 held to this position (F. J. A. Hort, as we shall see, believed the phrases modify "apostle" + "elect" rather than just "apostle").

13. Kelly, *Epistles of Peter and of Jude*, 42.

14. Michaels, *1 Peter*, 3.

15. Ibid., 6.

16. Schelkle, *Die Petrusbriefe, der Judasbrief*, 20 ("Die Erwählung ist begründet im Ratschluß Gottes, vermittelt durch die Wirkung des Geistes und hat zum Ziel die Gemeinschaft mit Christus").

17. Achtemeier, *1 Peter*, 86.

below), argues that Peter speaks to the readers' "discouragement because of the sociopolitical alienation they experience, which is a direct consequence of their relationship to God in Christ. Therefore, it is exegetically preferable to understand these three phrases as modifying the term that most fundamentally defines who these Christians are; the *eklektoi*, the chosen."[18] Likewise, Ellen Juhl Christiansen argues, "This passage describes election in terms of its origin, its means, and its cause."[19]

Interestingly, even divergent soteriological traditions take this same position with different results. For the Calvinist, "according to the foreknowledge of God" is seen as referring to either God's foreordination or his eternal relationship with his elect (or a combination of the two). Thus S. M. Baugh interprets πρόγνωσις in 1 Pet 1:2 on the basis of what he believes it means in 1 Pet 1:20, where "there can be no doubt that the idea of previous commitment is the only possible meaning of foreknowledge."[20] For Baugh, then,

> we can be confident from 1 Peter 1:1–2, as we were from Romans 8:29, that speaking about God's foreknowledge may be a way of expressing his eternal commitment to individuals as part of his determination to bring them to faith and to all the glories and benefits of Christ's work. God does foresee our faith, but this is not the point in these passages.[21]

Conversely, Ben Witherington III sees 1 Pet 1:2a as referring to the fact that believers "are chosen according to the foreknowledge of God, which is a way of saying they were not chosen arbitrarily or without foresight and insight into how they would respond."[22] Arminian scholar Robert Picirilli, on the other hand, seems to combine a sense of "foreplanning" with that of prescience: "Without any dogmatism, the meaning that strikes me as most likely is prescience, with a hint of wise foreplanning."[23] Consequently, God's election "is 'according to foreknowledge' (1 Pet 1:2), where 'foreknowledge'

---

18. Jobes, *1 Peter*, 67–68.

19. Christiansen, "Election as Identity Term in 1 Peter," 54; cf. also Bartlett, *NIB* 12:247.

20. Baugh, "Meaning of Foreknowledge," 196.

21. Ibid.; cf. also Davids, *First Epistle of Peter*, 48 (Davids follows the work of P. Jacobs and H. Krienke to argue that "foreknowledge" here essentially equals "personal relationship").

22. Witherington, *Socio-Rhetorical Commentary on 1–2 Peter*, 68. Witherington, like this writer, sees the term as a prescient term (see 69).

23. Picirilli, *Grace, Faith, and Free Will*, 79.

may mean either prescience, foresight, or foreplanning—or a blending of all three."[24]

Theologian James Oliver Buswell represents an exception to the rule. While taking "according to the foreknowledge" as modifying "elect," he gently chastens the views of both the Arminian and his fellow Calvinist. Against the Arminian of his day, he writes,

> The Arminian argument misconstrues the preposition *kata* as though it were *epi* with the dative, which means, "on the basis of," or *dia* with the accusative, which means, "on account of." These words by Peter cannot by any proper syntactical exegesis be made to indicate that the basis or ground or reason of election is the foreknowledge of God. The preposition employed here, *kata* with the accusative, simply indicates the harmony of the items mentioned—election, and foreknowledge—and this text has nothing to say one way or the other as to the question whether election depends upon foreknowledge or whether foreknowledge depends upon election. The text simply says that the two are harmonious and parallel.[25]

On the other hand, against his fellow Calvinists who argue that foreknowledge necessarily means "foreknowledge in fellowship" or is "identical with election and can mean nothing else," Buswell writes,

> Aside from the point of syntax, that *kata* with the accusative does not connect identity, but implies two distinct parallel items, I must object to a subtle assumption which usually accompanies the cliché which I am describing. It is frequently held that God's knowledge is a subordinate attribute, dependent upon His will . . . It is sometimes even argued that God is incapable of literal foreknowledge or prescience in the sense of cognitive apprehension of future events. Some so-called Calvinists have even taken the Thomistic position that for God to know and to do are identical. I wish to make it clear that in rejecting the Arminian interpretation of I Peter 1:1,2, I am by no means accepting the cliché which makes God's foreknowledge nothing but His decree of election. Divine election is one thing and divine foreknowledge is another thing. There is no disharmony between them and no dependence of one upon the other is indicated in the Scripture.[26]

---

24. Ibid., 84.
25. Buswell, *Systematic Theology of the Christian Religion* 2:140.
26. Ibid., 140–41.

Although Buswell somewhat overstates his case regarding κατά with the accusative (as will be discussed below), nonetheless it is this writer's opinion that, at the least, more attention should have been paid to his cautions.

A few scholars see the three prepositional phrases as referring to multiple words in verse 1. The first variant of this view sees "apostle" as part of that group. Thus Hort argues that ἐκλεκτοῖς "unmarked for special emphasis by order or particle, divided from *v.* 2 by eight words, and itself preceded by four words . . ." is unlikely to have "so much weight" (i.e., the three prepositional phrases) attached to it.[27] Likewise, E. G. Selwyn argues, "But ἀπόστολος is also virtually a verbal noun; and a fuller meaning is given if we reckon the clauses to be governed by this also."[28] Ernest Best similarly argues, ". . . the whole of verse 2 from this word onwards may qualify all of verse 1 so that the readers are not only set out as 'destined' to be believers but also to be exiles of the dispersion and Peter to be an apostle . . . ."[29] Finally, Francis Wright Beare writes,

> This threefold phrase cannot possibly be taken exclusively with ἐκλεκτοῖς "chosen," from which it is separated by no less than eight words in the Greek text. It is related to the entire salutation and has a measure of connection with each part of it—to the apostolate of Peter, to the election of the dispersed sojourners, and to the grace and peace which the writer prays may be theirs.[30]

Yet for the three prepositions to point to both a singular *and* a plural noun would surely be asking too much.[31] Indeed this writer is not aware of any prepositional phrase in the NT that, acting adjectivally, points to both a singular and plural noun, and most certainly this is not the case with phrases consisting of κατά with the accusative in non-Pauline epistles (see the analysis below).

---

27. Hort, *First Epistle of St. Peter*, 18.
28. Selwyn, *First Epistle of St. Peter*, 119.
29. Best, *I Peter*, 79.
30. Beare, *First Epistle of Peter*, 49–50.
31. Surely Kelly, *Commentary on the Epistles of Peter and of Jude*, 43, is correct in calling this theoretical construction "a needlessly complicated construction." The reader should also note that, although it is mostly irrelevant to this study's argument, one could also discuss whether or not ἐκλεκτοῖς is an adjective or an appositional noun. For a defense of the former, see Elliott, *I Peter*, 315; for the latter, see Jobes, *1 Peter*, 75.

A significantly stronger variant of this position holds that the three prepositional phrases modify all the words related to the readers, but not "apostle." Thus Grudem argues,

> Since verse 1 contains no verb, it is most natural to let "according to the foreknowledge of God the Father" modify the whole situation of the readers described in the first verse: they are "chosen sojourners of the Dispersion in Pontus, Galatia, *etc.*, *according to the foreknowledge of God the Father.*"[32]

Grudem's position will be defended later in this section.

Finally, one more position must be considered. It is certainly syntactically possible that the three prepositional phrases modify either παρεπιδήμος, διασπορᾶς, or both. This position is not even discussed by the vast majority of scholars and is dismissed outright by Hort as ". . . evidently inadequate to carrying the contents of *v.* 2."[33] Yet surely one must allow the author to say what he intends to say with the syntax and vocabulary he has chosen. Hort needlessly postulates an *a priori* decision as to what the author can and cannot say. A preferable alternative would be to analyze the use of κατά with the accusative within the New Testament and at least take this into consideration before making exegetical pronouncements. Whatever κατά modifies will most likely be the word or words that the preposition ἐν modifies. The last phrase beginning with εἰς, however, may either modify what the other two modify or the act of sanctification posited in the second phrase; this, however, is irrelevant to the general point of this section. The focus here will be on κατά with the accusative.

While plenty of discussion can be found on what κατά means and how it is used, virtually no scholar has examined what word or words κατά with the accusative is most likely to modify when ambiguity exists. Consequently, this writer has analyzed each occurrence of κατά with the accusative in the non-Pauline epistles. For the following analysis, this writer used *Accordance* 8.4 with the following command line: "=κατά <followed by> <within 3 Words> [noun accusative]."[34] This resulted in 97 hits (counting both the preposition and the accusative noun) in 44 different verses. Hebrews 8:4 has a noun that is not actually part of the prepositional phrase yet was counted as one of the hits; the results may thus be amended to 96 hits in 44 verses, which means that there are 48 total constructions. This analysis will list the following: the prepositional phrase, whether it is adjectival or adverbial, the

---

32. Grudem, *1 Peter*, 50 (emphasis is Grudem's); in 50–51, Grudem extends his reasoning to the other two prepositional phrases as well.

33. Hort, *First Epistle of St. Peter*, 18.

34. *Accordance* 8.4 (OakTree Software, 2009). The Greek text is the NA 27th ed.

The Concept of Foreknowledge in Three Key Texts in First Peter   139

word or words it is modifying, and the number of words separating the phrase from the word or words it modifies. The "words separating" column will measure the distance between the phrase *as a whole* from the word or words it modifies. In other words, either the preposition or *the last word* of the prepositional phrase will be the starting point of the count (depending on whether the prepositional phrase comes before or after the word it modifies). In the last column, the word "after" indicates that the word the phrase modifies follows rather than precedes it. Finally, this list does not take pronouns into consideration. The list is as follows:

Table 5.1: Analysis of Κατά with the Accusative Noun

Prepositional phrase	Adv. or adj.	Word modifying	Distance
Heb 1:10—κατ' ἀρχάς	Adv.	ἐθεμελίωσας	4 (after)
Heb 2:4—κατὰ τὴν αὐτοῦ θέλησιν	Adj.	μερισμοῖς	1
Heb 3:3—καθ' ὅσον πλείονα τιμήν	Adv.	ἠξίωται	1
Heb 3:8—κατὰ τὴν ἡμέραν τοῦ πειρασμοῦ ἐν τῇ ῥήμῳ	Uncertain	Uncertain: either σκληρύνητε or παραπικρασμῷ	8 or 1
Heb 3:13—καθ' ἑκάστην ἡμέραν	Adv.	παρακαλεῖτε	2
Heb 4:15 (#1)—κατὰ πάντα	Adv.	πεπειρασμένον	2
Heb 4:15 (#2)— καθ' ὁμοιότητα	Adv.	πεπειρασμένον	4
Heb 5:6—κατὰ τὴν τάξιν Μελχισέδεκ	Adj.	ἱερεύς	4
Heb 5:10— κατὰ τὴν τάξιν Μελχισέδεκ	Adj.	ἀρχιερεύς	1
Heb 6:20— κατὰ τὴν τάξιν Μελχισέδεκ	Adj.	ἀρχιερεύς	1 (after)
Heb 7:5—κατὰ τὸν νόμον	Adv.	ἀποδεκατοῦν	3
Heb 7:11 (#1)— κατὰ τὴν τάξιν Μελχισέδεκ	Adj.	ἱερέα	3 after
Heb 7:11 (#2)— κατὰ τὴν τάξιν Ἀαρών	Adj.	ἱερέα	3
Heb 7:15—κατὰ τὴν ὁμοιότητα Μελχισέδεκ	Adj.	ἱερέα	2 after
Heb 7:16 (#1)—κατὰ νόμον ἐντολῆς σαρκίνης	Adv./Adj.	γέγενον (but implied ἱερεύς)	1 after

Heb 7:16 (#2)—κατὰ δύναμιν ζωῆς ἀκαταλύτου	Adv./Adj.	γέγενον (but implied ἱερεύς)	2
Heb 7:17—κατὰ τὴν τάξιν Μελχισέδεκ	Adj.	ἱερεύς	4
Heb 7:27—καθ' ἡμέραν ἀνάγκην	Adv.	ἔχει	1
Heb 8:4—κατὰ νόμον	Uncertain	Uncertain: either προσφερόντων or δῶρα	1 or 2 (after)
Heb 8:5—κατὰ τὸν τύπον	Adv.	ποιήσεις	2
Heb 8:9—κατὰ τὴν διαθήκην	Adj.	διαθήκην (v. 8)	2
Heb 9:5—κατὰ μέρος	Adv.	λέγειν	1
Heb 9:9—κατὰ συνείδησιν	Adv.	τελειῶσαι	1 (after)
Heb 9:19—κατὰ τὸν νόμον	Uncertain	Uncertain: either λαληθείσῆς or ἐντολῆς	4 or 1
Heb 9:22—κατὰ τὸν νόμον	Adv.	καθαρίζεται	1
Heb 9:25—κατ' ἐνιαυτόν	Adv.	εἰσέρχεται	4
Heb 10:1 — κατ' ἐνιαυτόν	Adv.	προσφέρουσιν	5 (after)
Heb 10:3 — κατ' ἐνιαυτόν	Adj.	ἀνάμνησις	2
Heb 10:8—κατὰ νόμον	Adv.	προσφέρονται	1 (after)
Heb 10:11—καθ' ἡμέραν	Adv.	ἔστηκεν	1
Heb 11:7—κατὰ πίστιν	Adj.	δικαιοσύνης	1 (after)
Heb 11:13— κατὰ πίστιν	Adv.	ἀπέθανον	1 (after)
James 2:8—κατὰ τὴν γραφήν	Adv.	τελεῖτε	2
James 3:9— καθ' ὁμοίωσιν θεοῦ	Adv.	γεγονότας	1 (after)
1 Pet 1:2—κατὰ πρόγνωσιν θεοῦ πατρός	Adj.	Under debate	Uncertain
1 Pet 1:17—κατὰ τὸ ἑκάστου ἔργον	Adv.	κρίνοντα	1
1 Pet 3:7—κατὰ γνῶσιν	Adv.	συνοικοῦντες	1
1 Pet 4:6 (#1)—κατὰ ἀνθρώπους σαρκί	Adv.	κριθῶσι	2
1 Pet 4:6 (#2)—κατὰ θεόν	Adv.	ζῶσι	2
1 Pet 4:19—κατὰ τὸ θέλημα τοῦ θεοῦ	Adv.	πάσχονες	1
1 Pet 5:2—κατὰ θεόν	Adv.	ἐπισκοποῦντες[A]	5

2 Pet 3:3—κατὰ τὰς ἰδίας ἐπιθυμίας αὐτῶν	Adv.	πορευόμενοι	1 (after)
2 Pet 3:13—κατὰ τὸ ἐπάγγελμα αὐτοῦ	Adv.	προσδοκῶμεν	1 (after)
1 Jn 5:14—κατὰ τὸ θέλημα αὐτοῦ	Adv.	αἰτώμεθα	1
2 Jn 6—κατὰ τὰς ἐντολάς αὐτοῦ	Adv.	περιπατῶμεν	1
3 Jn 15—κατ' ὄνομα	Adv.	ἀσπάζου	3
Jude 16—κατὰ τὰς ἐπιθυμίας ἑαυτῶν	Adv.	πορευόμενοι	1 (after)
Jude 18—κατὰ τὰς ἑαυτῶν ἐπιθυμίας	Adv.	πορευόμενοι	1 (after)

A. Here there is a textual variant, with some doubt as to whether or not ἐπισκοποῦντες is original (if not, then the phrase might be modifying ποιμάνετε, a total distance of 11, the longest gap by far in this study). On the one hand, the UBS 4th ed. places it in brackets with a "C" rating. Yet the only significant Greek texts that lack this word are *Aleph**, 322, 323, and 1441, while the Byzantine text supports this inclusion of ἐπισκοποῦντες (Robinson-Pierpont, 2005). As such, we will here assume the presence of ἐπισκοποῦντες.

Some observations may be made. First of all, in 1 Pet 1:1-2, ἐκλεκτοῖς is 9 words removed from κατὰ πρόγνωσιν θεοῦ πατρός, which would be the most distance between a phrase consisting of κατά plus the accusative and the word it modifies. Indeed, the only construction that comes close is in Heb 3:8, and only if it is being used adverbially rather than adjectivally. Consequently, it must be stressed that *no other construction consisting of κατά + plus the accusative in non-Pauline epistles is ever separated by more than 8 words*, and out of those clearly used adjectivally, *no other construction is separated by more than 4 words, and there is no ambiguity in these cases* (i.e., in Heb 5:6 and 7:17 there is no other option for "according to the order of Melchizedek" to modify except for "priest"). In 1 Pet 1:2, however, there are at least two other words that, syntactically, would make sense for κατὰ πρόγνωσιν θεοῦ πατρός to modify, namely, παρεπιδήμοις and διασπορᾶς. The following question must be asked, then: would the readers and/or hearers of 1 Peter automatically link the prepositional phrase to the *farthest* word that would make sense? This question becomes all the more pertinent when one remembers that such hearers did not possess systematic or biblical theologies that would explain to them how best to understand Peter's theology; rather, they were forming their impression of Peter's theology as they heard it. To argue that "elect" would most likely be the word modified by κατὰ πρόγνωσιν on theological grounds alone seems to court the danger of special pleading (especially since this occurs at the very beginning of the epistle).

Secondly, within 1 Peter itself, only once does the distance between κατά with the accusative and its target word exceed a distance of 2 words, and that is in 1 Pet 5:2 (assuming both the UBS 4th and Byzantine/Majority text reading). Furthermore, in 1 Pet 5:2, there are no other nouns or verbs between the prepositional phrase and its target ἐπισκοποῦντες, and no other nouns or verbs after it for another 7 words (the participle κατακυριεύοντες in verse 3).

If one expands the search to accusative participles, however, 1 Pet 1:15 contains an adverbial phrase consisting of κατὰ τὸν καλέσαντα ὑμᾶς ἅγιον, which is potentially separated by 7 words from the word (γενήθητε) it modifies (the count beginning after ἅγιον, technically the last word of the prepositional phrase). Yet even here, between the phrase and its (possible) target verb, there is a predicative adjective the phrase might modify that is much closer (ἅγιοι). It must be stressed, however, that in this passage the overall sense of the verse remains the same whether the target is the verb or the predicate adjective. This stands in sharp contrast to 1 Pet 1:1–2, where a preference for one of the words over the others could potentially alter the meaning of the sentence.

The point is this: prepositional phrases with κατά + the accusative generally modify something closer than 9 words and generally do not suffer from ambiguity. In other words, it is normally a simple matter to determine which word it modifies, and when there is ambiguity, it is between a noun and a verb and never between two nouns. This, then, would argue against the idea that κατὰ πρόγνωσιν θεοῦ πατρός would modify a noun 9 words removed when closer options (other nouns) exist.

Yet all other instances of κατά + the accusative modify verbs in 1 Peter, and consequently it would be unusual for the construction to modify a noun at all. Grudem stresses this point when he argues, "Since verse 1 contains no verb, it is most natural to let 'according to the foreknowledge of God the Father' modify the whole situation of the readers . . ."[35] One could also point out than in the phrase ἐκλεκτοῖς παρεπιδήμοις διασπορᾶς, each word has verbal cognates within the NT, so no word is at an advantage.

In addition, at this point one could appropriate J. Ramsey Michael's logic (used against the "apostle" position) against the idea that the phrases modify "elect." Would it not have been more natural, had the author wished the phrases to modify "elect," to place the three prepositional phrases

---

35. Grudem, *1 Peter*, 50. I am not totally convinced by Grudem's argument here, but at the least it seems just as reasonable as the idea that the prepositional phrases modify "elect."

immediately after "elect"? Consequently, the author could have written, "Peter, an Apostle of Jesus Christ, to the elect according to the foreknowledge of God the Father, *etc.*, . . . even to those who are strangers of the Diaspora . . ." This would have dispensed with much of the ambiguity.

Finally, an argument could be made that "elect" is the most thematically prominent term and that the recipients would naturally attach the prepositional phrases to it. Martin Williams argues,

> The fact that ἐκλεκτός elsewhere in the New Testament functions as an important designation for the church suggests a certain priority for it here as well . . . Moreover, because ἐκλεκτοῖς is a word that points directly to the action of God, it (and not the entire phrase ἐκλεκτοῖς παρεπιδήμοις διασπορᾶς κτλ.) is best understood as the antecedent of the three prepositional phrases of v. 2 . . .[36]

It must be stressed once more, however, that arguing that the phrases modify "election" on theological grounds at the expense of syntactical discussion remains, to this writer at least, unconvincing. The issue is not "what best fits the theology of the NT," but rather "how the readers would have understood this construction," especially since this occurs at the beginning of the letter before they have had the opportunity to form their opinions of its theological themes. Furthermore, Williams' argument seems to run as follows: election indicates God's activity, and since the three prepositional phrases also point to God's activity, then consequently the phrases must modify election. The assumption seems to be that prepositional phrases describing the actions of God can only modify a noun describing the action of God, an assumption that Williams does not prove (this further assumes that "strangers of the Diaspora" is not the result of the action of God). Yet what if the three prepositional phrases were meant to *explain* how exactly the audience's situation related to the plan of God? In that case, the entire expression ἐκλεκτοῖς παρεπιδήμοις διασπορᾶς would be explained by the subsequent prepositional phrases; this is, at the least, a viable exegetical alternative to Williams' view.

Elsewhere, regarding the significance of the term "elect," Stephen Fagbemi draws from Eugene Boring to argue, "Although 1 Peter is smaller than most NT writings, it uses the term 'elect' more than any other NT document. Five of its twenty-three occurrences in the NT are found in 1 Peter."[37] Yet this statement must be corrected. First Peter includes only four occurrences of the word ἐκλεκτός (1 Pet 1:1; 2:4; 2:6; and 2:9). Furthermore, the

---

36. Williams, *Doctrine of Salvation in the First Letter of Peter*, 47.
37. Fagbemi, *Who Are the Elect in 1 Peter?*, 67; Boring, *1 Peter*, 53–54.

twenty-third occurrence of ἐκλεκτός (as opposed to the twenty-two occurrences in the NA 27th ed.) is dependent upon a textual variant in Matthew 20:16 (a variant supported by the Majority text but not by the Alexandrian text).[38] If Fagbemi and Boring wish to go with the twenty-three occurrences of the Majority text (a concession this writer is willing to make), then Matthew actually contains more occurrences of the word than 1 Peter. Nevertheless, since 1 Peter is smaller than Matthew, Fagbemi and Boring's point mostly stands, even if their data needs to be amended.[39]

Fagbemi, once more drawing from Eugene Boring, also argues, "It is the only NT document in which the election motif forms part of the salutation and thus a major theological theme from the outset."[40] Yet this might also need to be amended (depending on what is meant by "motif"), for at least two other epistles, Titus and 2 John, contain exactly the same word within their first verse (κατὰ πίστιν ἐκλεκτῶν and ἐκλεκτῇ κυρίᾳ, respectively), though one could support Fagbemi and Boring by arguing that 1 Peter is still the only one in which election is "a major theological theme from the outset." Yet even this would be debatable, for the Apostle Paul, in Rom 1:1, mentions his own calling as an apostle (κλητὸς ἀπόστολος), a word which is certainly being used synonymously with "election" (i.e., they share the same concept, that of divine choice), and most would argue that election is a major theme within Romans. Once could further argue that the *concept* of election (as opposed to the same word) appears in 1 Cor 1:1–2. Nevertheless, this study is prepared to acknowledge Fagbemi and Boring's point that election (as the broader concept "choice/determination") is probably a greater motif in 1 Peter than in any other NT writing except Romans.

Yet within the greeting of 1 Pet 1:1, however, this writer would suggest that the recipients might naturally be drawn to the rarer terminology, namely παρεπιδήμοις διασπορᾶς, for the latter word only occurs elsewhere in the NT in John 7:35 and the introduction to James while the former likewise occurs only two other places in the entire NT (one of them being 1 Pet 2:11). Furthermore, the former never occurs in an introduction to a NT book outside of 1 Peter. Thus, if the recipients were to chose only one word to attach the prepositional phrases to in light of its uniqueness, it would most likely be either παρεπιδήμοις or διασπορᾶς. Nevertheless, in this writer's opinion,

---

38. All searches conducted via *Accordance* 8.4.

39. It is possible that Fagbemi and Boring are both counting the term συνεκλεκτός (though neither state this). Yet this is a different word; if this were to be included then one might as well include the cognate noun ἐκλογή as well, which would yield a different set of data.

40. Fagbemi, *Who Are the Elect in 1 Peter?*, 67; Boring, *1 Peter*, 53–54.

this argument is not sufficient to demonstrate that either word by itself is the target of the three prepositions.

Of the various options, then, this writer concludes that "elect" by itself is an unlikely (though not impossible) candidate. Yet many, if not all, of the same arguments that were used against "elect" being the target of the prepositional phrase can now be used against παρεπιδήμοις, leaving διασπορᾶς as a favorable candidate (and at least once in the non-Pauline epistles a genitive noun is modified by κατά + the accusative). Yet even with διασπορᾶς, there is still the issue of ambiguity; in other words, would the average first-century hearer or listener likely have gravitated towards this word with two other viable options in close proximity?

This study, then, is forced into the following conclusion: rather than the readers/hearers having to choose between three possible options, it is most likely that the recipients would see the prepositional phrases as modifying the entirety of their own situation, as Grudem has argued.

Yet in none of the above examples in figure 5 does the prepositional phrase modify such a broad scope of concepts. Is there, then, any evidence that κατά + the accusative can actually function in this manner? At the syntactical level, this writer is unable to give a definitive answer. At the conceptual level, however, this is most definitely the case in Judith 11:19, where *the very same phrase* κατὰ πρόγνωσιν points back to the plural "ταῦτα" (basically referring to all the content of Judith's speech from Jdt 11:6–19a). Thus, in the closest syntactical parallel one can find between 1 Pet 1:2 and the texts of the time (including the LXX), one discovers that κατὰ πρόγνωσιν can indeed refer to a collection of concepts. Consequently, in support of Grudem, it is not unreasonable to suggest that the prepositional phrases, and especially κατὰ πρόγνωσιν θεοῦ πατρός, can point to a broader concept than just one word, namely, the "all these things" of the audience's situation. This also eliminates Hort's concern that one word is not enough to handle three prepositional phrases of this level of theological magnitude.

The second and third prepositional phrases would most likely modify whatever the first prepositional phrase modifies. This maintains both the parallelism and the focus on the recipients and their relationship to God.

What Is the Meaning of Κατὰ Πρόγνωσιν?

Having established that, as Grudem argues, the prepositional phrases refer to the entire situation the readers find themselves in (and not just their election), one can now turn to the meaning and significance of κατὰ πρόγνωσιν θεοῦ πατρός. Murray J. Harris, in *Prepositions and Theology in the Greek*

New Testament, gives four items that any analysis of a prepositional phrase should give heed to. They are as follows:

> 1. the primary meaning of the preposition itself (i.e., the local/spatial sense) and then its range of meaning when used with the particular case involved. 2. the basic significance of the case that is used with the preposition. 3. the indications afforded by the context as to the meaning of the preposition. 4. the distinctive features of prepositional usage in the NT that may account for seeming irregularities.[41]

Unfortunately, the last point is beyond the scope of this paper, though A. T. Robertson suggests, "On the whole, the N. T. use of the accusative with κατά corresponds pretty closely to the classic idiom."[42] Also assumed here is the fact that, as Edward R. Hope notes, "Some prepositions change their meaning with different types of reference point [sic] [i.e., the subsequent noun]."[43] Naturally, authorial style should also be considered.[44] One should not, of course, completely discount the possibility that an author uses the same preposition in two different ways simultaneously (e.g., perhaps, 1 Pet 3:20).[45] This, however, should most likely be the last resort in interpretation.

Initially, the various meanings of κατά may hearken back to its original opposition to ἀνά, with the former pointing down and the latter pointing up in adverbial usage.[46] Thus Silvia Luraghi can speak of the original meaning of κατά as "'downward,' from which a widespread abstract meaning develops, based on the notion of conformity ('according to')."[47] The nineteenth-century grammarian Gessner Harrison even goes so far as to suggest that the primary sense of κατά is "down," with all other senses related to or deriving from that sense.[48]

Κατά with the accusative, however, is the specific focus of this study. Nevertheless, as Daniel Wallace cautions, "*The use of a particular preposition*

---

41. Harris, *Prepositions and Theology*, 31; cf. Dana and Mantey, *Manual Grammar of the Greek New Testament*, 98—"Thus to understand the full significance of a preposition one needs to know the function of the case with which it is used in each instance, the meaning of the preposition absolutely, and, what is most difficult, learn what it means relatively in each context."

42. Robertson, *Grammar of the Greek New Testament*, 98.

43. Hope, "Translating Prepositions," 403.

44. Harris, *Prepositions and Theology*, 40; Black, *It's Still Greek to Me*, 87.

45. Harris, *Prepositions and Theology*, 42.

46. Adams, *The Greek Prepositions*, 11. Cf. also Porter, *Idioms of the Greek New Testament*, 162.

47. Luraghi, *On the Meaning of Prepositions and Cases*, 316–17.

48. Harrison, *Treatise on the Greek Prepositions*, 307–12.

The Concept of Foreknowledge in Three Key Texts in First Peter   147

with a particular case never exactly parallels—either in category possibilities or in relative frequency of nuances—the use of a case without a preposition."[49] Consequently, this section will not examine the basic usage of the accusative case in NT Greek. It will, however, examine both the general use of κατά in 1 Peter and its specific meaning when attached to the accusative.

A. T. Robertson suggests that the primary meaning of κατά with the accusative is "along, at, according to," but with the possibility for "with reference to, with respect to, pertaining to."[50] Harrison, focusing on classical usage, suggests that κατά with the accusative can also mean "as far as reaches" or "to the measure or extent of."[51] It is not clear, however, if this usage continued into the first century AD. Laurence Vance suggests that κατά with the accusative "usually signifies correspondence." When used adjectivally, however, "location, time, respect, and distribution" may all be legitimate meanings.[52]

Luraghi sees κατά with the accusative as "occurring in two types of context," namely "direction" and "Location or multidirectional Path on a surface."[53] In general, however, Luraghi suggests that "κατά with the accusative means 'regarding,' 'as to,' and denotes Area."[54] Harris, in his discussion of κατά in Col 1:11, seems to see three different options for κατά with the accusative: "conformity" (i.e., "in accordance with" or "according to"), "basis," and "cause" (i.e., "as a result of").[55]

Finally, Wallace provides one of the more comprehensive lists for the use of κατά with the accusative. His list is as follows:

a. Standard: *in accordance with, corresponding to*

b. Spatial: *along, through* (extension); *toward, up to* (direction)

c. Temporal: *at, during*

d. Distributive: "indicating the division of a greater whole into individual parts" [Wallace is quoting BAGD here]

e. Purpose: *for the purpose of*

f. Reference/Respect: *with respect to, with reference to*[56]

---

49. Wallace, *Greek Grammar Beyond the Basics*, 361–62 (emphasis is Wallace's).
50. Robertson, *Grammar of the Greek New Testament*, 107.
51. Harrison, *Treatise on the Greek Prepositions*, 330.
52. Vance, *Guide to Prepositions in the Greek New Testament*, 14–15.
53. Luraghi, *On the Meaning of Prepositions*, 200–201.
54. Ibid., 211.
55. Harris, *Prepositions and Theology*, 158.
56. Wallace, *Greek Grammar Beyond the Basics*, 377 (emphasis is Wallace's).

Within 1 Peter, κατά occurs 10 times: 1 Pet 1:2, 3, 15, 17; 2:11; 3:7; 4:6 (x2), 19; and 5:2. In every single occurrence except 1 Pet 1:2, the preposition is used adverbially. Within those uses, however, in 1:3 the prepositional phrase does seem to denote "cause" or "grounds of." In 1:15, the sense is similarity (i.e., "be holy *just as* the one calling you is holy"). In 1:7, the sense is once more "cause" or "grounds." In 1 Pet 2:11, the sense is "against." In 3:7, however, one could either argue for "conformity/correspondence to" (i.e., "live with your wives corresponding to knowledge") or "basis/grounds" (i.e., "live with your wives on the basis of knowledge"). In 4:6 the sense seems to be "in conformity with," as indicated by the New English Translation's "by human standards . . . by God's standards." In 4:19, the sense is once more causal ("according to God's will"), whereas in 5:2 it is clearly "in conformity to" or "in harmony with" ("overseeing . . . in conformity to God [i.e., his will]"). In summary, then, the evidence from κατά in 1 Peter is inconclusive.

Most, if not all, of the same scholars who view the prepositional phrase as pointing to "elect" also see κατά as possessing a determinative sense, the "grounds" for what it modifies. It other words, it represents election according to (i.e., grounded in or caused by) God's foreknowledge.[57] This interpretation is certainly a possibility even if one takes the phrase as pointing to the audience's entire situation. In other words, the recipients would see themselves as "elect strangers of the Diaspora caused by God's foreknowledge." In addition to those places in 1 Peter noted above, this sense of κατά (when modifying a noun) is clearly attested to in Heb 2:4 where the will of God is the cause of or grounds for the distribution of the Holy Spirit's gifts.

A viable alternative exists, however. As demonstrated, sometimes κατά means "in accordance with" (i.e., "consistent with" or "alongside of"). While Buswell overstates his case (κατά can mean "on the grounds of" or "the basis of," quite frequently), this writer believes his overall sentiments are correct regarding 1 Pet 1:2. Drawing from both Buswell and Wallace, "harmony," in the sense of "in accordance with" or "corresponding to," is a possibility that must be considered.[58] This sense of κατά may be seen, for example, in 1 Pet 5:2 where κατὰ θεόν seems to indicate not so much the determinative force behind the command to lead willingly, but rather something to be taken into account or considered. In other words, in 1 Pet 5:2 (where the preposition

---

57. E.g., Schelkle, *Die Petrusbriefe, der Judasbrief*, 20 ("Die Erwählung ist begründet im . . . ."). Cf. Thurén, *Argument and Theology in 1 Peter*, 92 (the first "Warrant" in Thurén's rhetorical interpretation of this passage is that "Foreknowledge and sanctification make one elect and a stranger").

58. Or, perhaps, the term "congruence" might be appropriate (see Abernathy, *Exegetical Summary of 1 Peter*, 13, where he states that κατά in verse 2 "indicates congruence with being chosen").

occurs with an accusative noun), overseers are to lead willingly in harmony with the will of God (and leading reluctantly would be in disharmony with the will of God). This use of κατά is in contrast to 1 Pet 1:3, where it is the Lord's rich mercy that is the *cause* of his gift of hope.

More importantly, however, the only exact occurrence of the phrase κατὰ πρόγνωσιν in the literature surveyed in chapter 4 gives precisely this sense. Not only does Jdt 11:19 clearly use the term πρόγνωσις in a strictly prescient sense, it also clearly uses the preposition κατά to mean "in accordance with" or "in harmony with." In other words, Judith's foreknowledge is not the *cause of* the events that (she claims) will take place; instead, those events are in harmony with her foreknowledge. Consequently, here foreknowledge acts as *a word of encouragement*. Judith is in essence saying to the villain, "You will totally dominate Jerusalem; trust me on this, for I have foreseen it."

When combined with the fact that πρόγνωσις is, in the literature of AD 1–100, used mostly (if not exclusively) in a prescient sense, one can then posit the following translation: "Peter, an apostle of Jesus Christ, to the elect strangers of the Diaspora . . . [whose circumstances are] in harmony with the foreknowledge of God." The significance of the three prepositional phrases can now be discussed.

What Is the Broader Significance of the Three Prepositional Phrases in 1 Peter 1:2?

What, then, is the author trying to accomplish with the three prepositional phrases? First of all, one must certainly agree with Roselyne Dupont-Roc that the phrases point to the interaction of the Trinity with the entirety of human history, including the "presence of God" in "salvation history."[59] Indeed, these phrases also point to the presence of God within the entire social-spiritual status of the readers, both their acceptance by God and their rejection by men. In other words, what is being portrayed is not so much the recipients' soteriology *per se* (though this is certainly a part of it), but their identity. They are displaced and dispersed strangers on the one hand, yet elect members of a new community on the other. The distressed readers would surely be wondering how their own situation fits in with the plan of God. To such a discouraged group, Peter responds that not only was their entire situation forever in the mind of God (and no surprise to him), but it was also brought about by the Holy Spirit and now functions as the impetus towards sacred obedience.

59. Dupont-Roc, "Le jeu des prepositions en 1 Pierre 1, 1–12," 203.

The first prepositional phrase, κατὰ πρόγνωσιν θεοῦ πατρός, indicates that, far from being an unexpected surprise to their Creator, both their status as outcasts and their newly discovered status as the chosen have existed forever within the mind of God. As Grudem articulates,

> This implies that their status as sojourners, their privileges as God's chosen people, even their hostile environment in Pontus, Galatia, *etc.*, were all known by God before the world began, all came about in accordance with his foreknowledge, and thus (we may conclude) all were in accordance with his fatherly love for his own people. Such foreknowledge is laden with comfort for Peter's readers.[60]

Grudem's interpretation makes perfect sense within the context of the trials and tribulations of the recipients (e.g., 1 Pet 1:7). The readers, despite their circumstances, draw comfort from the very beginning of the epistle by knowing that their situation comes as no surprise to the one watching over them, for he has destined them for something greater. The concept of foreknowledge then, functions (theologically, not syntactically) as the grounds of their "confidence" in God: whatever is happening to them now was foreknown by God.[61]

As for the phrase ἐν ἁγιασμῷ πνεύματος, two options exist. One could take the preposition in an instrumental sense (i.e., "*by* the Holy Spirit").[62] If this were the case, then it is the Spirit himself who is instrumental in bringing about the audience's circumstances. Grudem, however, offers an alternative:

> It is much easier, again, to see the phrase "in sanctification of the Spirit" as referring to the entire status of Peter's readers. This allows *en* to have its common sense "in": Peter is saying that his readers' *whole existence* as "chosen sojourners of the Dispersion . . ." is being lived "in" the realm of the sanctifying work of the Spirit. The unseen, unheard activity of God's Holy Spirit surrounds them almost like a spiritual atmosphere "in" which

---

60. Grudem, *1 Peter*, 50 (emphasis is Grudem's).

61. Schröger, *Gemeinde im 1. Petrusbrief*, 14–15.

62. See Elliott, *I Peter*, 318; Jobes, *1 Peter*, 69. Jobes, however, seems to base her conclusion on the belief that the phrase modifies only "elect." She states, "Both Selwyn and Grudem take the whole of verse 1 as the governing thought of these three prepositional phrases, but if *eklektois* is the more specific antecedent, though, then an instrumental dative is more apt here. To be chosen *by* the instrumental agency of the Spirit is a more natural thought than to be chosen *into* a location, even if the location is a 'spiritual' one" (p. 69).

they live and breathe, turning every circumstance, every sorrow, every hardship into a tool for his patient sanctifying work.⁶³

Either way, clearly the Spirit is involved in the social-spiritual circumstances of the readers.

Finally, the phrase εἰς ὑπακοὴν καὶ ῥαντισμὸν αἵματος Ἰησοῦ Χριστοῦ points to the ultimate destiny of these displaced sojourners, namely their obedience and sprinkling. Francis Agnew, however, has argued that this last phrase should be translated "'*because* of the obedience and the sprinkling of the blood of Jesus Christ'... [with] a causal sense [given] to the preposition *eis*."⁶⁴ This would result in each member of the Trinity having an active role in the three prepositions.⁶⁵

While Agnew's position is attractive (not least due to the parallelism it would maintain, with each member of the Trinity playing an active role), solid objections have been raised. Syndey Page points out that such a causal sense of εἰς is virtually nonexistent elsewhere; furthermore, "It is most natural to understand εἰς in 1 Pet 1:2 as expressing purpose and/or result, as it does three times in the following verses."⁶⁶ He later argues, "The awkwardness of attributing two functions to the genitive case of Ἰησοῦ Χριστοῦ is avoided if ὑπακοὴν is understood to be used absolutely and Ἰησοῦ Χριστοῦ is seen as qualifying only αἵματος."⁶⁷ As Witherington points out, a ὅτι would have been more appropriate than εἰς for Agnew's position, and one must not neglect the reference to Exodus 24 which indicates that the focus is on "what God has done for the audience."⁶⁸ For Jobes, "The phrase 'obedience and sprinkling of blood' can serve as a hendiadys to refer to God's covenant relationship with his people."⁶⁹ Consequently, "the Christians of Asia Minor have been chosen for a purpose, and that purpose is their own obedience after the example of Christ (cf. 1:14; 2:21)."⁷⁰ One could further add that their entire situation as elect strangers is meant to lead them towards obedience to Christ.⁷¹ Consequently, this particular phrase indicates

---

63. Grudem, *1 Peter*, 51–52.
64. Agnew, "1 Peter 1:2—An Alternative Translation," 69–70. Emphasis is Agnew's.
65. Ibid., 70.
66. Page, "Obedience and Blood-Sprinkling in 1 Peter 1:2," 294–95.
67. Ibid., 293.
68. Witherington, *Socio-Rhetorical Commentary on 1–2 Peter*, 73.
69. Jobes, *1 Peter*, 72.
70. Ibid., 71.
71. As Fagbemi, *Who Are the Elect in 1 Peter?*, 76, appropriately states, "In other words, the identity of the Christians through the act of the Holy Spirit is to lead them *into* the act of obedience to Christ and the sprinkling of the blood of Christ (no-one

God's purpose in the readers' present existence as "chosen sojourners" in their native lands: their lives ought to be leading "toward" (*eis*) increasing obedience to Christ (*cf.* Eph. 2:10; 1 Thes. 4:3; Jn. 14:15). What the Father plans and the Spirit empowers, Christ thus receives as exalted Saviour and ruling Lord . . . their lives are also leading toward (*eis*) *sprinkling with his blood*.[72]

In this way all three prepositional phrases qualify the readers' current social *and* spiritual status and begin to point the way forward to their ultimate destiny.

1 PETER 1:10–12

In keeping with the dichotomy of current versus future circumstances, 1 Pet 1:7 contrasts the current struggles the recipients face with the future glory awaiting them at the *parousia* of Christ, the one whom they do not yet see but nonetheless love (1:8). It is Christ who represents the culmination of their faith, their salvation. From here, the author launches into a key discussion of how this salvation was looked into from times past.[73] Regarding 1 Pet 1:10–12, William Schutter states, "Few NT texts compare favourably with the breadth and weight of this statement. The whole course of salvation history and the progress of revelation seem to be summed up in a skilful manoeuvre that draws the addressees simultaneously into its perspective."[74] Consequently, this passage can be linked to the mention of foreknowledge in 1:2 because here, like there, God's care and knowledge of the recipients of the letter plays a prominent role.[75] Before one can discuss the significance of this passage and its relation to social identity, however, the following two issues must be addressed: the identity of the passage's "prophets," and the meaning of the expression τίνα ἢ ποῖον καιρόν.[76]

---

who has not taken on Christ can obey him)." Emphasis is Fagbemi's.

72. Grudem, *1 Peter*, 52. Emphasis is Grudem's.

73. Joseph, *Narratological Reading*, 48–49, goes so far as to say, "Most scholars agree that 1 Pet. 1.3–12 contains in a nutshell the essence of the author's entire message to his audience."

74. Schutter, *Hermeneutic and Composition in I Peter*, 101.

75. Ibid., 102; note also p. 109, where Schutter calls this passage ". . . a hermeneutical key, since it not only gives unmatched insight into what by all appearances is at least a major aspect of the author's hermeneutical stance, but also allows for convenient access to his use of the OT elsewhere in the letter."

76. I have briefly discussed this passage in Himes, "Peter and the Prophetic Word," 233–37.

The Prophets of 1 Peter 1:10–12

The traditional view has held that the "prophets" discussed in this passage are Old Testament prophets. Yet if, as some argue, the prophets are actually contemporary Christian prophets, this study's thesis is weakened, for then their act of "foretelling" would actually be more along the lines of "proclamation/teaching."[77] This would effectively cut out a key text that supports this study. Fortunately, however, the former view still enjoys the preference of the majority of scholarship, although the minority view deserves fair consideration.

In his commentary on 1 Peter, Edward Gordon Selwyn objects to the standard view on the grounds that (a) "the 'seeking and searching' mentioned in verse 10 are not easily identifiable with what we know of the activities of the O.T. prophets" and (b) "the phrase 'the spirit of Christ' is without parallel if applied to the O.T. prophets."[78] He further argues that the lack of the article with προφῆται "is more natural if the reference were to men whose activities were well known to the readers."[79] Furthermore, he argues that contemporary (Christian) prophets were more likely to fit the description of "researching" the nature of "the sufferings of the Christian road."[80]

Julian Price Love defends Selwyn's interpretation in the following manner:

> It would seem unnatural to think of the prophets of the Old Testament as "searching and inquiring about salvation." While he could indeed speak of them as "predicting the sufferings of Christ," the word translated "predicting" occurs nowhere else and may just as well mean "publicly proclaiming." It seems rather far-fetched to think of the messages of the ancient prophets as things into which "angels long to look."[81]

In a more recent defense, Duane Warden suggests that the prophets in 1 Pet 1:10–12 are similar to those in Acts 13:1 and bolsters Selwyn's argument regarding the lack of the article by suggesting that Peter "uses the article quite frequently when he wishes to designate specific members of a class. We might have expected Peter to use the article if he had specific

---

77. See Love, "The First Epistle of Peter," 69, and Warden, "The Prophets of 1 Peter 1:10–12," 4–5.
78. Selwyn, *First Epistle of St. Peter*, 262.
79. Ibid., 262–63.
80. Ibid., 263.
81. Love, "The First Epistle of Peter," 69. Love does, however, seem to include both the OT prophets and the Christian prophets in the passage's description (see p. 69).

reference to Old Testament prophets."[82] For Warden, the expression "τὰ εἰς Χριστὸν παθήματα" indicates the sufferings Christians experience rather than those Christ experienced, for ". . . εἰς with the accusative may have the force of a genitive, but it is rare. . . . Why Peter should have chosen to use such an unusual construction [to indicate Christ's suffering] presents a difficult question."[83] Warden also draws a parallel with Peter's use of εἰς in 1:11 to its use later in 1:25 and 2:14 (i.e., as meaning "direction" in the former and "for the purpose of" in the latter).[84] This is significant, for both Warden and Selwyn view this particular interpretation ("the sufferings of the Christward road," in Selwyn's words) as more conducive to identifying the prophets as ministers contemporary to the epistle's audience.[85]

In response, one must first examine the expression "τὰ εἰς Χριστὸν παθήματα" in 1 Pet 1:11. Karen Jobes convincingly argues, "Elsewhere the prepositional phrase with *eis* adjectivally modifies its head noun by specifying the recipients of the verbal action by the noun."[86] She points out that in 2 Cor 1:11 (τὸ εἰς ἡμᾶς χάρισμα), "the closest syntactical parallel," the preposition ultimately points to "the recipients of the implied verbal action."[87] In other words, just as in 2 Cor 1:11 the "we" is receiving the "gift," so also in 1 Pet 1:11 the "Christ" is receiving the "suffering." For Jobes, Peter here "chooses a prepositional phrase with εἰς rather than the genitive because of the prophetic perspective of the immediate context."[88]

Secondly, it must be stressed that pre-Christian prophets are indeed portrayed by the NT as investigating the matters pertaining to the new age, especially to Christ. Reinhard Feldmeier aptly argues this by pointing to Luke 24:25–27 and Acts 3:18 while declaring that 1 Peter's link between "salvation history" (*Heilsgeschichte*) and the current situation is "typical" of "early Christian theology."[89] Similarly, Paul Achtemeier refers to other places such as Matt 13:16–17 and Acts 7:52 as evidence that early believers were indeed aware that the OT pointed somehow to Christ.[90] Finally, Norman Hillyer points out that Peter's discussion of "the prophets" elsewhere in

82. Warden, "The Prophets of 1 Peter 1:10–12," 4–5.
83. Ibid., 5–6.
84. Ibid., 6.
85. Selwyn, *First Epistle of St. Peter*, 263; Warden, "The Prophets of 1 Peter 1:10–12," 5.
86. Jobes, *1 Peter*, 99–100.
87. Ibid.
88. Ibid., 100–101.
89. Feldmeier, *Der erste Brief des Petrus*, 62.
90. Achtemeier, *1 Peter*, 108; cf. Kelly, *Commentary on the Epistles of Peter and of Jude*, 60.

Scripture (e.g., Acts 2–4) corresponds to OT prophets rather than Christian prophets (in contrast to Paul's writings, which speak of both).[91]

Thirdly, the most significant argument advanced against Selwyn and others lies in the nature of the contrast between these prophets and Peter's contemporaries. J. N. D. Kelly, in arguing against Selwyn's view, states, "Among the serious difficulties facing this exegesis is the fact that the prophets are manifestly contrasted with, and seem to belong to an earlier epoch than, the readers and those who evangelized them."[92] Along the same lines, Lewis Donelson points out that "the sense of future articulated in 1:11–12, which fits perfectly with OT prophets, makes little sense with Christian ones."[93] In other words, within 1:10–12 the epistle's audience is given a powerful contrast between their own status and those who preceded them (as evidenced by v. 12's expression ὅτι οὐχ ἑαυτοῖς ὑμῖν δὲ διηκόνουν αὐτά), a contrast which is lost if the "prophets" are their contemporaries (and fellow believers of the new era).

Finally, the word προμαρτυρόμενον must be briefly examined. Love has argued that the word is virtually nonexistent in the literature of the first century AD and could "just as well mean 'publicly proclaiming.'"[94] If the latter point is correct, Selwyn's argument is somewhat strengthened while that of this dissertation is hampered. Yet Love, while correct that προμαρτύρομαι is extremely rare, offers no evidence on behalf of the view that it refers to "publicly proclaiming."[95] Due to the rarity of the word, however, it is impossible to either conclusively refute or confirm Love's suggestion. Until someone offers better proof that προμαρτύρομαι would here mean "teach" or "publicly proclaim" rather than "witness ahead of time," however, the burden of proof lies on those who wish to argue for the former.

Nevertheless, it is worth noting 1 Peter's use of the cognates of προμαρτύρομαι within the epistle.[96] In 5:1, Peter presents himself as a "μάρτυς," somebody who ". . . could legitimately claim to be a witness to the sufferings of the Messiah."[97] Yet also, "Our author's identification of himself

---

91. Hillyer, *1 and 2 Peter*, 41.

92. Kelly, *Commentary on the Epistles of Peter and of Jude*, 59; cf. Davids, *First Epistle of Peter*, 60–61.

93. Donelson, *I & II Peter*, 36.

94. Love, "The First Epistle of Peter," 69.

95. This writer conducted a search for "προμαρτύρομαι" in the online database *Thesaurus Linguae Graecae* (University of California, 2009). This writer was unable to find any other occurrence of the word before the fourth century AD.

96. The argument in this paragraph stems from comments Dr. Gene L. Green made as the outside reader at my dissertation defense. I am grateful to him for directing me to the potential link between 1:10–12; 5:1; and 5:12.

97. Jobes, *1 Peter*, 301.

as 'witness' (*martys*), furthermore, relates to his stated aim in writing (5:12). There he employs a kindred verb . . . to indicate that, along with exhortation, his aim in this letter is to 'bear full witness' to the grace of God experienced by the believers. Here (5:1) his witness pertains to Christ's suffering, a reason for the grace experienced."[98] The use of ἐπιμαρτυρέω in 5:12, then hearkens back to 1:10–12, for "With his authoritative witness, the author thus confirms the proclamation of those who first announced the good news to the addressees in an earlier time (1:12)."[99] In this way one could view the prophetic word of 1:10–12 pointing ahead to what Peter himself will witness concerning both the suffering and the grace of God. Consequently, it would be consistent with the entire message of 1 Peter to view 1 Pet 1:10–12 as a passage that includes (among other motifs) the theme of foreknowledge (as possessed by the OT prophets).[100]

The Meaning of the Expression Τίνα ἢ Ποῖον Καιρὸν

Although the basic thrust of this chapter will not be altered either way, the meaning of τίνα ἢ ποῖον καιρὸν still impacts the significance of 1 Pet 1:10–12 to a certain degree. The issue is whether or not the first word is a pronoun or adjective; consequently, the phrase would either be translated "to whom or to what time" or "to what time or manner of time," respectively.[101]

G. D. Kilpatrick, in an examination of how both τίς and ποῖος are used throughout the NT, concludes, "The interpretation which treats τίνα as the interrogative pronoun and ποῖον as the corresponding interrogative adjective seems to be in agreement with general New Testament practice."[102] In addition, Kilpatrick notes that within 1 Peter itself τίς is used exclusively as a pronoun.[103]

98. Elliott, *I Peter*, 818.

99. Ibid., 878.

100. The argument from the lack of the article is, in this writer's opinion, the weakest part of Selwyn and Warden's case. Contra Warden, "contemporary prophets" would have just as much of a claim to be a "class" as OT prophets. Consequently, one is forced to conclude that the lack of the article here is irrelevant to the overall discussion. One could, however, agree with Beare, *First Epistle of Peter*, 65, that ". . . the omission of the article gives the noun a generic force . . . calling attention not to their persons, but to their function." This may be true, though this writer is slightly uncomfortable with what may be an overstatement on Beare's part. Regardless, it is beyond the scope of this study to discuss how the article is used in 1 Peter other than the preceding observation on Warden's argument.

101. Kilpatrick, "1 Peter 1:11," 91.

102. Ibid., 92.

103. Ibid., 91. Kilpatrick is supported by Grudem, *1 Peter*, 75.

In response, Jobes, Michaels, and Everett Harrison all suggest that a καί rather than an ἤ would have been the appropriate conjunction if the first word were a pronoun and the second were not.[104] In response to Kilpatrick's argument that τίς is used mostly as a pronoun, Jobes notes that it could still technically be viewed as a neuter pronoun (i.e., "what things" = "what circumstances") without necessarily referring to the identity of the Messiah.[105] Michaels further points out, "In many instances τίς and ποῖος are synonymous (BGD, 684, 819), and it is possible that Peter combines them merely for rhetorical effect."[106]

The arguments are very well balanced on each side. Kilpatrick's argument would be significantly more convincing if τίς actually occurred more than two other times in 1 Peter. In defense of Kilpatrick, however, it could be pointed out that occasionally the pre-Christian prophets did seem to concern themselves with the *identity* of the Messiah rather than simply the circumstances of his arrival (e.g., Simeon and Anna in Luke 2, though whether or not Simeon was technically a prophet may be debated). Yet since clearly τίς can mean either "who" or "what sort of," the final determination must come down to context. While both senses would be coherent, the identity of the Messiah does not seem to factor into the overall point of 1 Peter 1 as much as the nature of the current situation of the readers, both the positive (their new status in Christ) and the negative (rejection and persecution). This is bolstered by the fact that the overall scope of 1:10–12 hinges on the σωτηρία of verse 10—the nature of this salvation, not the identity of the Savior *per se*. Regardless, one may still conclude with Schutter that

> On any reading, however, some time reference is present, which is enough for immediate purposes. . . . The time when the vision or oracle would be fulfilled is prominent in these texts, as in many others, and the point of 1.11f. is to assert that the time of fulfillment associated with τὰ εἰς Χριστὸν παθήματα καὶ τὰς μετὰ ταῦτα δόξας has been inaugurated and includes the addressees.[107]

The focus, then, is on the arrival of a new era.

---

104. Jobes, *1 Peter*, 101; Michaels, *1 Peter*, 41–42; Harrison, "Exegetical Studies in 1 Peter," 71. Harrison suggests that the suitable expression for Kilpatrick's position would have been τίνα καὶ τίνα καιρόν.
105. Jobes, *1 Peter*, 103.
106. Michaels, *1 Peter*, 42.
107. Schutter, *Hermeneutic and Composition*, 106.

The Significance of 1 Peter 1:10–12 as a Word of Comfort

Clearly, then, foreknowledge plays a key role in 1 Pet 1:10–12. The OT prophets are looking towards the future, seeking for answers regarding the nature of that salvation spoken of in verse 9. Yet they are doing so on behalf of 1 Peter's audience. It is the circumstances of this audience that are in view, as indicated by the expression "ὅτι οὐχ ἑαυτοῖς ὑμῖν δέ" in v. 12; indeed, the focus of the prophets' work is "for your sake."[108] Peter makes it clear that the prophets' mantic knowledge is relevant to his audience's current situation (as indicated by the νῦν of v. 12). As Witherington notes, "The word 'now' is a refrain throughout this epistle as Peter tries to show how much God has now already given and done and is now announcing that he will yet do to encourage his suffering audience."[109] Consequently, the foreknowledge that the prophets received in earlier times functions as a word of comfort for these "strangers" of Asia Minor.[110] The epistle points out the "exclusive privilege" that the readers and hearers now possess, a privilege that makes the status of the OT prophets and even the angels themselves pale in significance.[111]

One must further stress that the epistle here also focuses on the role of the community within the last era. In other words, by describing the role of the OT prophets in terms of benefit for his audience, Peter is demonstrating ". . . the importance of this community within universal history as well as the epochal nature of the present."[112] These believers, ostracized strangers in both the past and present, are now destined to play a great role in the eschatological culmination of God's plan. In other words, by addressing a group of believers who live in this era as harassed strangers, Peter uses the foreknowledge of OT prophets as a means of demonstrating that this community possesses a significance far beyond what their present circumstances would seem to indicate. This community is ultimately linked to the identity of Christ and his plan, a link that will forge within them a new social identity as a holy nation.

---

108. This is stressed by the following (among others): Knopf, *Die Briefe Petri und Judä*, 77; Brox, *Der erste Petrusbrief*, 69; Elliott, *I Peter*, 353.

109. Witherington, *Socio-Rhetorical Commentary on 1–2 Peter*, 84–85.

110. Cf. also Elliott, *I Peter*, 353.

111. Ibid., 351.

112. Brox, *Der erste Petrusbrief*, 68 (". . . den Gemeinden ihren Stellenwert in der universalen Geschichte sowie den epochalen Charakter der Gegenwart zu illustrieren").

1 PETER 1:20

Foreknowledge in 1 Pet 1:20 has generally been viewed as referring to the foreordination of Christ as the means of redemption. Many scholars argue that simple prescience would not even make sense within the context. James, for example, suggests that since ". . . foreknowledge cannot act, and since the act of redemption is in view (vs. 18), . . ." then the participle προεγνωσμένου must naturally mean "foreordination."[113] Baugh bluntly states, "In this passage, there can be no doubt that the idea of previous commitment is the only possible meaning of foreknowledge."[114] Finally, Peter Davids argues, "To say 'chosen in advance' is not simply to say that God predicted it would happen (which is what the translation 'foreknown' might suggest), but to say that God planned and brought it about, for with God 'predict' and 'predestine' are not separate concepts."[115]

Yet all of the above statements seem to assume *a priori* that (1) "foreordination" automatically equals "foreknowledge" when the Divine is the subject and (2) it is impossible to discuss foreknowledge separately from foreordination. As argued in chapter 3, however, this does not logically follow and would not follow even if one could prove that divine foreknowledge exists because God has foreordained all things.[116] In response, it must be reiterated that if it cannot be conclusively demonstrated that προγινώσκω ever meant "foreordination" in the language of the day, then it is highly unlikely that 1 Peter's readers, still in the process of developing their theology, would necessarily have taken that Greek term to refer to the concept of "determining/choosing ahead of time." This is not to argue that God did not foreordain his Son to die for the sins of the world (this is made explicit in Acts 2:23). It is simply to point out that this is not necessarily the point of 1 Pet 1:20.

Within the context of 1 Pet 1:20, good reason exists for seeing προγινώσκω as a prescient term. To begin with, the epistle is creating here a grand contrast between προγινώσκω on the one hand and φανερόω on the other. This is made explicit by the "μέν . . . δέ" construction. While whether or not this verse forms part of a formal hymn may be debated, at least one

---

113. James, "Is Foreknowledge Equivalent to Foreordination?," 218.

114. Baugh, "Meaning of Foreknowledge," 196.

115. Davids, *First Epistle of Peter*, 74.

116. Whether or not this can be demonstrated is beyond the scope of this paper. For those who would wish to argue in this manner, however, they must also take into account that this would require God to actually foreordain every single choice to commit an evil act (not "foreordain to allow," which is a different concept altogether). As noted in chapter 1, however, even Augustine was leery of holding to this position. In the end, this writer will simply reiterate Buswell, who states, "Divine election is one thing and divine foreknowledge is another thing" (*Systematic Theology* 2:141).

can appreciate Jacob Prasad's observations when he states, "There is *parallelismus membrorum*; the two participles are anarthrous; the antithetical expressions are correlated with the participles μέν and δέ; the participial construction is made to modify Christ, there is the corresponding numbers of syllables in both lines; . . ."[117] Thus, as Witherington points out, "'Foreknown' parallels 'revealed' and refers to an activity of God the Father, who does both."[118]

Here, then, is the question: which of the following forms the more natural contrast: *foreordination* with revelation or *foreknowledge* with revelation? Since the second half of the μέν . . . δέ construction deals with what is *made known* to believers in the present era, this writer contends that it would naturally make sense for the first half of the construction to refer to what has been *known* by God from eternity past. Thus the contrast naturally involves the revelation of knowledge and places past knowledge in opposition to present knowledge (instead of foreordination in opposition to present knowledge). In other words, it is *"knowing* something now" compared to *"knowing* something all along," not *"knowing* something now" compared to *"determining* something in the past." Consequently, Peter is declaring that what God has known within himself all along (namely, the Messianic plan of redemption) has "now" (επ' ἐσχάτου τῶν χρόνων) been made known to the privileged community of strangers.[119]

Once again, this study does not deny that the NT teaches that God did indeed foreordain his Son to suffer and gain redemption for his people. That act of foreordination, however, is not what is in view in 1 Pet 1:20. Rather, in this text the focus is on the revelation of knowledge. In this way, 1 Pet 1:20 actually ties back to 1:10–12. In 1:10–12, the revelation given to the prophets was for the sake of the current generation. Now, in the same manner, the facts about Jesus and his redemption have been made known (φανερόω) to this same generation of strangers.[120] Furthermore, this generation can take

---

117. Prasad, *Foundations of the Christian Way of Life According to 1 Peter 1, 13–24*, 229. For more discussion on the hymn-like nature of verse 20, see Kelly, *Commentary on the Epistles of Peter and of Jude*, 75.

118. Witherington, *Socio-Rhetorical Commentary on 1–2 Peter*, 108. Like this writer, Witherington clearly takes προγινώσκω in a prescient sense. Following Witherington's interpretation, then, this writer has no problem with seeing "foreknowing" as constituting an activity, even when referring to simple prescience (contra James, "Is Foreknowledge Equivalent to Foreordination?," 218).

119. See Schelkle, *Die Petrusbriefe*, 50, and Bartlett, *NIB* 12:259 for a discussion of this point (though neither takes the term προγινώσκω in a strictly prescient sense as this writer does).

120. Thurén, *Argument and Theology in 1 Peter*, 115, when comparing the broader context of 1 Pet 1:20 with 1:10–12, states, "Both stress the extraordinary nature of

heart that "... this new thing that God has done and is doing in Christ is, in God's eyes at least, not a new thing at all."[121]

This new revelation of knowledge about Christ, then, is once again "for your sake" ("δι' ὑμας") in regards to this community of strangers (here that pronoun parallels the "ὑμῖν" of 1:12). Indeed, "All of this has been and is being done 'because of you.' This centering of the entire story of salvation upon 'you' is one of the central convictions of the letter."[122]

Thus this new revelation of knowledge to believers, contrasted with God's eternal foreknowledge, has ushered in a new era.[123] Furthermore, this new cosmic era is one that 1 Peter's audience has the privilege of being a part of. God's plan, foreknown before the foundation of the world, is not only revealed to them but also includes them as key participants. This fact naturally leads to the command to love each other in 1:22.

CONCLUSION

All three passages, 1 Pet 1:1–2; 1:10–12; and 1:20, contain the concept of foreknowledge. Furthermore, all three passages also focus on the readers/listeners and their current circumstances. In 1:1–2, they are "elect strangers," yet this is in complete harmony with the foreknowledge of the Father. In 1:10–12, the foreknowledge that the prophets received was actually for the benefit of this new community of elect strangers. Finally, in 1:20, what God the Father has foreknown is now revealed to these strangers, and this also is for their benefit. In this way, foreknowledge in all three texts functions as a word of comfort to these strangers, despite their social status as outcasts. The next step, then, is to see how both foreknowledge and social-spiritual identity function within the broader scope of 1 Peter's theology.

---

the addressees' situation." Similarly, Brox, *Der erste Petrusbrief*, 83, also links 1:20 to 1:10–12. Cf. also Donelson, *I & II Peter*, 48; and Bartlett, *NIB* 12:259.

121. Donelson, *I & II Peter*, 48.

122. Ibid., 49. Cf. Feldmeier, *Der erste Brief des Petrus*, 79, and Achtemeier, *1 Peter*, 132.

123. Feldmeier, *Der erste Brief des Petrus*, 79.

6

The Significance of Foreknowledge for a New Social Identity in 1 Peter

This chapter now begins with two key assumptions. First, in John Elliott's words,

> 1 Peter was directed to actual strangers and resident aliens who had become Christians. Their new religious affiliation was not the cause of their position in society though it did add to their difficulties in relating to their neighbors. It is precisely this combination of factors which best explains the disillusionment which the converts felt.[1]

In other words, a significant portion of 1 Peter's audience knew what it meant to be truly displaced.[2] This sense of displacement then also func-

---

1. Elliott, *Home for the Homeless*, 131.
2. It is this writer's contention (as argued, to a certain degree, in chapter 2) that "displacement" is a negative concept regardless of whether it is being used literally or figuratively/spiritually. Yet Green, in his essay "Living as Exiles: The Church in the Diaspora in 1 Peter," 319, suggests, "Rejection by others loses its power when one realizes one's status as strangers in a strange land" (Green takes a metaphorical view of the displacement language of 1 Peter). Yet this writer, having grown up as a literal foreigner in a Far Eastern country for almost all of his childhood, would partially differ. The self-aware state of "otherness" usually lingers as a negative feeling for foreigners in a distant land, and it is rarely ever something that is embraced. The only cure for the stigma of displacement is to be accepted by others as an equal, an experience that I was privileged to have received from my closest Japanese friends (and even then, one's own self-awareness of being a "stranger" rarely dissipates completely in the rest of one's daily life). Nevertheless, I am not necessarily unsympathetic to Green's overall point, better articulated in a later sentence where he states, "The loss of honor among men

The Significance of Foreknowledge for a New Social Identity in 1 Peter

tions as a paradigm through which to view the circumstances of the readers in relation to society (both spiritually and socially).[3]

Secondly, "foreknowledge" in 1 Peter may best be understood as a prescient concept and as such occurs in three places (1 Pet 1:2; 1:10–12; 1:20). In each of those passages, this concept acts as an encouragement to those readers and is linked to both their present and future circumstances.

With that in mind, this chapter will place both foreknowledge and social identity within the broader theological scope of the first major section of 1 Peter. This chapter will not argue that these two concepts are necessarily the primary themes of 1 Pet 1:1—2:10.[4] Rather, this study will simply focus on how these two concepts function in relation to each other within the broader realm of 1 Peter's theology, a correspondence that has never, to this writer's knowledge, been thoroughly explored.

The goal of this chapter, then, is to build on the social scientific criticism, the lexical semantics, and the exegesis of previous chapters and enter into a theological dialogue. Theologically, foreknowledge ultimately points towards a promised eschatological shift in social identity, a shift that is anchored within the person of the Lord Jesus himself.

CAUSE FOR DESPAIR: DISPLACEMENT AND PERSECUTION

Scholarship has widely acknowledged that 1 Peter confronts an audience suffering genuine persecution, and this persecution is assumed throughout the epistle.[5] Such suffering is clearly referred to throughout the epistle,

---

and women loses its sting when this loss is parried by the reception of honor from God" (p. 319). Interpreters of 1 Peter, however, must be careful not to diminish the negative effect of displacement.

3. As argued in chapter 2, I see no reason why the same term cannot be used both literally and also metaphorically.

4. A variety of views exist regarding the various themes in 1 Peter (see, for example, Joseph, *Narratological Reading of 1 Peter*, 69–70, and his opinion regarding the "four main elements that constitute the fabula of the letter," namely "election," "suffering," "faithful response," and "vindication").

5. See, for example, the following sources: Harink, *1 & 2 Peter*, 45–46; Köstenberger, et al, *The Cradle, the Cross, and the Crown*, 737; Chester and Martin, *Theology of the Letters of James, Peter, and Jude*, 88. Spicq, *Les Épitres de Saint Pierre*, 11, correctly points out that such poor treatment towards Jesus' disciples was prophesied by Christ himself. Nevertheless, it is worth asking how much these Anatolian Christians would have understood of Christ's teaching at this point (and, consequently, how much comfort they could draw from Christ's words). Ultimately, it is up to Peter to educate this new generation of Christians and show them that, as Meinertz and Vrede articulate,

including 1 Pet 1:6–7; 2:12, 20; etc. As David Horrell aptly observes, "the situation depicted in 1 Peter looks like a situation in which Christians are suffering verbal hostility and ridicule from their neighbours, who react negatively to this new faith and to those who convert to it."[6] Indeed, "The language of suffering permeates the letter."[7] Consequently, 1 Peter can, to a certain degree, be viewed as a letter of consolation or encouragement in the face of suffering.[8]

The nature of the recipients' suffering cannot be boiled down to just any one type of harassment, nor should one focus too much on an "informal," as opposed to a "formal," persecution (or vice versa).[9] Yet certainly one aspect of that persecution stemmed from the "otherness" of the Christian community in Anatolia. It was bad enough that the readers began their residence in Asia Minor as true strangers; accepting Christianity made it worse, accentuating their "otherness" even further until their outcast status became nearly unbearable. Consequently, Christians

> were at odds with society around them and feeling the sharp pricks of "persecution" from local officials and community pressures . . . Then, their social status was thrown into question by their acceptance of a new religion, and at least some of the letter reflects the felt need of an alienated social group whose underpinnings have been swept away as a direct consequence of their conversion to Christianity (2.10; 4.4).[10]

"The purpose of this suffering is the testing of their faith" (*Die Katholischen Briefe*, 92 ["Der Zweck dieser Leiden ist die Prüfung des Glaubens"; translation is this writer's]).

6. Horrell, *1 Peter*, 54. Cf. also all of pp. 54–58.

7. Joseph, *Narratological Reading*, 95.

8. See Guthrie, *New Testament Introduction*, 781–82; Kirk, "Endurance in Suffering in 1 Peter," 55. Furthermore, as Thompson, "Rhetoric of 1 Peter," 250, notes, "The repetition of the basic argument that runs from 1:13 to 5:5 further reinforces the call to endurance by an appeal to past witnesses and the community tradition." As a result, 1 Peter could be classified as "a persuasive work" (p. 250).

9. Williams, in his very recent monograph, *Persecution in 1 Peter*, has stressed this point. On p. 179 (and elsewhere) he cautions against drawing a "(false) dichotomy between 'official' and 'unofficial' persecution . . ." On p. 235, he argues, ". . . contrary to the opinions of many Petrine commentators, the detrimental downturn in the legal status of Christians took place during the time of Nero rather than during the second or third centuries CE." Instead, ". . . all Christians shared the same perilous legal status following the Neronian persecution." Yet on the other hand, Williams states, "Rather than approaching 1 Peter with the notion that all of its recipients were equally prone to and necessarily expectant of Christian martyrdom, we should be careful in drawing too grim a portrait of Christian circumstances simply on the basis of how they were viewed in the eyes of Roman authorities" (235–36).

10. Chester and Martin, *Theology of the Letters of James, Peter, and Jude*, 89. The

Furthermore, one must not only consider the fact that the Anatolian Christians were suffering, but also the fact that they were experiencing such "antagonism, slander, and social ostracism *from those amongst whom they lived.*"[11] Thus neighbors become strangers, friends become enemies, and those with whom they would normally enjoy all the normal social conventions of life shut them out from the basic privileges of communal hospitality. It is one thing to suffer; it is another thing altogether to suffer at the hands of those who at the least were neighbors and might even be their most intimate partners (e.g., 1 Pet 3:1).[12]

In this way, the background of 1 Peter seems to assume that the readers' situation went from bad to worse. What began as mere social displacement with the hope for a better life suddenly deteriorates further into both a social *and* a spiritual outcast status, complete with various kinds of persecution.[13] The path to social conformity did not lie parallel to the path of Christ. Rather, the two paths diverged, and the farther they diverged the greater the possibility for isolation and loneliness.

This sense of displacement, then, brought with it a grave spiritual threat. Joel Green states,

> For persons thus branded as "not at home," intimate with day-to-day cancerous slander and calamity, the temptations are several: to embrace the dispositions and practices conventional in the wider world (i.e., the threat of assimilation and defection) and to query one's status before God chief among them. (We do not easily correlate rejection within the human family with honorable status before God).[14]

Yet 1 Peter has a solution for its audience's situation. Their alien status will be alleviated by providing them an alternative "holy nation," a new social status in Christ.[15] In order to lay the groundwork for this resounding

---

situation of the readers, even their status as strangers, may be further discussed in terms of the concepts of "honor" and "shame." Although it is beyond the scope of this paper to offer much of an investigation, the reader is advised to especially examine the following two sources: Campbell, *Honor, Shame, and the Rhetoric of 1 Peter*; and Elliott, "Disgraced yet Graced," 166–78.

11. Horrell, *1 Peter*, 58 (emphasis added).

12. Furthermore, as Gene Green points out in "1 Peter," 347, "Particularly where close social ties existed, . . . there was the danger of physical hostility."

13. For a thorough discussion of the various kinds of persecution implied by 1 Peter and its background, see Williams, *Persecution in 1 Peter*, 300–316.

14. Joel Green, *1 Peter*, 17.

15. Although he ultimately holds to the standard metaphorical understanding of "strangers" in 1 Peter, nevertheless Martin, in his monograph *Metaphor and Composition*

theological theme in 1 Pet 2:4–10, the author paves the way with the concept of foreknowledge and the great revelation it portends.

CAUSE FOR HOPE: FOREKNOWLEDGE AS THE BRIDGE TO A NEW SOCIAL STATUS

As demonstrated in the last chapter, the concept of foreknowledge plays a key role in Peter's theology from the very beginning of the epistle. This foreknowledge, ultimately of a divine origin, is revealed to the readers themselves and points towards an eschatology in which they play a major role.

In 1 Pet 1:2, both the Christian's election and rejection (displacement) have been foreknown by God the Father. In other words, the entirety of their circumstances, both the positive and the negative, come as no surprise to God. In light of the negative circumstances of the readers (especially displacement, and all the woes that stem from it), "part of the comfort to be derived from this letter by readers who currently confront persecutions of various sorts comes from the fact that even such unfortunate circumstances are not beyond the control of the benevolent God who in Christ will rescue those who remain steadfast . . ."[16]

Later in the epistle, the circumstances of the readers come to the forefront, and the concept of foreknowledge addresses these circumstances. Thus, as Joel Green states regarding 1 Pet 1:3–12, "Throughout, Peter maintains an unwavering focus on the situation of his addressees: their new birth, their distress, their trials, their testing, their love, their faith, their joy, and the grace that had come to them."[17] Particularly in 1:10–12, foreknowledge is seen as functioning *on behalf of* the readers. Thus, what once looked like a bleak and dismal situation (displacement) turns out to be an enviable situation, a privileged status that even the OT prophets and angels wish to learn more of.

In 1 Pet 1:20, as argued in the previous chapter, what was divinely foreknown is now revealed to the Christians themselves. Foreknowledge, then, is not for the benefit of God but rather pivotal to the Christian's self-understanding.

---

in 1 Peter, 208, makes a profound theological statement regarding the "strangers" of 1 Peter. He states, "Furthermore, as aliens they stand under the direct protection of God." Martin here evidences a brilliant understanding of the OT treatment of aliens sojourning among the Israelites (e.g., Exod 22:21), an understanding that needs to be unpacked further in light of 1 Peter's theology.

16. Achtemeier, *1 Peter*, 101.
17. Green, *1 Peter*, 22–23.

In this way, three theological truths are gleaned from foreknowledge in 1 Pet 1:1–20. First, in 1:2, such foreknowledge is ever present with God the Father, a key characteristic of his interaction with the elect of his creation. Secondly, such foreknowledge, mediated through the prophets, reveals the privileged status of the recipients (1:10–12). Finally, what was foreknown by God about His Son is now revealed to the Christians themselves.

Consequently, the concept of foreknowledge informs 1 Peter's eschatology, since the latter is naturally related to the former. Thus, despite their displacement as homeless strangers, Peter's audience is promised an eschatological "inheritance" in 1:4. Significantly, however, this "inheritance" itself is partially located in the "here and now" rather than representing a "spiritual" kingdom that 1 Peter's audience is headed for (i.e., "pilgrim" theology).[18] On the one hand, as Douglas Harink argues, "The inheritance kept (literally) 'in the heavens' is given to God's people when God himself comes in power to deliver and purify his people, to establish the new Jerusalem in the midst of the nations, and to make creation the home of his own righteousness."[19] Yet as Harink further clarifies, Jesus often spoke of the kingdom of heaven as if it were already present in some form, and Peter seems to suggest a similar idea in much of his epistle (especially the second chapter, as will be demonstrated). Thus, for Harink, the phrase "kept in the heavens . . . is not a statement about where the inheritance is located; it is a statement about its divine origin and quality—God's eternal life, glory, and reign is itself our inheritance."[20] The significance of this for the audience of 1 Peter, as Elliott notes, is that "For strangers and resident aliens who would also be ineligible to inherit land where they currently reside, this promise of an inheritance preserved in heaven thus had a double appeal."[21]

---

18. Harink, *1 & 2 Peter*, 45.

19. Ibid.

20. Ibid. It should, of course, be acknowledged that there is a sense in which this "inheritance" possesses an eschatological force (see Williams, *Doctrine of Salvation in the First Letter of Peter*, 157; Prasad, *Foundations of the Christian Way of Life according to 1 Peter 1, 13–25*, 258). Yet this eschatological force does not exclude the fact that, as Harink argues above, the inheritance is also present in some sense within the church (in the same way that salvation is also "already-not-yet"). Furthermore, in light of the fact that 1 Peter (and the NT as a whole) uses "family" and "household" language, and in light of the fact that "inheritance" is a family matter, surely it would be in keeping with the broader rhetoric of 1 Peter to argue that this "inheritance" is partially realized within the new family and new nation that is the community of believers (without necessarily denying its eschatological culmination). For more on the eschatological sense of "inheritance" in this passage, however, see Beale, *New Testament Biblical Theology*, 325–26.

21. Elliott, *I Peter*, 336.

It is difficult to dispute that a sense of "already-not-yet" permeates the epistle. On the one hand, in 1 Pet 1:5 the recipients are privy to "a salvation ready to be revealed in the last time" (ESV). This future salvation, then, is allowed to be foreknown by them. In this way, foreknowledge is linked to eschatological salvation. Consequently, their current sorrows (including displacement) can fade away in light of the "eschatological joy" of 1:6.[22]

Yet on the other hand, clearly this salvation is of present benefit, more than just a future hope "by and by." Both the soteriological future and the present go hand in hand. Gene Green aptly sums up this fact when he states,

> Christians have become participants in this saving plan: salvation is "to/for" them (1:10, 12, 20, 25; 2:7, 9) and is "now" realized in the time of fulfillment (1:12; 2:10; 3:21) . . . 1 Peter also links the present and the future. Future salvation is one with present salvation (1:5, 9, 10–12; 3:21).[23]

Thus, regardless of the intricacies of 1 Peter's eschatology, it is clear that the epistle's readers and hearers themselves possess foreknowledge of a forthcoming future, a future vastly superior to their present status as displaced strangers. Furthermore, this revelation of the future stems from the trustworthy, enduring word of God that has been proclaimed to this audience. As D. A. Carson notes, the citation of Isa 40:6–8 in 1 Pet 1:24–25 would probably have brought the entire context of Isaiah 40 to the mind of the readers; in that case,

> then the word preached to them is doubtless the word promising the visitation by Yahweh, the promised worldwide theophany—manifested in the gospel itself *and still to be fulfilled at the end of the age*. Precisely because God's word is reliable, Peter's readers can rest assured that *the fulfillment that has not yet taken place will come*—and "this is the word that was preached to you."[24]

This foreknowledge of the future fulfillment of God's word is cause for hope. No matter their current circumstances, God himself has promised them a much superior status, an elect status that stands in stark contrast to their current rejection by those around them.

Finally, the foreknowledge that the epistle's recipients benefit from and partake in is inexorably linked to the person and revelation of Jesus Christ in 1 Pet 1:20. In other words, whatever foreknown destiny awaits 1 Peter's

---

22. Goppelt, *Der erste Petrusbrief*, 99. Cf. also Kendall, "Literary and Theological Function of 1 Peter 1:3–12," 107.

23. Green, "1 Peter," 347.

24. Carson, "1 Peter," 1022 (emphasis added).

The Significance of Foreknowledge for a New Social Identity in 1 Peter 169

audience is made possible only because of the work of Christ, a work now revealed to them. It is Christ that anchors both the eschatological and present hope.[25]

CAUSE FOR IDENTIFICATION: SOCIAL IDENTITY TIED TO CHRIST

The act of linking foreknowledge and eschatological knowledge to the person of Christ in 1 Pet 1:20 is a calculated rhetorical strategy on the part of the author. This ultimately paves the way for building his audience's new social status on the "rejected-yet-elected" status of Jesus Christ. In other words, foreknowledge gives hope to the audience by first pointing to Christ, the foundation of their own elect status as a new kingdom.[26]

The ecclesiological significance of Christ's work does not begin with 1 Pet 1:20, however. As Earl Richard states, "The first section of the letter with its emphasis upon the soteriological function of the Christ-event serves to establish the basis for the community's new life . . . From the outset the author puts the traditional Jesus material at the service of his ecclesiological task."[27] As early as 1 Pet 1:3, the eschatological and ecclesiological hope of the epistle is linked to the resurrection of Jesus Christ. Indeed, in 1:3–12 as a whole (the "groundwork for the rest of the letter," in the words of Chester and Martin), we see that "The believers' new existence is grounded in Christ's resurrection. This is the basis for hope and points to God's guaranteed future."[28] Immediately after that section, in 1:13, the grace made available to the audience is tied directly to the revelation of Jesus Christ.

Between 1 Pet 1:17 and 1:20, then, the link between Christology and eschatology (and, consequently, foreknowledge) is further intensified. As Green notes, "The juxtaposition of these two descriptions [the "χρόνος" of these two verses] is parabolic of the deeper reality to which his audience must attend. This is that the last days inaugurated by the death and resurrection of Jesus can only be a time of living as strangers and never really at

---

25. Schreiner, *New Testament Theology*, 403, aptly notes the tight connection between Christology and eschatology in 1 Pet 1:20 when he states, "The last days have dawned in Jesus Christ, and the age of fulfillment has begun."

26. See Schröger, *Gemeinde im 1 Petrusbrief*, 19, and his discussion of how 1 Peter's description of God's work in the Christian *Gemeinde* parallels its description of God's work in Jesus Christ.

27. Richard, "Functional Christology of First Peter," 135.

28. Chester and Martin, *Theology of the Letters of James, Peter, and Jude*, 102. Cf. Cothenet, "Le réalisme de l'espérance chrétienne selon 1 Pierre," 564, who also links the community's hope to the resurrection of Jesus.

home for those who have been born anew."[29] In 1 Pet 1:20, Christ's foreknown role in God's plan anchors the eschatological hope of his audience.

Shortly thereafter, Peter brings his audience to the rhetorical peak of the epistle, the great Christological and ecclesiological discourse of 1 Pet 2:4–10.[30] In this section, Peter explicitly links his own audience's new social identity to the identity of Christ. In fact, as Lauri Thurén points out, "An extra purpose with 2.1–10, which also has occurred before, is to show how important Christ is to the addressees: Through him they have obtained their new status."[31]

First, in 1 Pet 2:1–3, "Peter joins theology to ethics . . . , forming a transition between his teaching on the eternal, imperishable seed that has made his readers children of God (1:22–25) and his subsequent teaching in verses 2:9–11 on the nature of the people of God that they have become."[32] This new identity of God's people is linked closely to their desire for "milk," which Karen Jobes defines as "God's life-sustaining grace in Christ." This is "appropriate to Peter's goal of redefining his reader's self-identity in light of the new reality into which they have come through the new birth."[33]

At this point, Peter immediately launches into a discussion on the identity of this Christ. Yet in 2:4 and the following discussion, just as in 1:13—2:3, the focus is also on "the *relationship between the believers and Jesus* . . ."[34] The Christology of the entire first half of 1 Peter 2 will be closely tied to both the conduct and the identity of the believers.

Significantly, much of the Christology of 1 Peter 2 focuses on the Messiah's suffering (briefly hinted at in 1:11 and 1:19) or, to be more precise, "The juxtaposition of rejection (suffering) and election . . ."[35] Consequently, identification with the suffering of Jesus naturally encourages those readers who themselves are experiencing persecution.[36] In other words,

29. Joel Green, "Narrating the Gospel in 1 and 2 Peter," 273.

30. For a helpful discussion of the structure and vocabulary of this section, see Chevallier, "I Pierre 1/1 à 2/10," 136–37. See also the discussion by Williams, "A Case Study in Intertextuality," 37–55, for a comprehensive discussion of 1 Peter's use of Isaiah in this section. Williams argues, "Peter uses Isaiah first and foremost to expound his Christology" (rather than *primarily* ecclesiology), but she further states that Peter's purpose in this passage is also ecclesiological (in a secondary sense).

31. Thurén, *Argument and Theology in 1 Peter*, 131.

32. Jobes, "Got Milk? Septuagint Psalm 33 and the Interpretation of 1 Peter 2:1–3," 13.

33. Ibid., 14. Jobes' thesis in this article is somewhat controversial, but it does seem to make sense within the context of the passage.

34. Elliott, *Elect and the Holy*, 214 (emphasis is Elliott's).

35. Joseph, *Narratological Reading of 1 Peter*, 101.

36. Elliott, *I Peter*, 443.

The Significance of Foreknowledge for a New Social Identity in 1 Peter 171

Jesus' suffering is not an end in itself. Jesus' suffering is only one aspect of the overall story of his relationship with God, whose scope extends from before the creation of the world until the last times, and whose end is the "glory" that God will bestow (1.19–21). In 1 Peter, the sufferings of Christ are never discussed in isolation.[37]

Yet it is also Christ's divine election that is in view (contrasted with human rejection), a motif that will prove crucial to 1 Peter's discussion of the Christian community.[38] Elliott appropriately notes,

> The form and content of I P 2:4–10 reveals that this section was an attempt to describe via the motif of *election* the character and responsibility of the eschatological People of God, her bond with Jesus Christ, her infusion with the Spirit, her holiness, and her task of witness through the holy life and the proclamation of the saving deeds of God.[39]

In 1 Pet 2:4, then, Peter develops the image of Christ as a stone—rejected on the one hand by humans, but elect by God on the other. Jobes aptly summarizes this passage (2:4–5) in the following manner:

> Peter describes the Lord Jesus Christ, to whom his readers come, as the Living Stone and thereby introduces a dominant image in this passage that has both Christological and ecclesiastical significance. The Living Stone was rejected as worthless by "the builders" but was chosen and precious to God . . . Here Peter reintroduces the theme of election (cf. 1 Pet. 1:1–2) and associates the rejection of the Living Stone with the rejection of those who come to him. The parity of Jesus' experience with the experience of Peter's readers is a conceptual structure throughout the book. Moreover, this passage also introduces the soteriological concept that one's response to the Living Stone—rejecting him or coming to him—determines one's relationship to God and, consequently, one's destiny.[40]

Thus Christ is held up as the paradigm of both election and rejection. Significantly, the fate of the Christian community is bound up with him, and "the rejected, suffering, and yet elect Christ" is inextricably tied to "his

37. Joseph, *Narratological Reading of 1 Peter*, 105.
38. Elliott, *I Peter*, 411.
39. Elliott, *Elect and the Holy*, 219. The reader will remember that "election" and "foreknowledge" appear in close proximity at the very beginning of 1 Peter, vv. 1:1–2 (though not as identical concepts).
40. Jobes, *1 Peter*, 146.

rejected, suffering, and elect followers."[41] Thus, "To call Jesus the cornerstone means that he determines the orientation and direction of the church, the new covenant community."[42]

Naturally, then, these "stone" passages in 1 Pet 2:4-10 demonstrate that

> the movement from Christ as elect and precious living stone to his followers who because of their relationship to him are also elect and precious stones constituted into a people special to God, sums up the thought begun in 1:13 that has concerned the relationship of Christians to God through Christ (e.g., 1:18-21, 23-25) and the duties such a relationship makes incumbent upon them (e.g., 1:13-17, 22; 2:1-3). The topic of election, encountered in the opening verse of the letter, here becomes thematic, but it is now clear that God's election of the Christian community (2:9) depends entirely on God's prior election of Christ (2:4, 6; cf. 1:20).[43]

This close tie between the destiny of Christ and the destiny of believers consequently becomes a word of comfort to Peter's audience.[44]

Here, then, is where foreknowledge, Christology, and ecclesiology join together in one grand harmony. Both the circumstances of Christ's life (his rejection, death, election, and resurrection) and the circumstances of the epistle's audience (their rejection and election) have been foreknown by God, and their significance is now revealed to this audience. Consequently, none of the audience's situation is outside of God's plan, and all of this plays a key role in the great meta-narrative of redemption. All this is done "for you."[45] It is in this new people, 1 Peter's audience, that God will perform something incredible, namely affect a reversal of circumstances anchored upon the election of Jesus Christ. The result is a new community, built upon the death and resurrection of Jesus Christ, which demonstrates the love of God towards all of humanity. For this community, "Christ is both the focal

---

41. Elliott, *I Peter*, 411.

42. Helyer, *Life and Witness of Peter*, 138.

43. Achtemeier, *1 Peter*, 152. For more discussion on the link between Christ and the fate of the community, see Goldstein, "Das Gemeindeverständnis des ersten Petrusbriefs," 131. The converse of the positive elements of identification with Christ is, as Dryden has pointed out in *Theology and Ethics*, 120, the fact that "Just as Jesus was rejected, so also the church will be rejected. Identity breeds difference."

44. Achtemeier, *1 Peter*, 170.

45. Donelson, *I & II Peter and Jude*, 49.

The Significance of Foreknowledge for a New Social Identity in 1 Peter 173

point and the foundation of this spiritual house in Zion. He is the living stone who summons individuals to become part of this grand edifice."[46]

CAUSE FOR REJOICING AND OBEDIENCE: THE STRANGERS BECOME A NEW NATION

With 1 Pet 2:4 and 2:9-10, the theological focus of the epistle now turns to the ultimate destiny of the Christian community, their new social identity in Christ. Yet this new social identity has already been hinted at earlier in the epistle. Commenting on 1 Pet 1:3-12, Paul Achtemeier points out how this section "functions as the *prooemium* for the discussion to follow, showing how the triune God has established the church as a community of hope by reason of the resurrection of Jesus .... In that way the major themes of the ensuing discussion of the present and future fate of the new people of God are announced in these opening verses."[47] Similarly, J. De Waal Dryden states,

> The theme of the great ἔλεος of God, which opened this section in 1:3, is reiterated in the identification of the readers as those who have been shown mercy in 2:10. The story of this mercy, having just focused on conversion, now devotes itself to God's creation of a new community of the redeemed. The movement here is from individual conversion to corporate identity.[48]

The focus on social identity especially intensifies with the description of a building in 1 Pet 2:5. Jobes writes,

> The image of living stones being built into a spiritual house whose cornerstone is Christ also speaks of the unity, significance, and purpose of all believers, concepts essential for Christian self-understanding ... The imagery of the living stones being built into a single unity implies that the significance and purpose of the individual Christian cannot be realized apart from community with other believers. Coming to Christ means coming into relationship with others, not only in one's own generation but also by being united with believers of every generation, who likewise have been built into God's grand building project.[49]

---

46. Helyer, *Life and Witness of Peter*, 193.
47. Achtemeier, *1 Peter*, 91.
48. Dryden, *Theology and Ethics*, 119.
49. Jobes, *1 Peter*, 149.

Thus the "rock" becomes the basis for the "stones" of the great building. As W. Edward Glenny writes, "The purpose of this section is to establish the identity or self-understanding of the recipients of the epistle as the people of God, and this identity, described in verses 9–10, is based upon their relationship with the stone in verses 6–8."[50] At this point, election is the key concept that links ecclesiology to Christology.[51]

Finally, then, the reader is led to the great culmination of the social transformation awaiting 1 Peter's audience (1 Pet 2:9). The strangers are now given a new set of titles, namely, that of "a chosen race, a royal priesthood, a holy nation, a people for his own possession" (ESV).

As true, literal strangers, the audience of 1 Peter had lost one of the key elements of a "normal" life in any generation: the sense of belonging, of having a home. In a masterful stroke, Peter draws on a flurry of OT passages to give them the following alternative: social identity within a new nation, a new family. In the words of Chester and Martin, "The social identity they fear to be lost is replaced by a new sense of belonging to the 'people of God,' stretching back to Abraham and Sarah (3. 5, 6) and onward to the complete 'household of faith' one day to be realized (2.4–10; 4.17–19)."[52] As Gene Green similarly states, "Though rejected by their contemporaries, the Christians have a new social identity which is in continuity with that of the OT people of God and based on their new faith in God."[53] Finally, David Horrell aptly notes,

> What the author of 1 Peter is doing, then, is using the resources of Jewish scripture and identity to give a positive sense of identity to the recipients of the letter, who are hard-pressed due to their negative experience of hostility and suffering, and the criticism and slander they receive from their neighbours. In social-psychological terms, the author is pursuing a certain strategy to reverse this negative evaluation of the believers' identity. While those around them may condemn them as evildoers, and

---

50. Glenny, "Israelite Imagery of 1 Peter 2," 161. Cf. also Fanning, "Theology of Peter and Jude," 453.

51. Glenny, "Israelite Imagery," 169. Glenny states, "The connection between the stone (λίθος) quotations in verses 6–8 and the people (λαός) allusions in verses 9–10 is based on the fact that both the stone and the people are elect."

52. Chester and Martin, *Theology of the Letters of James, Peter, and Jude*, 90. Here Chester and Martin aptly balance out eschatology with the "here-and-now" of 1 Peter's theology.

53. Green, "1 Peter," 349.

criticize their faith and conduct, the author insists that they have a glorious and highly valued identity as God's special people.[54]

The terminology of 2:9 is loaded with both theological and social significance. As the only verse in the NT where γένος, ἔθνος, and λαός all simultaneously appear, one could conclude that this represents ". . an almost deliberate attempt to pack the verse with ethnic identity labels."[55] In his recent article discussing these particular terms, David Horrell points out, "These ethnic terms are, as we have also seen, taken over from the language of Jewish self-identity, such that they acquire a particular resonance in early Christian literature; and this raises the further question about whether, and in what ways, Christian identity itself should be seen as ethnic or ethnoracial in character."[56]

On the one hand, Horrell acknowledges that ethnic differences within the early Christian community did not completely disappear (as seen in Gal 2:15 and Rom 9:3).[57] Yet significantly,

> None of this contradicts the fact that the early Christians, and the author of 1 Peter in particular, used ethnoracial language to describe and construct "Christian" identity. And once we see ethnic identity as socially constructed through discourse, as something *believed* more than objective or factual, then early Christian identity is as "really" ethnic as are other forms of ethnic identity in the ancient and indeed the modern world.[58]

In light of the early designation of the epistle's audience as "strangers," then, 1 Peter "represents the first move to designate Christians explicitly as a γένος, a move that was of considerable significance in the evolution of Christian identity discourse."[59]

In this way, 1 Peter balances out the dismal state of displacement with the hope of a new social identity. The expression "holy nation" is especially significant, for membership in such is the exact opposite of being a displaced alien, a stranger. The latter concept means that one is without a true home and a true people. The former, however, affects a change of circumstances,

---

54. Horrell, *1 Peter*, 72.

55. Horrell, "'Race,' 'Nation,' 'People,'" 129. Horrell also points out how 1 Pet 2:9 and Matt 21:43 are the only places in the New Testament that refer to the church as an ἔθνος.

56. Ibid., 135.

57. Ibid., 140–41.

58. Ibid., 141 (emphasis is Horrell's).

59. Ibid., 143. For more discussion on "social dialect" in 1 Peter (albeit regarding different terminology than what is discussed here), see Trebilco, *Self-designations and Group Identity in the New Testament*, 11.

for now the "stranger" has a nation of his or her own, a nation that will never be farther away than the distance of that believer to his or her closest fellow Christian.

This new designation of Christians as a "holy nation" has another effect, however. It forces Christians to think of the theological and practical ramifications of their new identity in reference to the Roman empire. Thus,

> Precisely because they were an international "people" and "race" and "nation" who were without the kind of territory that was part of being a "nation" in the eyes of the Romans (and in the assumption of OT writers), Christians found themselves in an eschatological tension that has been both an unavoidable challenge and a glorious privilege throughout two millennia of church history.[60]

Finally, Peter concludes this major ecclesiological discussion with a reference to Hos 1:6—2:1 (1 Pet 1:10); here, Peter once more takes what was originally referring to ethnic Israel and applies it to his own audience of believers.[61] This provides a powerful capstone to his overall argument. The community was once displaced but is now given placement inside a new kingdom; the community, at the same time, was without mercy yet now receives mercy from the great Cornerstone.

The powerful, comforting nature of these verses is difficult to overemphasize. Peter here begins "to counteract the demoralizing and disintegrating impact [of the audience's circumstances] by reassuring its members of their distinctive communal identity . . ."[62] In other words, the way in which Peter counters the displaced social status of his audience "is not [by means of] an ephemeral 'heaven is our home' form of consolation but the new home and social family to which the Christians belong here and now; namely, the *oikos tou theou*."[63]

Fika van Rensburg aptly sums up the theological and social force of this passage:

---

60. Carson, "1 Peter," 1033. Similarly, on p. 1032, Carson notes, "One of the effects [of Peter's rhetoric], of course, was to make them sufficiently different as a 'people' or 'race' or 'nation' that first-century pagan society would not be long in resenting them."

61. van Rensburg, "Metaphors in the Soteriology in 1 Peter," 428.

62. Elliott, *Home for the Homeless*, 148.

63. Ibid., 130. Significantly, however, Elliott does *not* deny the eschatological significance of 1 Peter. On p. 130 he states, "The orientation of 1 Peter is indeed eschatological . . . . At the same time, the achievement of that future reward (5:4) is everywhere linked to, and dependent upon, the believers' maintenance of the bonds of their brotherhood here and now."

The Significance of Foreknowledge for a New Social Identity in 1 Peter 177

The believers were aliens and strangers, scattered individuals without security, without a sense of belonging and without being integrated into a nation. Now, since having become not only God's family and part and parcel of his household, they have become not just "a" nation, but the *chosen* people, the *holy* nation, the people *of God*![64]

In this way, the concept of a new nation, a positive social identity, balances out the negative displaced status that the readers have been in. The ultimate comfort for a displaced stranger is a new home and a new country, especially one that is vastly superior to his or her old one.

CONCLUSION

The recipients of 1 Peter faced debilitating circumstances. Initially suffering from a displaced status within Asia Minor, they are comforted by the fact that their circumstances are foreknown by God. Not only that, but the foreknowledge of God and the prophets points to a superior status preserved for them, a status anchored within the foreknown Lamb of God who is now revealed. This Lamb has become the chosen Cornerstone for the foundation of a new community. This community is spoken of in specific, ethnoracial terms, terms which are drawn from Jewish *Heilsgeschichte* yet applied to the present community of multi-ethnic believers.[65]

In this way, the concept of foreknowledge (linked closely with eschatology) plays an important role in the theology of 1 Peter. In one sense, it functions as a thematic bridge between the negative and positive circumstances of the readers (displacement vs. nationhood). Peter essentially declares to

---

64. Van Rensburg, "Metaphors in the Soteriology in 1 Peter," 432 (emphasis is Rensburg's).

65. Horrell, "'Race,' 'Nation,' 'People,'" 130, 135. It is worth noting, however, that this does not necessarily mean that the new community has *replaced* Israel. Rather, as Glenny argues in "Israelite Imagery of 1 Peter 2," 179, Peter at this point ". . . shows that they are the *people of God*, whose salvation and spiritual benefits under the new covenant follow a pattern established in God's promised relationship with his chosen people, the nation of Israel." In addition, there is a key difference between Peter's reference to the people of Israel and his application of their terminology to this new community. As Rensburg, "Metaphors in the Soteriology in 1 Peter," 426, states, "Here, however,—and this differs from the Exodus text—there are no conditions for becoming the holy nation. It is something that God has already done, out of own [sic] volition." It is God's initiative, then, that creates the community and its ministry. Consequently, in Elliott's words (*Elect and the Holy*, 168), "The Church is not a 'body of priests' because she offers sacrifice, but she offers sacrifice because she is a 'body of priests.' According to vv. 5 and 9, the Church's nature prescribes her function and not vice versa."

the readers, "Both your current social circumstances and your newfound social identity in Christ are foreknown by God and part of his plan." In this way, the epistle emphasizes the fact that the readers are the *recipients* of this revelation concerning their ultimate destiny. On the one hand, the OT prophets of the past have been the recipients of foreknowledge concerning this community, and this revelation is mediated through them to the present group via the various OT texts cited in 1 Peter (and, perhaps, within the oral Gospel material handed down to them). On the other hand, the present community itself directly receives revelation of God's foreknowledge concerning the Son, and it is the Son's work that ultimately anchors their own newfound identity as a holy nation. The concepts of foreknowledge and social identity are thus intertwined.

Furthermore, this foreknowledge acts as a word of comfort.[66] If all their circumstances are foreknown, and if Christ's work is also foreknown, then 1 Peter's audience can rest assured that nothing has caught God by surprise. Consequently, God is able to work on their behalf through the Son without any danger of being blindsided by circumstances. The result of God's work, foreknown before the foundation of the world and now revealed to the Anatolian community, is nothing less than the creation of a new nation founded on Christ. Membership in this new, yet eternally foreknown, community offers hope and comfort, for ". . . it is within the Christian communities that the letter expects its readers to discover the answer to the problem of their suffering."[67] Indeed, ". . . since believers have been reborn they now belong to a loving community that supports them in their suffering."[68] The stranger added to this new community is no longer alone.[69]

Finally, it is no coincidence that 1 Pet 2:11, the transition to the next major section, introduces a very specific series of practical exhortations.[70] By using the phrase "παρακαλῶ ὡς παροίκους καὶ παρεπιδήμους," the author brings his audience full circle back to their displaced status. Here, then, ". . . Peter is calling his readers to recognize that they are living in an alien place

---

66. This does not mean that 1 Peter 1–2 cannot also contain a word of warning, as well (see the discussion in Stewart, "When Are Christians Saved and Why Does It Matter?," 232). Yet the focus of this study is more on comfort than warning.

67. Bechtler, *Following in His Steps*, 177.

68. Kendall, "Literary and Theological Function of 1 Peter 1:3–12," 110.

69. Philipps, *Kirche in der Gesellschaft nach dem ersten Petrusbrief*, 22. Cf. also Jobes, *1 Peter*, 149, "Even if Peter's readers find themselves alienated from their society and suffering loss of status, Peter assures them that they have become part of a much grander and everlasting community."

70. See the discussion in Thurén, *Argument and Theology in 1 Peter*, 131, and Elliott, *I Peter*, 476.

that has different values and practices than those appropriate for the people of God's holy nation."[71] In other words, neither foreknowledge nor social identity are abstract theological principles imprisoned in an ivory tower. Rather, they are a rallying cry for a new life dedicated to the glory of God (1 Pet 2:9b).

---

71. Jobes, 1 Peter, 16

7

Conclusion

THESIS AND CHAPTER SUMMARIES

The thesis of this study has been the following: *from the introduction to the beginning of the second major section of the epistle, 1 Peter uses the concept of "foreknowledge" as a word of comfort to offset his readers' status as socially-displaced strangers and to thus emphasize their new-found social identity in Christ.* Inherent within this thesis is two key assumptions. First, this study has (mostly) followed John Elliott in arguing that a significant portion of the recipients of the epistle had been (and continued to be) literal strangers and foreigners within Asia Minor. This allowed Peter's use of social identity language (both negative and positive) to possess greater rhetorical and spiritual force. Secondly, this study has argued that "foreknowledge" in 1 Peter exists as a prescient concept instead of referring to "choice" ("foreordination," etc.) or the state of loving beforehand. These two assumptions are, in the opinion of this study, important for a better understanding of 1 Peter's theology.

The first chapter of this study began by discussing the need for this study and the lack of academic work dealing with both foreknowledge in 1 Peter and the relationship of foreknowledge and social identity. Chapter 1 proceeded to give a general overview of the contents of this study's chapters followed by the thesis statement and the clarification of certain key terms.

Chapter 1 then briefly examined introductory matters relevant to 1 Peter, paying special attention to background, outline, and the identity of the recipients. The chapter then spent a significant amount of time surveying both modern and ancient scholarship on foreknowledge (in general) and social identity (in reference to 1 Peter). Within the limited nature of this chapter, three key points came to the forefront. First, the terminology of 1 Pet 2:4–10 was quite frequently applied to believers in the early church, but it later came to be applied by some to either the clergy or the church as a corporate entity. Secondly, there is little evidence that the earliest church consistently equated the concept of "foreknowledge" with either "foreordination" or "loving beforehand." In fact, Augustine himself stressed the distinction between foreknowledge and foreordination. Finally, so far as this writer was able to discover, no scholar has yet performed a complete lexical analysis of either πρόγνωσις or προγινώσκω within the literature of New Testament times.

Chapter 1 concluded with an examination of texts dealing with foreknowledge in the first century and with an overview of social scientific criticism. For the latter, both its history and its relevance for New Testament interpretation were stressed, and this writer suggested that SSC "models" could be utilized to examine key texts so long as certain precautions were taken.

Chapter 2 then applied social scientific criticism to the exploration of the social status of the recipients of 1 Peter. The first section of this chapter surveyed the various views on the social status of the recipients, paying special attention to John Elliott's *A Home for the Homeless* and the various reactions to his work. The second section examined the concept of "stranger" in New Testament times, including an examination of the specific words πάροικος and παρεπίδημος. Finally, this chapter interacted with Elliott and his critics and defended Elliott's argument that 1 Peter was addressing literal "strangers" in Asia Minor. This chapter did, however, disagree with Elliott in one area by preferring to see πάροικος and παρεπίδημος as synonymous terms (i.e., Peter did not intend to draw much, if any, of a distinction between them).

Chapter 3 delved into the realm of lexical semantics in order to justify the methodology of chapter 4. While various linguistic issues were discussed, chapter 3 focused especially on the following two key topics: the difference between a "concept" and a "word," and the role of semantic range and context in determining meaning. This writer argued that a word's semantic range in the literature of AD 1–100, together with the LXX, was important to understanding what a word meant in the New Testament. The NT writers did not create meaning *ex nihilo*. The NT writers, like any normal communicator, used both the semantic range of a word (in contemporary usage) and context to delineate meaning at a particular point.

Drawing on the linguistic arguments of the previous chapter, chapter 4 then proceeded to examine every single occurrence of the words πρόγνωσις and προγινώσκω in the LXX and the literature of AD 1–100. Having done so, this writer argued the following: (1) the words πρόγνωσις and προγινώσκω overwhelmingly possess a prescient sense; (2) there is no clear instance of either word meaning "foreordination," "election," "predestination," or any other choice-related concept (though there are a few instances where one of the words *might* mean that); and (3) out of all the occurrences of πρόγνωσις and προγινώσκω in the literature surveyed, only one instance clearly means "possessing a relationship with [somebody]." In light of those facts, this writer concluded that the burden of proof is on those who wish to argue that 1 Peter's audience would have understood either πρόγνωσις or προγινώσκω to mean something other than "foreknowledge" and "to foreknow," respectively.

Chapter 5 examined the following three key texts in 1 Peter where the concept of foreknowledge appears: 1 Pet 1:1–2, 10–12, and 20. For the first passage, this writer argued the following: first, following Wayne Grudem, the three prepositional phrases in v. 2 modify the entire situation of the readers. In other words, they are "elect strangers of the Dispersion" in accordance with God's foreknowledge, etc. Secondly, the preposition κατά is best understood as "in accordance with." The circumstances of the readers, then, are "in accordance with" God's foreknowledge. Finally, πρόγνωσις in 1 Pet 1:2 is a prescient term, referring to God's knowledge of the future. First Peter's audience can take comfort in the fact that their circumstances, both positive and negative, have been known by the Father all along and are part of his plan.

Regarding 1 Pet 1:10–12, this writer argued that the "prophets" in this passage are OT prophets. Thus the concept of foreknowledge here plays a key role (as opposed to the interpretation that "prophets" are contemporary Christian prophets). Here the prophetic foreknowledge is "for your sake," i.e., to the benefit of the readers. Here, too, foreknowledge acts as a word of comfort.

Finally, chapter 5 examined the word προγινώσκω in 1 Pet 1:20. This writer argued that even though Scripture declares that Christ's death was foreordained, this is not the point of this particular text. Rather, Peter is saying that although Christ and his role in redemption have always been foreknown by God, this is now revealed to the epistle's audience. Once again, then, God's foreknowledge functions as a word of comfort, transforms into revelation of the future, and assures the audience of their place in the plan of God.

Chapter 6 placed the concept of foreknowledge within the broader scope of 1 Peter's theology. First, this chapter examined how the negative circumstances of 1 Peter's audience, including displacement (the state of being removed from one's home), created a situation that needed to be addressed. Then this chapter discussed foreknowledge in 1 Peter and how it functioned on behalf of the audience, pointing the audience towards brighter circumstances (namely, a new social identity in Christ). Thirdly, foreknowledge is linked to the work of Christ, and Christ himself provides the anchor for a new social identity for the believers. Finally, this chapter examined the creation of this new social identity, a new people and nation, emphasizing how this naturally served to counteract the demoralizing effect of the displacement of the epistle's audience.

Here, then, is how these chapters have argued for the thesis statement. First, this writer attempted to establish that displacement was a literal and negative social circumstance that the readers were intimately familiar with. Secondly, this writer attempted to demonstrate that "foreknowledge" in 1 Peter refers to simple knowledge of the future. Finally, building on both those points, this writer suggested that knowledge of the future in 1 Peter implies God's overall mastery over the circumstances of both his readers and his Son, Jesus Christ. Consequently, nothing takes God by surprise, and 1 Peter's audience can rest assured that both their current displaced status and the holy kingdom into which they are transforming have forever existed in the mind of God. If this is the case, they can rest assured of the outworking of God's plan for them in Jesus Christ.

CONTRIBUTIONS OF THIS STUDY

This study has attempted to contribute to scholarship in the following areas. First of all, this study has furthered the discussion of social scientific criticism in 1 Peter, providing an in-depth examination of Elliott's thesis, his critics, and alternative interpretations. Secondly, this study has attempted to provide a more thorough justification, via lexical semantics, of why the semantic range of a word is important for determining its meaning in a particular context. Thirdly, this study provided an exhaustive examination of πρόγνωσις and προγινώσκω within the literature of the time of the New Testament, something that has not, to this writer's knowledge, ever been done. Finally, this study attempted to demonstrate the role that foreknowledge, as a concept, plays in the theology of 1 Peter (also a topic that has not, to this writer's knowledge, been adequately pursued).

RESPONSE TO POTENTIAL OBJECTIONS

Based on a survey of scholarship (and personal conversations), this writer anticipates two major objections to this study. First of all, many will object to the idea that divine foreknowledge could be considered separately from divine foreordination; in other words, for some, foreknowledge *necessarily* means foreordination. Yet regardless of whether or not God foreordains everything, such a statement confuses two entirely distinct concepts. In other words, the question is not, "Does God foreordain *everything*?" but rather, "Does God foreknow *anything*?" If such a concept as divine foreknowledge (i.e., knowledge of the future) legitimately exists, then to a certain extent it can be discussed separately from any other divine attributes. One does not, for example, refuse to discuss divine justice by itself simply because (in theory) it cannot exist apart from divine wrath. Rather, most scholars would recognize that justice and wrath are two separate (though potentially related) concepts. None would say, "Justice *must* mean wrath whenever it is discussed in Scripture."

This makes it all the more inexplicable (to this writer) why many scholars often refuse to consider foreknowledge as a distinct concept in its own right. Even if God foreordains all things (a theological assumption that even Augustine refused to embrace), should not the scholar still be free to discuss what God *knows* as a separate concept from what he *ordains*? This, then, is all we ask of the reader: freedom to discuss foreknowledge on its own terms in 1 Peter without automatically equating it with foreordination (or any related concept).

Secondly, many would object to this study's partial defense of John Elliott's views regarding the social status of Peter's audience. Nobody, unfortunately, has done a thorough examination of the social status of foreigners in Asia Minor during the first century (to this writer's knowledge). Yet surely it would make sense that at least *some* of 1 Peter's audience consisted of literal foreigners. From there, one could suggest that such people would have been the most likely to be attracted to the Gospel in the first place.[1] In this way, it makes sense for Peter to uphold literal strangers (now converted) as the paradigm for understanding the Christian's status before God and humanity. As argued in chapter 2, a metaphor makes the most sense when one is intimately acquainted with the reality.[2] It is, of course, possible for this study's thesis to be defended without following Elliott. Nevertheless, this

---

1. This writer, having grown up on the mission field, can speak from personal observation that quite often it is the outcasts of society that are [initially, at least] attracted to the gospel.

2. See especially Jobes, *1 Peter*, 25–27, on this point.

writer believes that the theology of 1 Peter makes the most sense if much of its audience consisted of literal strangers/foreigners.

SUGGESTIONS FOR FUTURE STUDY

To begin with, the concept of foreknowledge (both human and divine) and its role in a particular book's theology need to be further explored. Generally, in the sources this writer has cited, foreknowledge is assumed to be equivalent to foreordination; consequently, some of what a particular NT author is trying to say may be missed. While some scholars do examine foreknowledge (in a prescient sense) throughout Scripture, these works often focus on God's foreknowledge in relation to the Open Theism debate or within the broader "Calvinism vs. Arminianism" dialogue rather than studying foreknowledge for its own sake.[3] At a narrower level, the specific words πρόγνωσις and προγινώσκω have not received a fair treatment within NT scholarship (nor, for that matter, have any of their synonyms).

In addition, more work needs to be done on a theology of foreknowledge within the early church. Augustine's work on foreknowledge is too often neglected, in this writer's opinion, despite the fact that his views may represent the best opportunity for rapprochement between various views on divine sovereignty and human will.

Regarding social scientific criticism, much work has already been done in 1 Peter. Some areas, however, could be further explored. For example, an area of research called "social identity theory" is just coming to the forefront in biblical studies (though many of its elements have already been present in social scientific criticism). In particular, a recent article in *Biblical Theology Bulletin* by Coleman Baker attempts to introduce this field to biblical scholarship.[4] David Horrell's recent article on 1 Pet 2:9 (though published just before Baker's article) deals with social identity theory in its discussion of Christian self-understanding in 1 Peter.[5] This presents some new opportunities for scholarship.

For 1 Peter in general, more work needs to be done on the history of Asia Minor at this time, especially regarding the relationship between its inhabitants (including foreigners) and the Roman Empire (and how this would have affected Christians). While an overwhelming amount of work

---

3. See, for example, Roy, *How Much Does God Foreknow?*, who provides a very comprehensive overview but seems to be mostly reacting to the Open Theism debate. See also Beilby and Eddy, ed., *Divine Foreknowledge: Four Views*.
4. Baker, "Social Identity Theory and Biblical Interpretation," 129–38.
5. Horrell, "'Race,' 'Nation,' 'People,'" 123–43.

has been done on the New Testament use of the Old Testament in 1 Peter, this writer wishes to see somebody discuss the concept of "stranger" and "foreigner" in 1 Peter in light of the existence of "strangers" and "foreigners" within the nation of Israel in OT times, something that Troy Martin hints at but does not unpack in his monograph.[6]

Finally, in light of 1 Peter's shift from "strangers" to "holy nation," the time is ripe for a thorough work on 1 Peter's ecclesiology (how Peter views the church). In this way, social scientific criticism and exegesis would pave the way for biblical theology (and, perhaps, even Petrine theology) and practically benefit the church as a whole.

THEOLOGICAL AND PRACTICAL IMPLICATIONS

The stranger and foreigner in Asia Minor declares, "This is not my home." To such an outcast, 1 Peter offers a new home, the church of Jesus Christ. The significance of this for the modern church cannot be overstated, for Christians in the United States (and other countries) have often taken one of two theologically incorrect approaches.

First, while correctly acknowledging that their citizenship is kept in heaven (Phil 3:20), some Christians have nevertheless forgotten that they do indeed have a home on earth, namely, the church. According to 1 Peter, as Elliott pointed out years ago, the Christian belongs to "a familial-like community or brotherhood (1:22; 2:5, 17; 5:9) defined by a unique faith in Jesus as the Christ, as the agent of the salvation for which they hope (1:2, 3, 6–8, 13, 18–21; 2:3, 4–10) and an ethic which prescribes religious allegiance, 'fear' (1:17; 2:17; cf. 3:6, 14) and 'obedience' (cf. 2:8; 3:20; 4:17) to the will of God alone (2:15; 3:17; 4:2, 19)."[7] The Christian's citizenship stems from heaven and ultimately awaits its culmination in the appearing of Jesus Christ (as Phil 3:20 indicates), but it is also manifested in the "here-and-now" of the "new nation" which is the church.

Consequently, there is no excuse for a "holy" withdrawal from engagement with the world. In 1 Pet 2:9, the whole point of this "holy nation" is to declare the glory of God to a lost world. According to 1 Pet 2:11–12, the Christian is to simultaneously fight personal sin while winning over the sinner through his or her good works. In order for the "holy nation" to be truly doing the work of God, then, it needs simultaneously to be internally holy and externally missional, the latter including both the proclamation

---

6. Martin, *Metaphor and Composition in 1 Peter*, 208.
7. Elliott, *Home for the Homeless*, 75.

of the gospel and the performance of good works within society.⁸ In other words, the church is not functioning as the church unless it is working out the Gospel in kindness and mercy to those around them.⁹ While there needs to be much more discussion on how exactly the church and individual believers "work out" the Gospel, the point is that the church is called to make a positive impact within society along with its proclamation of the gospel.

Secondly, from this writer's personal experience, too many Christians have created a rival to the kingdom of heaven in the form of the United States. While this writer is grateful for the freedoms and privileges that both of my national homes (the US and Japan) have offered, it is one thing to ask God to bless a nation and another thing altogether to extol the virtues of that nation in corporate worship, as has often been done within the United States. In other words, when any secular nation, even the United States, is exalted within corporate worship among Christians, *such a nation becomes a rival to the church*, for *there is only room for one "Holy Nation" in 1 Peter!*¹⁰

Yet, sadly, when Christians meet together to worship God (especially around certain times of the year), too often it is the American founding fathers, American democracy, and the American constitution that are praised. The founding fathers are promoted as "Christian" heroes and the constitution is given almost as much modern significance as Scripture (this writer once heard a Sunday sermon where Prov 22:28 was directly applied to the US constitution). Even worse, traditional American democracy is somehow given prominence as the outworking of God's plan in the modern age, thus (perhaps inadvertently) giving place to an "accommodationist" theology that "assumes[s] wrongly that the American church's primary social task is to underwrite American democracy."¹¹ When this happens, nationalism and politics are inadvertently set up as idols against the God who alone deserves the praises of the Church.¹²

---

8. As Goppelt (*Der erste Petrusbriefe*, 154) points out, the church declares the "great work of God" ("große Tat Gottes") both in its preaching on the one hand and in its existence and conduct on the other ("Dies geschieht durch die Predigt, von der die Gemeinde getragen ist, und weit darüber hinaus durch deren Sein und Verhalten").

9. For a provocative discussion of how, in light of 1 Peter's theology, the church should be engaging the world, see Elliott, "The Church as Counterculture," 176–85. I am grateful to Prof. Elliott for personally sending me a copy of this essay.

10. Black, *Christian Archy*, 1, articulates it best when he states, "There is perhaps no clearer example of the church's misguided appropriation of the world than the god of nationalism."

11. Hauerwas and Willimon, *Resident Aliens*, 32.

12. In fact, while there is nothing in scripture to suggest that Christians cannot be involved in politics, this writer would tentatively suggest that in most churches there is too much political rhetoric and not enough social engagement.

The American Christian of the twenty-first century, then, must realize two things drawn from 1 Peter's theology. First of all, in light of the transition from "strangers" to "holy nation" within the context of the Roman empire in 1 Peter, it is time to embrace the fact that, as Stanley Hauerwas and William Willimon state, "[I]t is the nature of the church, at any time and in any situation, to be a colony."[13] Consequently, there is no such thing as an "American" church or a "Japanese" church. There is only *the* Church, a holy nation of sanctified believers with its colonies scattered throughout the world.

Secondly, in the words of Douglas Harink, "There is a stark contrast between Peter's vision of justice for the church and the world and that often represented by, for example, champions of a vision of 'Christian America' and the claim of the church to a privileged place in the American empire."[14] This writer would consequently suggest that the time has come to stop looking to America (especially an idealized America of the glorified founding fathers) as one's country of origin and remember that Christ demands that we put aside both family and nationalistic ties and join him in a new community of holiness. In other words, it is the Church, not the United States, that is truly "home" for the Christian. When this is realized, missional engagement will naturally flow out from the church, for then other tribes and tongues become just as important as America in God's plan.

The cure for displacement is placement within a new nation, and the cure for being a stranger is to be admitted into a new home. This new home is God's method of reaching the world in this era, but this also means that Christians are not called to act alone. "Nothing the gospel asks of us—compassion, promise-keeping, childbearing, healing—is expected of us as loners. We exist as family, as a colony . . . ."[15] In this way, God's mighty plan, foreknown for all eternity and now showing the outworking of his grace in Jesus Christ, manifests itself in a new family and, to once more borrow Elliott's phrase, "a home for the homeless."

---

13. Hauerwas and Willimon, *Resident Aliens*, 12.
14. Harink, *1 & 2 Peter*, 59.
15. Hauerwas and Willimon, *Resident Aliens*, 136.

Bibliography

Abernathy, David. *An Exegetical Summary of 1 Peter.* Dallas: SIL International, 2007.
Accordance Bible Software 8.4. OakTree Software, 2009.
Achtemeier, Paul J. *1 Peter.* Hermeneia. Minneapolis: Fortress, 1996.
———. "Review of John H. Elliott, *A Home for the Homeless: A Sociological Exegesis of 1 Peter, Its Situation and Strategy.*" *JBL* 103 (1984) 130–33.
Adams, F. A. *The Greek Prepositions, Studied from Their Original Meanings as Designations of Space.* New York: Appleton, 1885.
Agnew, Francis H. "1 Peter 1:2—An Alternative Translation." *CBQ* 45 (1983) 68–73.
Aland, Barbara, Kurt Aland, Johannes Karavidopoulos, Carlo M. Martini, and Bruce Metzger, eds. *Novum Testamentum Graece.* 28th rev. ed. Stuttgart: Deutsche Bibelgesellschaft, 2012.
Aland, Barbara, Kurt Aland, Johannes Karavidopoulos, Carlo M. Martini, and Bruce Metzger, eds. *The Greek New Testament.* 4th rev. ed. Stuttgart: Deutsche Bibelgesellschaft: 1998.
Antiochus. *Fragmenta (e cod. Neapolitano 19).* From *Codices Italici.* Edited by D. Bassi, F. Cumont, A. Martini, and A. Olivieri. Catalogus Codicum Astrologorum Graecorum 4. Brussels: Lamertin, 1903. Online: http://www.tlg.uci.edu.
———. *Fragmenta (e cod. Paris).* From *Codices Parsini.* Edited by P. Boudreaux. Catalogus Codicum Astrologorum Graecorum 8.3. Brussels: Lamertin, 1912. Online: http://www.tlg.uci.edu.
"Appianus." In *Dictionary of Greek and Roman Biography and Mythology,* edited by William Smith, 1:247. 3 vols. Boston: Little, Brown, 1867. Online: http://books.google.com.
Aristonicus. *De signis Iliadis.* From *Aristonici Περὶ σημείων Ἰλιάδος reliquiae emendatiores.* Göttingen: Dieterich, 1853. Online: http://www.tlg.uci.edu.
Aristophanes. *Fragmenta (Nauck).* In *Aristophanis Byzantii grammatici Alexandrini fragmenta.* Edited by A. Nauck. 2nd ed. Halle: Lippert & Schmid, 1848. Cited 2011–2012 (various dates). Online: http://www.tlg.uci.edu.
———. *Nomina aetatum (fragmentum).* In E. Miller, "Opscule divers." In *Lexica Graeca Minora.* Hildesheim: Olms, 1965. Online: http://www.tlg.uci.edu.
———. *Nomina aetatum (fragmentum Parisinum).* In *Aristophanis Byzantii grammatici Alexandrini fragmenta.* Edited by A. Nauck. 2nd ed. Halle: Lippert & Schmid, 1848. Online: http://www.tlg.uci.edu.
Augustine. *City of God.* Cambridge Texts in the History of Political Thought. Edited and translated by R. W. Dyson. Cambridge: Cambridge University Press, 1998.

Bibliography

―――. *City of God*. In *The Nicene and Post-Nicene Fathers*, ser. 1, vol. 2. Edited by Philip Schaff. 14 vols. 1886–1889. Reprinted, Peabody, MA: Hendrickson, 1999.

―――. *Enchiridion*. In *The Nicene and Post-Nicene Fathers*, ser. 1, vol. 3. Edited by Philip Schaff. Translated by J. F. Shaw. 14 vols. 1886–1889. Reprinted, Peabody, MA: Hendrickson, 1999.

―――. *Exposition on the Psalms*. In *The Nicene and Post-Nicene Fathers*, ser. 1, vol. 8. Edited by Philip Schaff. 14 vols. 1886–1889. Reprinted, Peabody, MA: Hendrickson, 1999.

―――. *Homilies on the Gospel of John*. In *The Nicene and Post-Nicene Fathers*, ser. 1, vol. 7. Edited by Philip Schaff. Translated by John Gibb and James Innes. 14 vols. 1886–1889. Reprinted, Peabody, MA: Hendrickson, 1999.

―――. *On Baptism, Against the Donatists*. In *The Nicene and Post-Nicene Fathers*, ser. 1, vol. 4. Edited by Philip Schaff. Translated by J. R. King. 14 vols. 1886–1889. Reprinted, Peabody, MA: Hendrickson, 1999.

―――. *On the Catechising of the Uninstructed*. In *The Nicene and Post-Nicene Fathers*, ser. 1, vol. 3. Edited by Philip Schaff. Translated by S. D. F. Salmon. 14 vols. 1886–1889. Reprinted, Peabody, MA: Hendrickson, 1999.

―――. *Reply to Faustus the Manichæan*. In *The Nicene and Post-Nicene Fathers*, ser. 1, vol. 4. Edited by Philip Schaff. Translated by Richard Stothert. 14 vols. 1886–1889. Reprinted, Peabody, MA: Hendrickson, 1999.

Badilita, Smaranda. "Philon d'Alexandrie et l'exégèse allégorique." *Foi et vie* 107 (2008) 63–76.

Baker, Coleman A. "Social Identity Theory and Biblical Interpretation." *Biblical Theology Bulletin* (2012) 129–138.

Balbillus. *Fragmenta*. From *Codices Parisini*. Edited by W. Kroll and A. Olivieri. Catalogus Codicum Astrologorum Graecorum 8.3. Brussels: Lamertin, 1912. Online: http://www.tlg.uci.edu.

Bandy, Alan S. "Persecution and the Purpose of Revelation with Reference to Roman Jurisprudence." *BBR* 23 (2013) 377–398.

Barr, James. *The Semantics of Biblical Language*. 1961. Reprinted, Eugene, OR: Wipf & Stock, 2004.

Barrow, R. H. *Plutarch and His Times*. Bloomington: Indiana University Press, 1967.

Bartlett, David L. "First Peter: Introduction, Commentary, and Reflections." In *Hebrews, James, 1 & 2 Peter, 1, 2, & 3 John, Jude, Revelation. The New Interpreter's Bible*, 12:229–361. Nashville: Abingdon, 1998.

Barton, Stephen C. "Historical Criticism and Social-Scientific Perspectives in New Testament Studies." In *Hearing the New Testament: Strategies for Interpretation*, edited by Joel B. Green, 61–89. Grand Rapids: Eerdmans, 1995.

Baugh, S. M. "The Meaning of Foreknowledge." In *Still Sovereign: Contemporary Perspectives on Election, Foreknowledge, and Grace*, edited by Thomas R. Schreiner and Bruce W. Ware, 183–200. Grand Rapids: Baker, 2000.

Baxter, Benjamin J. "The Meaning of Biblical Words." *McMaster Journal of Theology and Ministry* 11 (2009–2010) 89–120.

Beale, G. K. *A New Testament Biblical Theology: The Unfolding of the Old Testament in the New*. Grand Rapids: Baker Academic, 2011.

Beare, Francis Wright. *The First Epistle of Peter: The Greek Text with Introduction and Notes*. 2nd rev. ed. Oxford: Blackwell & Mott, 1958.

Bechtler, Steven Richard. *Following in His Steps: Suffering, Community, and Christology in 1 Peter*. Society of Biblical Literature Dissertation Series 162. Atlanta: Scholars, 1998.
Bede the Venerable. *Commentary on the Seven Catholic Epistles*. Translated by Dom David Hurst. Kalamazoo, MI: Cistercian, 1985.
Berding, Kenneth. "The Hermeneutical Framework of Social-Scientific Criticism: How Much Can Evangelicals Get Involved?" *Evangelical Quarterly* 75 (2003) 3–22.
Bernabé Ubieta, Carmen. "'Neither *Xenoi* nor *paroikoi*, *sympolitai* and *oikeioi tou theou*' (Eph 2:19). Pauline Christian Communities: Defining a New Territorality." In *Social Scientific Models for Interpreting the Bible: Essays by the Context Group in Honor of Bruce J. Malina*, edited by John J. Pilch, 260–80. Biblical Interpretation Series 53. Leiden: Brill, 2001.
Best, Ernest. *I Peter*. New Century Bible. London: Marshall, Morgan & Scott, 1971.
Black, David Alan. *Christian Archy*. Areopagus Critical Christian Issues 1. Gonzalez, FL: Energion, 2009.
———. *It's Still Greek to Me: An Easy-to-Understand Guide to Intermediate Greek*. Grand Rapids: Baker Academic, 87.
———. *Linguistics for Students of New Testament Greek: A Survey of Basic Concepts and Applications*. 2nd ed. Grand Rapids: Baker, 1995.
Blackburn, Perry L. *The Code Model of Communication: A Powerful Metaphor for Linguistic Metatheory*. Dallas: SIL International, 2007.
Bloom, Paul. *How Children Learn the Meanings of Words*. Cambridge, MA: MIT Press, 2000.
Boman, Thorleif. "Review of James Barr, *The Semantics of Biblical Language* and *Biblical Words for Time*." *Scottish Journal of Theology* 15 (1962) 319–24.
Boring, M. Eugene. *1 Peter*. Abingdon New Testament Commentary. Nashville: Abingdon, 1999.
Brandis, Christian A. "Epictetus." Pages 31–33 in volume 2 of *Dictionary of Greek and Roman Biography and Mythology*. Edited by William Smith. 3 vols. Boston: Little, Brown, 1867. Online: http://books.google.com.
Bréal, Michael. *Essai de sémantique (science des significations)*. 3rd ed. Paris: Librairie Hachette, 1904.
Beilby, James K., and Paul R. Eddy, eds. *Divine Foreknowledge: Four Views*. Downers Grove, IL: InterVarsity, 2001.
Brox, Norbert. *Der erste Petrusbrief*. Evangelisch-katholischer Kommentar zum Neuen Testament. Zürich: Benziger, 1979.
———. "Situation und Sprache der Minderheit im Ersten Petrusbrief." *Kairós* 19 (1977) 1–13.
———. "The Strangers in Early Christianity." *Theology Digest* 41 (Spring 1994) 47–52.
Burge, Gary M., Lynn H. Cohick, and Gene L. Green. *The New Testament in Antiquity: A Survey of the New Testament Within Its Cultural Contexts*. Grand Rapids: Zondervan, 2009.
Buswell, James Oliver, Jr. *A Systematic Theology of the Christian Religion*. 2 vols. Grand Rapids: Zondervan, 1962.
Butler, Jim. "Grace Suffering: A Study in 1 Peter." *Notes on Translation* 10 (1996) 58–60.
Caird, G. B. *The Language and Imagery of the Bible*. Grand Rapids: Eerdmans, 1980.
Calvini, Ioannis. *Epistola ad Hebraeos. Epistolae Petri, Ioannis, Iacobi et Iudae*. Novum Testamentum Commentarii 8. Edited by Al Tholuck. Berlin: Eichler, 1865.

Campbell, Barth L. *Honor, Shame, and the Rhetoric of 1 Peter*. Society of Biblical Literature Dissertation Series 160. Atlanta: Scholars, 1998.

Caragounis, Chrys C. *The Development of Greek and the New Testament: Morphology, Syntax, Phonology, and Textual Transmission*. Grand Rapids: Baker Academic, 2004.

Carroll, Lewis. *Through the Looking-Glass and What Alice Found There*. Edited by Florence Milner. Chicago: Rand McNally, 1917.

Carson, D. A. "1 Peter." In *Commentary on the New Testament Use of the Old Testament*. Edited by G. K. Beale and D. A. Carson, 1015-45. Grand Rapids: Baker Academic, 2007.

Carston, Robyn. *Thoughts and Utterances: The Pragmatics of Explicit Communication*. Malden, MA: Blackwell, 2002.

Charles, J. Daryl. "1 Peter." In *Hebrews–Revelation*, edited by Tremper Longman III and David E. Garland, 275-356. The Expositor's Bible Commentary 13. Rev. ed. Grand Rapids: Zondervan, 2006.

Chester, Andrew, and Ralph P. Martin. *The Theology of the Letters of James, Peter, and Jude*. New Testament Theology. Cambridge: Cambridge University Press, 1994.

Chevallier, Max-Alain. "Conditionet vocation des chrétiens en diaspora: remarques exégétiques sur la 1re Épitre de Pierre." *Revue des sciences religieuses* 48 (1974) 387-400.

———. "I Pierre 1:1 à 2:10: structure littéraire et consequences exégétiques." *Revue d'histoire et de philosophie religieuses* 51 (1971) 129-42.

Chin, Moses. "A Heavenly Home for the Homeless: Aliens and Strangers in 1 Peter." *Tyndale Bulletin* 42 (1991) 96-112.

Cicero, Marcus Tullius. *De divinatione*. Translated by William Armistead Falconer. *Cicero* vol. 19. LCL. Cambridge: Harvard University Press, 1923.

———. *De natura deorum*. Translated by H. Rackham. *Cicero* vol. 19. LCL. Cambridge: Harvard University Press, 1933. Rev. ed., 1951.

Chomsky, Noam. *Language and Mind*. New York: Harcourt, Brace & World, 1968.

Christiansen, Ellen Juhl. "Election as Identity Term in 1 Peter with a View to a Qumran Background." *Svensk exegetisk årsbok* 73 (2008) 39-64.

Chrysostomus. *In Primam S. Petri Epistolam*. Patrologia graeca 64. Edited by J.-P. Migne. 162 vols. Paris, 1857-1886.

Church, Alonzo. "The Need for Abstract Entities." *American Academy of Arts and Sciences Proceedings* 80 (1951) 100-113. Repr. as "Intensional Semantics." In *The Philosophy of Language*, edited by A. P. Martinich, 61-68. 4th ed. New York: Oxford University Press, 2001.

Clement of Alexandria. *Fragments of Clemens Alexandrinus*. In *The Ante-Nicene Fathers*, vol. 2. Edited by Alexander Roberts and James Donaldson. 10 vols. 1885-1887. Reprinted, Peabody, MA: Hendrickson, 1999.

Clement of Rome. *1 Clement*. In *The Apostolic Fathers: Greek Texts and English Translations*. Edited by Michael W. Holmes. Grand Rapids: Baker, 1999. In *Accordance* 8.4. OakTree Software, 2009.

Clementine Homilies, The. In *Ante-Nicene Fathers*, vol. 8. Edited by Alexander Roberts and James Donaldson. 10 vols. 1885-1887. Reprinted, Peabody, MA: Hendrickson, 1999.

Cobb, John W. "Election is Based on Foreknowledge." *Review and Expositor* 51 (1954) 22-28.

Constitution of the Holy Apostles. In the *Ante-Nicene Fathers*, vol. 7. Edited by Alexander Roberts and James Donaldson. 10 vols. 1885–1887. Reprinted, Peabody, MA: Hendrickson, 1999.

Corritore, Alfio. "Pietro agli eletti della diaspora: Identità storico-teologiche e dinamismi ecclesiali nella 'Prima Petri.'" PhD diss., di Sicilia S. Giovanni Evangelista, 2001.

Cothenet, Abbé Edouard. "Le realism de l'espérance chrétienne selon 1 Pierre." *NTS* 27 (1981) 564–72.

Cotterell, Peter, and Max Turner. *Linguistics and Biblical Interpretation*. Downers Grove, IL: InterVarsity, 1989.

Craffert, Pieter F. "More on Models and Muddles in the Social-Scientific Interpretation of the New Testament: The *Sociological Fallacy* Reconsidered." *Neotestamentica* 26 (1992) 217–39.

———. "Towards an Interdisciplinary Definition of the Social-scientific Interpretation of the New Testament." *Neotestamentica* 25 (1991) 123–44.

Cook, L. Stephen. *On the Question of the "Cessation of Prophecy" in Ancient Judaism*. Texts and Studies in Ancient Judaism 145. Tübingen: Mohr/Siebeck, 2011.

Crook, Zeba A. "Reflections on Culture and Social-Scientific Models." *JBL* 124 (2005) 515–20.

Cruse, D. A. "The Lexicon." In *The Handbook of Linguistics*, edited by Mark Aronoff and Janie Rees-Miller, 238–64. Malden, MA: Blackwell, 2001.

Cyril of Jerusalem. *Catechetical Lectures*. In *The Nicene and Post-Nicene Fathers*, ser. 2, vol. 7. Edited by Philip Schaff and Henry Wace. Translated by Edwin Hamilton Gifford. 14 vols. 1885. Reprinted, Peabody, MA: Hendrickson, 1999.

Dana, H. E., and Julius R. Mantey. *A Manual Grammar of the Greek New Testament*. New York: MacMillan, 1927.

Davids, Peter H. *The First Epistle of Peter*. New International Commentary on the New Testament. Grand Rapids: Eerdmans, 1990.

Davidson, A. B. *Old Testament Prophecy*. Edited by J. A. Patterson. Edinburgh: T. & T. Clark, 1912.

Davidson, Donald. "Truth and Meaning." *Synthese* 17 (1967) 304–23. Reprinted in *The Philosophy of Language*, edited by A. P. Martinich, 98–109. 4th ed. New York: Oxford University Press, 2001.

de Clorivière, Pierre-Joseph Picot. *Explication des Épitres de Saint-Pierre*. Paris: Société Typographique, 1809.

de Saussure, Ferdinand. *Troisième cours de linguistique générale (1910–1911): d' après les cahiers d'Emile Constantin*. Edited and translated by Eisuke Komatsu and Roy Harris. Oxford: Pergamon, 1993.

Deissmann, Adolf. *Licht vom Osten: Das Neue Testament und die neuentdeckten Texte der hellenistisch-römischen Welt*. 4th ed. Tübingen: Mohr/Siebeck, 1923.

———. *Light from the Ancient East: The New Testament Illustrated by Recently Discovered Texts of the Graeco-Roman World*. Translated by Lionel R. M. Strachan. 2nd ed. London: Hodder & Stoughton, 1911.

den Bok, Nico. "In vrijheid voorzien: Een systematisch-theologische analyse van Augustinus' teksten over voorkennis en wilsvrijheid." *Bijdragen: Tijdschrift voor filosofie en theologie* 56 (1995) 40–60.

Deterding, Paul E. "Exodus Motifs in First Peter." *Concordia Journal* 7 (1981) 58–64. Online: http://www.scribd.com/doc/50766118/Exodus-Mitif-in-1-Peter.

Didymi Alexandrini. *Epistolam S. Petri Primam Enarratio*. In *Patrologia graeca* 39. Edited by J.-P. Migne. 162 vols. Paris, 1857–1886.

Diogenes Laertius. *Lives of Eminent Philosophers*. Translated by R. D. Hicks. 2 vols. LCL. Cambridge: Harvard University Press, 1925.

Dio Chrysostom. *Discourses*. Translated by J. W. Cohoon and H. Lamar Crosby. 5 vols. LCL. Cambridge: Harvard University Press, 1971–1985.

Diodorus Siculus. *Bibliotheca historica*. From *Diodori bibliotheca historica*. Edited by K. T. Fischer and F. Vogel. 3rd ed. 5 vols. Leipzig: Teubner, 1888–1906. Online: http://www.tlg.uci.edu.

Donelson, Lewis R. *I & II Peter and Jude: A Commentary*. New Testament Library. Louisville: Westminster John Knox, 2010.

Dorotheus. *Fragmenta Graeca*. From *Dorothei Sidonii carmen astrologicum*. Edited by D. Pingree. Leipzig: Teubner, 1976. Online: http://www.tlg.uci.edu.

Dryden, J. De Waal. *Theology and Ethics in 1 Peter: Paraenetic Strategies for Christian Character Formation*. Wissenschaftliche Untersuchungen zum Neuen Testament, Second Series 209. Tübingen: Mohr/Siebeck, 2006.

du Buit, F. M. "'Voici votre vocation': Le message de Pierre." In *La Première Épitre de Saint Pierre*, 37–96. Évangile 50. Paris: Ligue Catholique de L'Évangile, 1963.

Dummett, M. A. E. "What Is a Theory of Meaning?" In *Mind & Language: Wolfson College Lectures 1974*, edited by Samuel Guttenplan, 97–138. Oxford: Oxford University Press, 1975.

Dunning, Benjamin H. *Aliens and Sojourners: Self as Other in the Rhetoric of Early Christianity*. Philadelphia: University of Pennsylvania, 2009.

Dupont-Roc, Roselyne. "Le jeu des prepositions en 1 Pierre 1, 1–12: De l'espérance finale à la joie dans les épreuves présents." *Estudios bíblicos* 53 (1995) 201–12.

Dvorak, James D. "John H. Elliott's Social-Scientific Criticism." *Trinity Journal* 28 (2007) 251–78.

Elliott, John H. "The Church as Counterculture: A Home for the Homeless and a Sanctuary for Refugees." *Currents in Theology and Mission* 25 (1998) 176–85.

———. "Disgraced yet Graced: The Gospel according to 1 Peter in the Key of Honor and Shame." *BTB* 25 (1995) 166–78.

———. *The Elect and the Holy: An Exegetical Examination of I Peter 2:4–10 and the Phrase βασίλειον ἱεράτευμα*. 1966. Reprinted, Eugene, OR: Wipf & Stock, 2006.

———. *A Home for the Homeless: A Social-Scientific Criticism of 1 Peter, Its Situation and Strategy*. With a new introduction. 1990. Reprinted, Eugene, OR: Wipf & Stock, 2005.

———. *1 Peter*. AB 37B. New Haven: Yale University Press, 2000.

———. "From Social Description to Social-Scientific Criticism. The History of a Society of Biblical Literature Section 1973–2005." *BTB* 38 (2008) 26–36.

———. "The Rehabilitation of an Exegetical Step-Child: 1 Peter in Recent Research." *JBL* 95 (1976) 243–54.

———. "Social-Scientific Criticism of the New Testament and Its Social World." *Semeia* 35 (1986) 1–33.

———. *What Is Social-Scientific Criticism?* Guides to Biblical Scholarship: New Testament Series. Minneapolis: Fortress, 1993.

Epictetus. "The Discourses." No pages. Translator unknown. Online: http://classics.mit.edu/Epictetus/discourses.2.two.html.

———. *Dissertationes ab Arriano digestae.* From *Epicteti dissertationes ab Arriano digestae.* Edited by H. Schenkl. Leipzig: Teubner, 1916. Online: http://www.tlg.uci.edu.

Erasmus. *Erasmus' Annotations on the New Testament: Galatians to the Apocalypse.* Edited by Anne Reeve. Studies in the History of Christian Thought. Leiden: Brill, 1993.

Erotianus. *Fragmenta.* From *Erotiani vocum Hippocraticarum collectio cum fragmentis.* Edited by E. Nachmanson. Göteborg: Eranos, 1918. Cited June–December 2012. Online: http://www.tlg.uci.edu.

———. *Vocum Hippocraticarum collection.* From *Erotiani vocum Hippocraticarum collection cum fragmentis.* Edited by E. Nachmanson. Göteborg: Eranos, 1918. Cited June–December 2012. Online: http://www.tlg.uci.edu

Esler, Philip F. "Models in New Testament Interpretation: A Reply to David Horrell." *JSNT* 28 (2000) 107–13.

———. *The First Christians in Their Social Worlds: Social-scientific Approaches to New Testament Interpretation.* London: Routledge, 1994.

ESV Study Bible, The. Wheaton, IL: Crossway, 2008.

Fagbemi, Stephen Ayodeji. "Living for Christ in a Hostile World: The Christian Identity and Its Present Challenges in 1 Peter." *Transformation* 26 (January 2009) 1–22.

———. *Who Are the Elect in 1 Peter? A Study in Biblical Exegesis and Its Application to the Anglican Church of Nigeria.* Studies in Biblical Literature 104. New York: Lang, 2007.

Fanning, Buist M. "A Theology of Peter and Jude." In *A Biblical Theology of the New Testament,* edited by Roy B. Zuck and Darrell L. Bock, 437–71. Chicago: Moody, 1994.

Feldmeier, Reinhard. *Der erste Brief des Petrus.* Theologischer Handkommentar zum Neuen Testament 15. Leipzig: Evangelische Verlagsanstalt, 2005.

———. "Die Außenseiter als avant-garde Gesellschaftliche Ausgrenzung als Missionarische Chance nach dem 1. Petrusbrief." Pages 161–178 in *Persuasion and Dissuasion in Early Christianity, Ancient Judaism, and Hellenism.* Edited by Pieter W. van der Horst, M. J. J. Menken, J. F. M. Smit, and Geert Van Oyen. Contributions to Biblical Exegesis and Theology 33. Leuven: Peeters, 2003.

———. *Die Christen als Fremde: Die Metapher der Fremde in der antiken Welt, im Urchristentum und im 1. Petrusbrief.* Wissenschaftliche Untersuchungen zum Neuen Testament 64. Tübingen: Mohr/Siebeck, 1992.

Filson, Floyd V. "Partakers with Christ: Suffering in First Peter." *Interpretation* 9 (1955) 400–412.

Furnish, Victor Paul. "Elect Sojourners in Christ: An Approach to the Theology of 1 Peter." *Perkins Journal* 28 (Spring 1975) 1–11.

Gager, John G. "Religion and Social Class in the Early Roman Empire." In *The Catacombs and the Colosseum: The Roman Empire as the Setting of Primitive Christianity,* edited by Stephen Benko and John J. L'Rourke, 99–120. Valley Forge, PA: Judson, 1971.

Gibson, Arthur. *Biblical Semantic Logic: A Preliminary Analysis.* 2nd ed. Biblical Seminar 75. London: Sheffield Academic, 2001.

Glenny, W. Edward. "The Israelite Imagery of 1 Peter 2." In *Dispensationalism, Israel and the Church: The Search for Definition,* edited by Craig A. Blaising and Darrell L. Bock, 156–87. Grand Rapids: Zondervan, 1992.

Goldstein, Horst. "Das Gemeindeverständnis des ersten Petrusbriefs: Exegetische Untersuchungen zur Theologie der Gemeinde im 1 Pet." PhD diss., Münster University, 1973.

Goppelt, Leonhard. *Der erste Petrusbrief. Kritisch-exegetischer Kommentar uber das Neue Testament.* 8th ed. Göttingen: Vandenhoeck & Ruprecht, 1978.

Gréaux, Eric James, Sr. "'To the Elect Exiles of the Dispersion . . . from Babylon': The Function of the Old Testament in 1 Peter." PhD diss., Duke University, 2003.

Green, Gene L. "'As for Prophecies, They Will Come to an End': 2 Peter, Paul and Plutarch on 'The Obsolescence of Oracles.'" *JSNT* 8 (2001) 107–22.

———. "First Peter." Pages 346–349 in *New Dictionary of Biblical Theology.* Edited by T. Desmond Alexander, Brian S. Rosner, D. A. Carson, and Graeme Goldsworthy. London: InterVarsity, 2003.

———. "Lexical Pragmatics and Biblical Interpretation." *Journal of the Evangelical Theological Society* 50 (2007) 799–812.

———. "Lexical Pragmatics and the Lexicon." *BBR* 22 (2012) 315–333.

———. "The Use of the Old Testament for Christian Ethics in 1 Peter." *Tyndale Bulletin* 41 (1990) 276–89.

Green, Joel B. *1 Peter.* Two Horizons New Testament Commentary. Grand Rapids: Eerdmans, 2007.

———. "Living as Exiles: The Church in the Diaspora in 1 Peter." In *Holiness and Ecclesiology in the New Testament,* edited by Kent A. Brower and Andy Johnson, 311–25. Grand Rapids: Eerdmans 2007.

———. "Narrating the Gospel in 1 and 2 Peter." *Interpretation* 60 (2006) 262–77.

Greenhill, William Alexander. "Erotianus." In *Dictionary of Greek and Roman Biography and Mythology,* edited by William Smith, 2:51. 3 vols. Boston: Little, Brown, 1867. Online: http://books.google.com.

Gregory of Nazianzen. *Orations.* In *The Nicene and Post-Nicene Fathers,* ser. 2, vol. 7. Translated by Charles Gordon Browne and James Edward Swallow. Edited by Philip Schaff and Henry Wace. 14 vols. 1885. Reprinted, Peabody, MA: Hendrickson, 1999.

Gregory the Great. *The Book of Pastoral Rule.* In *The Nicene and Post-Nicene Fathers,* Series 2, vol. 12. Edited by Philip Schaff and Henry Wace. 14 vols. 1885. Translated by James Barmby. Reprinted, Peabody, MA: Hendrickson, 1999.

Grice, H. P. "Meaning." *Philosophical Review* 66 (1957) 377–88. Reprinted in *The Philosophy of Language,* edited by A. P. Martinich, 92–97. 4th ed. New York: Oxford University Press, 2001.

Grubel, James. "Australian 'Misogyny' Speech Prompts Change to Dictionary." Edited by Nick Macfie. No pages. Online: http://news.yahoo.com/Australian-misogyny-row-prompts-change-dictionary-081326107.html.

Grudem, Wayne. *1 Peter.* Tyndale New Testament Commentaries. Grand Rapids: Eerdmans, 1988.

Guthrie, Donald. *New Testament Introduction.* 4th. ed. Downers Grove, IL: InterVarsity, 1990.

Gutt, Ernst-August. *Relevance Theory: A Guide to Successful Communication in Translation.* Dallas: Summer Institute of Linguistics, 1992.

Hale, Edward Everett. *The Man Without a Country.* Westwood, NJ: Revell, 1959.

Harink, Douglas. *1 & 2 Peter.* Brazos Theological Commentary on the Bible. Grand Rapids: Brazos, 2009.

Bibliography 197

Harmon, G. M. "Peter: The Man and the Epistle." *JBL* 17 (1898) 31–39.
Harris, Murray J. *Prepositions and Theology in the Greek New Testament: An Essential Reference Resource for Exegesis*. Grand Rapids: Zondervan, 2012.
Harrison, Everett Falconer. "Exegetical Studies in 1 Peter." *BibSac* 98 (1941) 69–77.
Harrison, Gessner. *A Treatise on the Greek Prepositions and on the Cases of Nouns with Which These Are Used*. Philadelphia, PA.: Lippincott, 1858.
Hauerwas, Stanley, and William H. Willimon. *Resident Aliens: Life in the Christian Colony*. Nashville: Abingdon, 1989.
Helyer, Larry R. *The Life and Witness of Peter*. Downers Grove, IL: IVP Academic, 2012.
Hemer, Colin J. "Address of 1 Peter." *Expository Times* 89 (May 1978) 239–43.
———. "Asia Minor." In *ISBE*, edited by Geoffrey W. Bromiley, 1:322–29. 4 vols. Grand Rapids: Eerdmans, 1979.
———. "Review of John H. Elliott, *A Home for the Homeless: A Sociological Exegesis of 1 Peter, Its Situation and Strategy*." *JSNT* 24 (1985) 443–45.
Hill, David. *Greek Words and Hebrew Meanings: Studies in the Semantics of Soteriological Terms*. Cambridge: Cambridge University Press, 1967.
Hillyer, Norman. *1 and 2 Peter, Jude*. New International Biblical Commentary. Peabody, MA: Hendrickson, 1992.
Himes, Paul A. "Peter and the Prophetic Word: The Theology of Prophecy Traced through Peter's Sermons and Epistles." *BBR* 21 (2011) 227–43.
Hirsch, E. D., Jr. *Validity in Interpretation*. New Haven: Yale University Press, 1967.
Holden, James Herschel. *History of Horoscopic Astrology: From the Babylonian Period to the Modern Age*. 2nd ed. Tempe, AZ: American Federation of Astrologers, 2006. Cited 2012–2013 (various dates). Online: http://books.google.com.
Hope, Edward R. "Translating Prepositions." *The Bible Translator* 37 (1986) 401–12.
Horrell, David G. *1 Peter*. New Testament Guides. London: T. & T. Clark, 2008.
——— "Models and Methods in Social-Scientific Interpretation: A Response to Philip Esler." *JSNT* 78 (2000) 83–105.
———. "'Race,' 'Nation,' 'People': Ethnic Identity-Construction in 1 Peter 2:9." *NTS* 58 (2012) 123–43.
———. "Social-Scientific Interpretation of the New Testament: Retrospect and Prospect." In *Social-Scientific Approaches to New Testament Interpretation*. , edited by David G. Horrell, 3–27. Edinburgh: T. & T. Clark, 1994.
———. "The Product of a Petrine Circle? A Reassessment of the Origin and Character of 1 Peter." *JSNT* 86 (2002) 29–60.
Horsley, G. H. R., S. R. Llewelyn, and J. R. Harrison, eds. *New Documents Illustrating Early Christianity*. 10 vols. Sydney, Australia: The Ancient History Documentary Research Centre (Macquarie University), 1981–2002; and Grand Rapids: Eerdmans, 2012.
Hort, F. J. A. *The First Epistle of Peter: I.1–II. 17*. London: MacMillan, 1898.
Howard, Douglas A. *The History of Turkey*. Greenwood Histories of the Modern Nations. Westport, CT.: Greenwood, 2001.
Ignatius. *Epistle of Ignatius to the Ephesians*. In *The Anti-Nicene Fathers* 1. Edited by Alexander Roberts and James Donaldson. 10 vols. 1885–1887. Reprinted, Peabody, MA: Hendrickson, 1999.
———. *Epistle of Ignatius to the Philadelphians*. In *The Anti-Nicene Fathers* 1. Edited by Alexander Roberts and James Donaldson. 10 vols. 1885–1887. Reprinted, Peabody, MA: Hendrickson, 1999.

Jaillard, Dominique. "Plutarque et la divination: la piété d'un prêtre philosophe." *Revue de l'histoire des religions* 224 (2007) 149–69.
James, Edgar C. "Is Foreknowledge Equivalent to Foreordination?" *BibSac* 122 (1965) 215–19.
Jerome. *The Dialogue against the Luciferians*. In *The Nicene and Post-Nicene Fathers*, ser. 2, vol. 6. Edited by Philip Schaff and Henry Wace. 14 vols. 1885. Reprinted, Peabody, MA: Hendrickson, 1999.
Jobes, Karen H. *1 Peter*. Baker Exegetical Commentary on the New Testament. Grand Rapids: Baker Academic, 2005.
―――. "Got Milk? Septuagint Psalm 33 and the Interpretation of 1 Peter 2:1–3." *Westminster Theological Journal* 63 (2002) 1–14.
―――. "The Syntax of 1 Peter. Just How Good is the Greek?" *BBR* 13 (2003) 159–73.
John of Damascus. *Expositions of the Orthodox Faith*. In *The Nicene and Post-Nicene Fathers*, ser. 2, vol. 9. Translated by S. D. F. Salmon. Edited by Philip Schaff and Henry Wace. 14 vols. 1885. Reprinted, Peabody, MA: Hendrickson, 1999.
Jones, C. P. "Plutarch." In *Lucretius to Ammianus Marcellinus*. In *Ancient Writers: Greece and Rome*, edited by T. James Luce, vol. 2. 2 vols. New York: Scribner, 1982.
Jorgenson, James. "Predestination according to Divine Foreknowledge in Patristic Tradition." In *Salvation in Christ: A Lutheran-Orthodox Dialogue*. Edited by John Meyendorff and Robert Tobias, 159–70. Minneapolis: Augsburg, 1992.
Joseph, Abson Prédestin. *A Narratological Reading of 1 Peter*. Library of New Testament Studies 440. New York: T. & T. Clark, 2012.
Josephus, Flavius. *Antiquitates Judaicae*. In vols. 1–4 of *Flavii Iosephi opera*. Edited by B. Niese. Berlin: Weidmann, 1885–1892. Online: http://www.tlg.uci.edu.
―――. *Contra Apionem*. In vol. 5 of *Flavii Iosephi opera*. Edited by B. Niese. Belin: Weidmann, 1889. Online: http://www.tlg.uci.edu.
―――. *De bello Judaico libri vii*. From vol. 6 of *Flavii Iosephi opera*. Edited by B. Niese. Berlin: Weidmann, 1895. Online: http://www.tlg.uci.edu.
―――. *Jewish Antiquities*. Translated by H. St. J. Thackeray. 6 vols. LCL. Cambridge: Harvard University Press, 1963–1990.
―――. *Josephi vita*. From vol. 4 of *Flavii Iosephi opera*. Edited by B. Niese. Berlin: Weidmann, 1890. Cited June–December 2012. Online: http://www.tlg.uci.edu.
―――. *The Jewish War*. Translated by H. St. J. Thackeray. 2 vols. LCL. Cambridge: Harvard University Press, 1984–1990.
―――. *The Works of Flavius Josephus*. Translated by William Whiston. Peabody, MA: Hendrickson, 1987. In *Accordance* 8.4. OakTree Software, 2009.
―――. *Works of Flavius Josephus*. [Greek text based on the 1890 Niese edition]. In *Accordance* 8.4. OakTree Software, 2009.
Judge, E. A. "The Social Identity of the First Christians: A Question of Method in Religious History." *Journal of Religious History* 11 (1980) 201–17.
Judith. From vol. 1 of *Septuaginta*. Edited by A. Rahlfs. 9th ed. Stuttgart: Württemberg Bible Society, 1935. Online: http://www.tlg.uci.edu.
Justinus Martyr. *Apologia prima pro Christianis*. In vol. 6 of *Patrologia graeca*. Edited by J.-P. Migne. 162 vols. Paris, 1857–1886.
Katz, Jerrold J. *Semantic Theory*. New York: Harper & Row, 1972.
Kelly, J. N. D. *A Commentary on the Epistles of Peter and of Jude*. Harper's New Testament Commentaries. New York: Harper & Row, 1969.

Kempson, Ruth. "Pragmatics: Language and Communication." In *The Handbook of Linguistics*, edited by Mark Aronoff and Janie Rees-Miller, 394–427. Malden, MA: Blackwell, 2001.
Kendell, David W. "The Literary and Theological Function of 1 Peter 1:3-12." In *Perspectives on First Peter*. Edited by Charles H. Talbert, 103–20. National Association of Baptist Professors of Religion Special Studies 9. Macon, GA: Mercer University Press, 1986.
Kilpatrick, G. D. "1 Peter 1:11 τίνα ἢ ποῖον χαιρὸν." *Novum Testamentum* 28 (1986) 91–92.
Kirk, Gordon E. "Endurance in Suffering in 1 Peter." *BibSac* 138 (January–March 1981) 46–56.
Kirkpatrick, William David. "The Theology of First Peter." *Southwestern Journal of Theology* 25 (Fall 1982) 58–81.
Kistemaker, Simon J. *James, Epistles of John, Peter, and Jude*. New Testament Commentary. Grand Rapids: Baker, 1986.
Koldon, Marc. "Are You Serious? First Peter on Christian Life in a Complicated World." *Word & World* 24 (2004) 421–29.
Köstenberger, Andreas J., L. Scott Kellum, and Charles L. Quarles. *The Cradle, the Cross, and the Crown: An Introduction to the New Testament*. Nashville: B&H Academic, 2009.
Knopf, Rudolf. *Die Briefe Petri und Judä*. Kritisch-exegetischer Kommentar über das Neue Testament 12. Göttingen: Vandenhoeck & Ruprecht, 1912.
Lea, Tommy. "I Peter—Outline and Exposition." *Southwestern Journal of Theology* 25 (Fall 1982) 17–45.
Lee, Clarence L. "Social Unrest and Primitive Christianity." In *The Catacombs and the Colosseum: The Roman Empire as the Setting of Primitive Christianity*, edited by Stephen Benko and John J. O'Rourke, 121–38. Valley Forge, PA: Judson, 1971.
Lee, John A. L. *A History of New Testament Lexicography*. Studies in Biblical Greek 8. New York: Lang, 2003.
Leighton, Robert. *A Practical Commentary upon the First Epistle of St. Peter*. 2 vols. London: Society for Promoting Christian Knowledge, 24. Online: http://books.google.com.
Leo the Great. Letters. In *The Nicene and Post-Nicene Fathers*, ser. 2, vol. 12. Translated by Charles Lett Feltoe. Edited by Philip Schaff and Henry Wace. 14 vols. 1885. Reprinted, Peabody, MA: Hendrickson, 1999.
———. Sermons. In *The Nicene and Post-Nicene Fathers*, ser. 2, vol. 12. Translated by Charles Lett Feltoe. Edited by Philip Schaff and Henry Wace. 14 vols. 1885. Reprinted, Peabody, MA: Hendrickson, 1999.
Lescelius, Robert H. "Foreknowledge: Prescience or Predestination?" *Reformation and Revival* 12 (Spring 2003) 25–39.
Levick, Barbara. *Roman Colonies in Southern Asia Minor*. Oxford: Clarendon, 1967.
Liddell, Henry George, and Robert Scott. *A Greek-English Lexicon*. 9th ed. Oxford: Oxford University Press, 1940 and 1996 (with rev. supplement).
Liebengood, Kelly. "'Don't Be Like Your Fathers': Reassessing the Ethnic Identity of 1 Peter's 'Elect Sojourners.'" Paper presented at the annual meeting of the SBL. New Orleans, LA, November, 2009.
Lloyd, Seton. *Ancient Turkey: A Traveler's History*. Berkeley: University of California Press, 1989.

Longinus. *De sublimitate*. From *Longinus' On the Sublime*. Edited by D. A. Russell. Oxford: Clarendon, 1964. Online: http://www.tlg.uci.edu.
———. *On the Sublime*. Translated by H. L. Havell. London: MacMillan, 1890. Online: http://www.gutenberg.org/files/17957/17957-h/17957-h.htm.
———. *On the Sublime*. Translated by W. Rhys Roberts. No pages. Online: http://classicpersuasion.org/pw/longinus/desub002.htm.
Louw, Johannes P. "How Do Words Mean—If They Do?" *Filologia Neotestamentaria* 4 (November 1991) 125–42.
———. *Semantics of New Testament Greek*. Philadelphia: Fortress, 1982.
Love, Julian Price. "The First Epistle of Peter." *Interpretation* 8 (1954) 63–87.
Luraghi, Silvia. *On the Meaning of Prepositions and Cases*. Studies in Language Companion Series 67. Amsterdam: Benjamins, 2003.
Lyons, John. *Introduction to Theoretical Linguistics*. Cambridge: Cambridge University Press, 1968.
———. *Language and Linguistics: An Introduction*. Cambridge: Cambridge University Press, 1981.
Malherbe, Abraham J. *Social Aspects of Early Christianity*. 1977. Reprinted, Eugene, OR: Wipf & Stock, 2003.
Malina, Bruce J. *The New Testament World: Insights from Cultural Anthropology*. 3rd ed. Louisville: Westminster John Knox, 2001.
———. "Rhetorical Criticism and Social-Scientific Criticism: Why Won't Romanticism Leave Us Alone?" In *The Social World of the New Testament*, edited by Jerome H. Neyrey and Eric C. Stewart, 5–21. Peabody, MA: Hendrickson, 2008.
———. "Why Interpret the Bible with the Social Sciences?" *Baptist Quarterly* 2 (1983) 119–33.
Marrow, Stanley B. "Review of *A Home for the Homeless: A Sociological Exegesis of 1 Peter, Its Situation and Strategy*." *CBQ* 45 (1983) 483–84.
Marshall, I. Howard. *1 Peter*. IVP New Testament Commentary Series. Downers Grove, IL: InterVarsity, 1991.
Martin, Troy. *Metaphor and Composition in 1 Peter*. Society of Biblical Literature Dissertation Series 131. Atlanta: Scholars, 1992.
Mbuvi, Andrew M. *Temple, Exile and Identity in 1 Peter*. Library of New Testament Studies 345. London: T. & T. Clark, 2007.
McCall, Tom, and Keith Stanglin. "S. M. Baugh and the Meaning of Foreknowledge: Another Look." *Trinity Journal* 26 (Spring 2005) 19–31.
McKnight, Scot. "Aliens and Exiles: Social Location and Christian Vocation." *Word & World* 24 (2004) 378–86.
McKnight, Scot. *1 Peter*. NIV Application Commentary. Grand Rapids: Zondervan, 1996.
Meinertz, Max, and Wilhelm Vrede. *Die Katholischen Briefe*. Die Heilige Schrift: Des Neuen Testaments 9. Bonn: Hanstein, 1932.
Merriam-Webster. Online: http://www.merriam-webster.com/dictionary/emic.
———. No pages. Online: http://www.merriam-webster.com/dictionary/mantic.
Methodius. *Oration Concerning Simeon and Anna on the Day That They Met in the Temple*. In *The Anti-Nicene Fathers*, vol. 6. Edited by Alexander Roberts and James Donaldson. 10 vols. 1885–1887. Reprinted, Peabody, MA: Hendrickson, 1999.
Metzger, Bruce M. *A Textual Commentary on the Greek New Testament*. 2nd ed. Stuttgart: Deutsche Bibelgesellschaft, 1994.

Michaels, J. Ramsey. *1 Peter*. Word Biblical Commentary 49. Waco, TX: Word, 1988.
Mitchell, Stephen. *The Celts and the Impact of Roman Rule*. Vol. 1 of *Aanatolia: Land, Men, and Gods in Asia Minor*, vol. 1. 2 vols. Oxford: Clarendon, 1993.
Moffett, Samuel Hugh. *Beginnings to 1500*. Vol. 1 of *A History of Christianity in Asia*. 2 vols. New York: HarperCollins, 1992.
Moo, Douglas. *The Epistle to the Romans*. New International Commentary on the New Testament. Grand Rapids: Eerdmans, 1996.
Moore, Carey A. *Judith: A New Translation with Introduction and Commentary*. AB 40. Garden City, NY: Doubleday, 1985.
Morris, Leon. *The Apostolic Preaching of the Cross*. Grand Rapids: Eerdmans, 2001.
———. *The Epistle to the Romans*. Pillar New Testament Commentary. Grand Rapids: Eerdmans, 1988.
Moule, C. F. D. "The Nature and Purpose of 1 Peter." *NTS* 3 (1956) 1–11.
Moulton, James Hope. *Prolegomena*. Vol. 1 of *A Grammar of New Testament Greek*. 3rd corrected ed. Edinburgh: T. & T. Clark, 1949.
Mulholland, M. Robert, Jr. "Sociological Criticism." In *Interpreting the New Testament: Essays on Methods and Issues*, edited by David Alan Black and David S. Dockery, 170–86. Nashville: Broadman & Holman, 2001.
Neyrey, Jerome H. "The Form and Background of the Polemic in 2 Peter." *JBL* 99 (1980) 407–31.
Nida, Eugene A., and Johannes P. Louw. *Lexical Semantics of the Greek New Testament: A Supplement to the Greek-English Lexicon of the New Testament Based on Semantic Domains*. Society of Biblical Literature Resources for Biblical Study 25. Atlanta: Scholars, 1992.
Obermann, Andreas. "Fremd im eigenen Land: Die Heimatkonzeption frühchristlicher Gemeinden nach dem 1. Petrusbrief und ihre praktische Implikationen heute." *Kerygma und Dogma* 51 (2005) 263–89.
Olson, C. Gordon. "A Lexical Study of Foreknowledge and Predestination." Paper presented at the annual meeting of the Eastern Region of the ETS, Philadelphia, PA, April 2, 1993.
Origin. *Against Celsus*. In *The Anti-Nicene Fathers*, vol. 4. Edited by Alexander Roberts and James Donaldson. 10 vols. 1885–1887. Reprinted, Peabody, MA: Hendrickson, 1999.
———. *Contra Celsum*. In *Patrologia graeca* 11. Edited by J.-P. Migne. 162 vols. Paris, 1857–1886.
Ortwein, Gudrun Guttenberger. *Status und Statusverzicht im Neuen Testament und seiner Umwelt*. Novum Testamentum et Orbis Antiquus 39. Göttingen: Vandenhoeck & Ruprecht, 1999.
Osiek, Carolyn. *What Are They Saying about the Social Setting of the New Testament?* Rev. ed. New York: Paulist, 1992.
Page, Sydney H. T. "Obedience and Blood-Sprinkling in 1 Peter 1:2." *Westminster Theological Journal* 72 (2010) 291–298.
Pervo, Richard I. *Acts: A Commentary*. Hemeneia. Minneapolis: Fortress, 2009.
Peterson, David G. *The Acts of the Apostles*. Pillar New Testament Commentary. Grand Rapids: Eerdmans, 2009.
Philipps, Karl. *Kirche in der Gesellschaft nach dem ersten Petrusbrief*. Augsburg: Gütersloh, 1971.

Philo Judaeus. *De somniis (lib. i–ii).* From vol. 3 of *Philonis Alexandrini opera quae supersunt.* Berlin: Reimer, 1898. Online: http://www.tlg.uci.edu.

———. *The Works of Philo: Complete and Unabridged.* Translated by C. D. Yonge. New and updated ed. Peabody, MA: Hendrickson, 1993. In Accordance 8.4. OakTree Software, 2009.

———. *The Works of Philo* (Greek text). Edited by Peder Borgen, Kåre Fuglseth, and Roald Skarsten. The Norwegian Philo Concordance Project, 2005. In Accordance 8.4. OakTree Software, 2009.

Picirilli, Robert E. *Grace, Faith, and Free Will—Contrasting Views of Salvation: Calvinism & Arminianism.* Nashville: Randall House, 2002.

Piper, John. *The Future of Justification: A Response to N. T. Wright.* Wheaton, IL: Crossway, 2007.

———. "Hope as the Motivation of Love: 1 Peter 3:9–12." *NTS* 26 (1980) 212–231.

Plutarchus. *Alcibiades.* From vol. 1.2 of *Plutarchi vitae parallelae.* Edited by K. Ziegler. 3rd ed. Leipzig: Teubner, 1964. Online: http://www.tlg.uci.edu.

———. *Comparatio Periclis et Fabii Maximi.* From vol. 1.2 of *Plutarchi vitae parallelae.* Edited by K. Ziegler. 3rd ed. Leipzig: Teubner, 1964. Online: http://www.tlg.uci.edu.

———. *De curiositate.* From vol. 3 of *Plutarchi moralia.* Edited by M. Pohlenz. Leipzig: Teubner, 1929. Online: http://www.tlg.uci.edu.

———. *De defectu oraculorum.* From vol. 3 of *Plutarchi moralia.* Edited by W. Sieveking. Leipzig: Teubner, 1929. Online: http://www.tlg.uci.edu.

———. *De E apud Delphos.* From vol. 3 of *Plutarchi moralia.* Edited by W. Sievekign. Leipzig: Teubner, 1929. Online:http://www.tlg.uci.edu.

———. *De sera numinis vindicta.* From vol. 3 of *Plutarchi moralia.* Edited by M. Pohlenz. Leipzig: Teubner, 1929. Online: http://www.tlg.uci.edu.

———. *De Pythiae oraculis.* From vol. 3 of *Plutarchi moralia.* Edited by W. Sievekign. Leipzig: Teubner, 1929. Online: http://www.tlg.uci.edu.

———. *De sollertia animalium.* From vol. 6 of *Plutarchi moralia.* Edited by C. Hubert. Leipzig: Teubner, 1954. Online:http://www.tlg.uci.edu.

———. *Dion.* From vol. 2.1 of *Plutarchi vitae parallelae.* Edited by K. Ziegler. 2nd ed. Leipzig: Teubner, 1964. Online: http://www.tlg.uci.edu.

———. *Fragmenta.* From vol. 7 of *Plutarchi moralia.* Edited by F. H. Sandbach. Leipzig: Teubner, 1967. Online:http://www.tlg.uci.edu.

———. *Fragments.* Translated by E. H. Sandbach. Vol. 15 of *Moralia.* LCL. Cambridge: Harvard University Press, 1987.

———. *Lives.* Translated by Bernadotte Perrin. 11 vols. LCL. Cambridge: Harvard University Press, 1982.

———. *Moralia.* Translated by Phillip H. de Lacy and Benedict Einarson. Vol. 7 of LCL. Cambridge: Harvard University Press, 1959.

———. *Moralia.* Translated by Frank Cole Babbitt. 16 vols. LCL. London: Heinemann, 1986.

———. *Moralia.* Translated by Harold Cherniss and William C. Helmbold. Vol. 12 of LCL. Cambridge: Harvard University Press, 1957.

———. *Moralia.* Translated by Lionel Pearson. Vol. 11 of LCL. Cambridge: Harvard University Press, 1965.

———. *Mulierum virtutes (242e–263c).* From vol. 2.1 of *Plutarchi moralia.* Edited by W. Nachstädt. Leipzig: Teubner, 1935. Online: http://www.tlg.uci.edu.

———. *Pyrrhus*. From vol. 3.1 of *Plutarchi vitae parallelae*. Edited by K. Ziegler. 2nd ed. Leipzig: Teubner, 1971. Online: http://www.tlg.uci.edu.

———. *Sulla*. From vol. 4 of *Plutarch's Lives*. Edited by B. Perrin. Cambridge: Harvard University Press, 1916. Online: http://www.tlg.uci.edu.

Poh, C. L. E. "The Social World of 1 Peter: Socio-historical and Exegetical Studies." PhD diss., University of London, King's College, 1998.

Polybius. *Histories*. From *Polybii historiae*. Edited by T. Büttner-Wobst. 4 vols. Leipzig: Teubner, 1889–1905. Online: http://www.tlg.uci.edu.

Porter, Stanley E. *Idioms of the Greek New Testament*. 2nd ed. Biblical Languages: Greek 2. London: Sheffield Academic, 1999.

Prasad, Jacob. *Foundations of the Christian Way of Life according to 1 Peter 1, 13–24: An Exegetico-Theological Study*. Analecta Biblica 146. Rome: Pontifical Biblical Institute Press, 2000.

Price, S. R. F. *Rituals and Power: The Roman Imperial Cult in Asia Minor*. Cambridge: Cambridge University Press, 1984.

Radermacher, Ludwig. *Koine*. Vienna: Holzhausens, 1947.

Ramsay, Sir William Mitchell. *The Historical Geography of Asia Minor*. Royal Geographical Society Supplementary Papers. London: Murray, 1890.

Reed, Jeffrey T. "Language of Change and the Changing of Language: A Sociolinguistic Approach to Pauline Discourse." In *Diglossia and Other Topics in New Testament Linguistics*, edited by Stanley E. Porter, 121–53. JSNTSup 193. Sheffield: Sheffield Academic, 2000.

Reicke, Bo. *The Epistles of James, Peter, and Jude*. AB 37. Garden City, NY: 1965.

———. *The New Testament Era: The World of the Bible from 500 B.C. to A.D. 100*. Translated by David E. Green. Philadelphia: Fortress, 1968.

Reider, Joseph. *The Book of Wisdom: An English Translation with Introduction and Commentary*. Jewish Apocrypha Literature Series. New York: Harper & Brothers, 1957.

Richard, Earl J. "The Functional Christology of First Peter." In *Perspectives on First Peter*, edited by Charles H. Talbert, 121–39. National Association of Baptist Professors of Religion Special Studies 9. Macon, GA: Mercer University Press, 1986.

———. "Honorable Conduct among the Gentiles—A Study of the Social Thought of 1 Peter." *Word & World* 24 (2004) 412–20.

Robertson, A. T. *A Grammar of the Greek New Testament in the Light of Historical Research*. Nashville: Broadman, 1934.

Robinson, Maurice A., and William G. Pierpont, eds. *The New Testament in the Original Greek: Byzantine Textform 2005*. Southborough, MA: Chilton, 2005.

Rohrbaugh, Richard L. "'Social Location of Thought' as a Heuristic Construct in New Testament Study." *JSNT* 30 (1987) 103–19.

Roy, Steve C. *How Much Does God Foreknow? A Comprehensive Biblical Study*. Downers Grove, IL: InterVarsity, 2006.

Rufus. *Quaestiones medicinales*. From *Rufus von Ephesos: Die Fragen des Arztes an den Kranken*. Edited by H. Gärtner. Corpus medicorum Graecorum supplement 4. Berlin: Akademie, 1962. Online: http://www.tlg.uci.edu.

Sawyer, John F. A. *Semantics in Biblical Research: New Methods of Defining Hebrew Words for Salvation*. Studies in Biblical Theology 2/24. Naperville, IL: Allenson, 1972.

Scharfe, Ernst. *Die Petrinische Strömung der Neutestamentlichen Literatur.* Berlin: Reuther & Reichard, 1893.
Schelkle, Karl Hermann. *Die Petrusbriefe, der Judasbrief.* Herders Theologischer Kommentar zum Neuen Teestament. Freiburg: Herder, 1970.
Schmitz, Leonhard. "Aristonicus." In *Dictionary of Greek and Roman Biography and Mythology*, edited by William Smith, 1:312. 3 vols. Boston: Little, Brown, 1867. Online: http://books.google.com.
———. "Longinus Dionysius Cassius." In *Dictionary of Greek and Roman Biography and Mythology*, edited by William Smith, 2:803–5. 3 vols. Boston: Little, Brown, 1867. Online: http://books.google.com.
Schrage, Wolfgang. "Der erste Petrusbrief." In *Die Katholischen Briefe*, 59–117. Das Neue Testament Deutsch 10. Göttingen: Vandenhoeck & Ruprecht, 1973.
Schreiner, Thomas R. *1, 2 Peter, Jude.* New American Commentary 37. Nashville: Broadman & Holman, 2003.
———. *New Testament Theology: Magnifying God in Christ.* Grand Rapids: Baker Academic, 2008.
———. *Romans.* Baker Exegetical Commentary on the New Testament. Grand Rapids: Baker Academic, 1998.
Schröger, Friedrich. *Gemeinde im 1. Petrusbrief: Untersuchungen zum Selbstverständnis einer christlichen Gemeinde an der Wende vom 1. zum 2. Jahrhundert.* Katholische Theologie 1. Passau: Passavia Universitätsverlag, 1981.
Schutter, William L. *Hermeneutic and Composition in I Peter.* Wissenschaftliche Untersuchungen zum Neuen Testament 2/30. Tübingen: Mohr/Siebeck, 1989.
Schweizer, Eduard. *Der erste Petrusbrief.* Zürcher Bibelkommentare. Zürich: Theologischer, 1972.
Seland, Torrey. "πάροικος καὶ παρεπίδημος: Proselyte Characterizations in 1 Peter?" *BBR* 11 (2001) 239–68.
Selwyn, Edward Gordon. *The First Epistle of St. Peter.* 2nd ed. London: Macmillan, 1955.
Sharp, Granville. *Remarks on the Uses of the Definitive Article in the Greek New Testament.* London: Sharp, 1803.
Shepherd of Hermas, The. In *Apostolic Fathers: Greek Texts and English Translations.* Edited by Michael W. Holmes. Grand Rapids: Baker, 1999. In *Accordance* 8.4. OakTree Software, 2009.
Silva, Moisés. *Biblical Words and Their Meaning: An Introduction to Lexical Semantics.* Rev. and expanded ed. Grand Rapids: Zondervan, 1994.
Smith, Craig A. "The Development of Style (Fifth Century BCE to Second Century CE) and the Consequences for Understanding the Style of the New Testament." *Journal of Greco-Roman Christianity and Judaism* 7 (2010) 9–31.
Smith, Kevin Gary. "Bible Translation and Relevance Theory: The Translation of Titus." DLitt diss., University of Stellenbosch, 2000.
Smith, William. *A New Dictionary of Greek and Roman Biography, Mythology, and Geography Partially Based upon the Dictionary of Greek and Romany Biography and Mythology.* Rev. ed. New York: Harper & Brothers, 1850. Online: http://books.google.com.
Soucek, Josef B. "Das Gegenüber von Gemeinde und Welt nach dem ersten Petrusbrief." In *Bibelauslegung als Theologie*, 199–209. Wissenschaftliche Untersuchungen zum Neuen Testament 100. Tübingen: Mohr/Siebeck, 1997

Sperber, Dan, and Deirdre Wilson. *Relevance: Communication and Cognition*. 2nd ed. Oxford: Blackwell, 1995.
Spicq, Ceslas. *Les Épitres de Saint Pierre*. Sources Bibliques. Paris: Gabalda, 1966.
Spörri, Theophil. *Der Gemeindegedanke im ersten Petrusbrief: Ein Beitrag zur Struktur des urchritlichen Kirchenbergriffs*. Untersuchungen zum Kirchenproblem des Urchristentums. Gütersloh: Rufer, 1925.
Staden, P. van, and A. G. van Aarde. "Social Description or Social-scientific Interpretation? A Survey of Modern Scholarship." *Hervormde teologiese studies* 47 (1991) 55–87.
Starwalt, Ervin Ray. "A Discourse Analysis of 1 Peter." PhD diss., University of Texas at Arlington, 2005.
Steenberg, Pierre Francois. "The Reversal of Roles as the Reasoning for Remaining Christian in the Face of Hardship." PhD diss., University of Pretoria, 2001.
Steiger, Wilhelm. *Der erste Brief Petri mit Berücksichtigung des ganzen biblischen Lehrbegriffs*. Berlin: Dehmigke, 1832.
Stewart, Alexander E. "When Are Christians Saved and Why Does It Matter? An Investigation into the Rhetorical Force of First Peter's Inaugurated Soteriology." *Trinity Journal* 32 (2011) 221–35.
Stover, Michael. "The Dating of First Clement." ThM thesis, Southeastern Baptist Theological Seminary, 2012.
Taber, Charles R. "Exegesis and Linguistics." *The Bible Translator* 20 (1969) 150–53.
Talbert, Charles H. "Once Again: The Plan of 1 Peter." In *Perspectives on First Peter*, edited by Charles H. Talbert, 141–51. National Association of Baptist Professors of Religion Special Studies Series 9. Macon, GA: Mercer University Press, 1986.
Tånberg, K. Arvid. "Linguistics and Theology: An Attempt to Analyze and Evaluate James Barr's Argumentation in *The Semantics of Biblical Language* and *Biblical Words for Time*." *The Bible Translator* 24 (1973) 301–10.
Tertullian. *An Answer to the Jews*. In *The Anti-Nicene Fathers*, vol. 3. Edited by Alexander Roberts and James Donaldson. 10 vols. 1885–1887. Reprinted, Peabody, MA: Hendrickson, 1999.
Thesaurus Linguae Graecae. University of California, 2009. No pages. Online: http://tlg.uci.edu.
Thomas, Robert L. "Modern Linguistics Versus Traditional Hermeneutics." *The Master's Seminary Journal* 14 (Spring 2003) 23–45.
Thompson, James W. "The Rhetoric of 1 Peter." *Restoration Quarterly* 36 (1994) 237–50.
"Thoughts on the Fore-Knowledge of God, with Reference to Those Passages of Scripture Where It Occurs." [Author unknown]. *Methodist Review* 3 (1820) 11–14, 49–53. Online: http://books.google.com.
Thurén, Lauri. *Argument and Theology in 1 Peter: The Origins of Christian Paraenesis*. JSNTSup 114. Sheffield: Sheffield Academic, 1995.
Trebilco, Paul. *Self-designations and Group Identity in the New Testament*. Cambridge: Cambridge University Press, 2012.
Trobisch, David. *The First Edition of the New Testament*. Oxford: Oxford University Press, 2000.
Usteri, Johann Martin. *Wissenschaftlicher und Praktischer Commentar über den Ersten Petrusbrief*. Zurich: Höhr, 1887.

Van Aarde, Andries G. "Inleiding tot die sosiaal-wetenskaplike kritiese eksegese van Nuwe-Testamentiese tekste: die metodologiese aanloop in die navorsingsgeskiedenis." *Hervormde teologiese studies* 63 (2007) 49–79.

Van Rensburg, Fika J. "Christians as 'Residents and Visiting Aliens': Implications of the Exhortation to the Πάροικοι and Παρεπίδημοι in 1 Peter for the Church in South Africa." *Neotestamentica* 32 (1998) 573–83.

———. "Metaphors in the Soteriology in 1 Peter: Identifying and Interpreting the Salvific Imageries." In *Salvation in the New Testament: Perspectives on Soteriology*, edited by Jan G. van der Watt, 409–35. Supplements to Novum Testamentum 121. Leiden: Brill, 2005.

Vance, Laurence M. *Guide to Prepositions in the Greek New Testament*. Pensacola, FL: Vance, 2007.

Verhaar, W. M. "Language and Theological Method." *Continuum* 7 (Winter–Spring 1969) 3–29.

Volf, Miroslav. "Soft Difference: Theological Reflections on the Relation between Church and Culture in 1 Peter." *Ex Auditu* 10 (1994) 15–30.

Wallace, Daniel B. *Granville Sharp's Canon and Its Kin: Semantics and Significance*. Studies in Biblical Greek 14. New York: Lang, 2009.

———. *Greek Grammar Beyond the Basics: An Exegetical Syntax of the New Testament*. Grand Rapids: Zondervan, 1996.

Warden, Preston Duane. "Alienation and Community in 1 Peter." PhD diss., Duke University, 1986.

———. "Imperial Persecution and the Dating of 1 Peter and Revelation." *Journal of the Evangelical Theological Society* 34 (June 1991) 203–12.

———. "The Prophets of 1 Peter 1:10–12." *Restoration Quarterly* 31 (1989) 1–12.

Whitaker, Richard E. "Concordances and the Greek New Testament." In *Biblical Greek and Lexicography: Essays in Honor of Frederick W. Danker*, edited by Bernard A. Taylor, John A. L. Lee, Peter R. Burton, and Richard E. Whitaker, 94–107. Grand Rapids: Eerdmans, 2004.

Wilckens, Ulrich. *Der Brief an die Römer (Röm 6–11)*. Evangelisch-katholischer Kommentar zum Neuen Testament 6/2. Zürich: Benziger, 1980.

Wilkenhauser, Alfred, and Josef Schmid. *Einleitung in das Neue Testament*. Freiburg: Herder, 1973.

Williams, Jocelyn A. "A Case Study in Intertextuality: The Place of Isaiah in the 'Stone' Sayings of 1 Peter 2." *Reformed Theological Review* 66 (April 2007) 37–55.

Williams, Martin. *The Doctrine of Salvation in the First Letter of Peter*. Society for New Testament Studies Monograph Series 149. Cambridge: Cambridge University Press, 2011.

Williams, Travis B. *Persecution in 1 Peter: Differentiating and Contextualizing Early Christian Suffering*. Supplements to Novum Testamentum 145. Leiden, Brill: 2012.

Winer, George Benedict. *A Grammar of the Idiom of the New Testament, Prepared as a Solid Basis for the Interpretation of the New Testament*. 7th ed. Enlarged and Improved by Gottlieb Lünemann. Rev. by Gottlieb Lünemann. Translated from the 6th ed. by Masson. Andover, MA: Draper, 1892.

Winston, David. *The Wisdom of Solomon: A New Translation with Introduction and Commentary*. AB 43. Garden City, NY: Doubleday, 1979.

Wisdom of Solomon. From vol. 2 of *Septuaginta*. Edited by A. Rahlfs. 9th ed. Stuttgart: Wüttemberg Bible Society, 1935. Online: http://www.tlg.uci.edu.

Wise, Michael, Martin Abegg Jr., and Edward Cook, trans. *The Dead Sea Scrolls: A New Translation*. New York: HarperCollins, 2005.
Witherington, Ben, III. *A Socio-Rhetorical Commentary on 1-2 Peter*. Vol. 2 of *Letters and Homilies for Hellenized Christians*. Downers Grove, IL: IVP Academic, 2006.
Wolff, Christian. "Christ und Welt im 1. Petrusbrief." *Theologische Literaturzeitung* 100 (1975) 333-42.
———. "Review of John H. Elliott, *A Home for the Homeless: A Sociological Exegesis of 1 Peter, Its Situation and Strategy*." *Theologische Literaturzeitung* 109 (1984) 443-45.
Wright, F. A. *A History of Later Greek Literature: From the Death of Alexander in 323 B.C. to the Death of Justinian in 565 A.D.* London: Routledge & Kegan Paul, 1932.
Wright, N. T. *Justification: God's Plan and Paul's Vision*. Downers Grove, IL: InterVarsity, 2009.

Index of Scripture and Other Ancient Works

OLD TESTAMENT/ HEBREW BIBLE

Genesis

12:10	62
15:13	56, 58, 69
21:1	62
23:4	40, 55, 56, 69

Exodus

2:22	69
6:4	62
12:45	69
18:13	69
22:21	166
24	151

Leviticus

22:12	69
25:6	69
25:23	69
25:35	69
25:40	69
25:45	69
25:47	69

Numbers

16:5	24
35:15	69

Deuteronomy

14:21	69
18:21–22	27
23:7	69

Ruth

1:1	62

1 Samuel

12	124

1 Kings

12–13	103

1 Chronicles

29:14–15	47, 68
29:14	56, 57
29:15	69

Ezra

8:35 (LXX)	58

Psalms

5:4 (LXX)	62
30:14 (LXX)	62
33 (LXX)	49, 68
33:5 (LXX)	58
36:13 (LXX)	88
38:12 (LXX)	40, 55
38:13–14 (LXX)	47, 69
94	124
118:19 (LXX)	47, 69
138:3 (LXX)	88

Proverbs

22:28	187

Isaiah

40	168
40:6–8	168
41:22–23	102
42:9	102n
43:9	102n
44:7	102n
46:9f	102n
53	83

Hosea

1:6–2:1	176
1:10	13

Amos

3:2	21

~

APOCRYPHA

Judith

5:8	62
5:9	58
9:6	24, 101–2, 126
10–11	102

11:6–19a	144
11:19	101, 102, 145, 149

Wisdom of Solomon

6:9–22	110
6:13	110–11, 129
8:8	111
18	111
18:6	111

Sirach

16:8	58

~

NEW TESTAMENT

Matthew

13:16–17	154
20:16	144
25:12	21

Luke

2	157
24:18	62
24:25–27	154

John

7:35	144
14:15	152

Acts

2–4	155
2:23	109–110
3:18	154
7:52	154
8:34	83
13:1	153
13:17	58
13:48	97
26:5	122–23, 124, 129

Romans

1:1	144
8:28–30	123–24
8:28	123–24, 129
8:29–30	97
8:29	16
9:3	175
11	124
11:2	124–25, 129
11:3–15	125
11:3	124

1 Corinthians

1:1–2	144

2 Corinthians

1:11	154

Galatians

2:15	175

Ephesians

1:4–5	16
1:5	97
2:10	152
6:5–6	65

Philippians

3:20	186

Colossians

1:11	147
4:1	65
4:12	65
4:16	79

1 Thessalonians

4:3	152

Titus

2:14	16

Hebrews

1:10	139
2:4	139, 148
3:3	139
3:8	139
3:13	139
4:15	139
5:6	139, 141
5:10	139
6:20	135
7:5	139
7:11	139
7:15	139
7:16	139, 140
7:17	140, 141
7:27	140
8:4	140
8:5	140
8:9	140
9:5	140
9:9	140
9:19	140
9:22	140
9:25	140
10:1	140
10:3	140
10:8	140
10:11–16	39n
10:11	140
11:7	140
11:9	62
11:13	12, 140

James

2:8	140
3:9	140

1 Peter

1:1–2:10/11	5, 163
1:1–20	167
1:1–12	41, 63
1:1–2	66, 131–52, 153, 171, 182

1 Peter (continued)

Reference	Pages
1:1	3, 12, 38, 41, 44, 48n, 49, 55, 63, 67, 73, 133, 143–44
1:2	5, 15, 16, 17, 20–25, 37, 64, 66, 109, 127, 130, 131, 135, 140, 141, 148, 166
1:3–2:10	11, 12, 66
1:3–12	152, 166, 169, 173
1:3–5	66
1:3	66, 148–49, 169, 173
1:4	44, 167
1:5	72, 168
1:6	168
1:6–8	66
1:6–7	72, 164
1:7	150, 152
1:8	152
1:9	168
1:10–12	3, 5, 6, 15, 25, 27, 37, 66, 88, 131, 152–58, 160, 163, 166–68, 182
1:10	157, 168, 176
1:11–12	155
1:11	154, 157, 170
1:12	155, 158, 161, 168
1:13–2:3	170
1:13–17	172
1:13	66, 169, 172
1:14	151
1:15	142, 148
1:16	63
1:17	38, 43, 45, 57, 140, 148, 169
1:18–21	15, 66, 172
1:18	48
1:19–21	171
1:19–20	24
1:19	170
1:20	3, 5, 15, 20, 24–25, 37, 122, 130, 131, 135, 159–161, 163, 166, 168–169, 170, 172, 182
1:22–25	170
1:22	66, 161, 172
1:23–25	172
1:24–25	168
1:25	168
2	13, 63, 65
2:1—4:11	11
2:1–10	170
2:1–3	68n, 170, 172
2:3	66
2:4–10	66, 132, 143, 166, 170–72, 174, 181
2:4–5	171
2:4	171–73
2:5	13, 14, 66, 173
2:6–8	174
2:6	143, 172
2:7	168
2:9–11	170
2:9–10	14, 65, 174
2:9	13, 14, 15, 39, 63, 73, 143, 168, 172–75, 179, 185–86
2:10	13, 64, 168, 173
2:10/11	12
2:10	12, 164
2:11–12	186
2:11	12, 16, 38, 40, 43, 48, 63, 64, 67, 144, 148, 178
2:12	67, 72, 132, 164
2:13–17	46n
2:17	66
2:18	72
2:20	10, 17, 164
2:21–23	72
2:21	151
3:1	165
3:5–6	174
3:6	67
3:7	140, 148
3:9–19	10
3:21	168
4:3	132
4:4	164
4:6	140, 148
4:12	12
4:12–19	10
4:16	66
4:17–19	174
4:19	140, 148
5:1	155, 156
5:2	140, 142
5:4	44, 176
5:9	66
5:12	3, 148, 156
5:13	49

2 Peter

3:3	141
3:13	141
3:17	125

1 John

5:14	141

2 John

6	141

3 John

15	141

Jude

16	141
18	151

DEAD SEA SCROLLS

4Q339	27
4Q410	27

GRECO-ROMAN WRITINGS

Antiochus

Fragmenta (e cod. Napolitano 19)

4.154	107
4.155	107

Fragmenta (e cod. Paris)

8.3.108	107–108
8.3.119	108

Aristonicus

De signis Iliadis

23.857	118–19
234	57

Aristophanes

Nomina aetatum (fragmentum)

279	55n

Nomina aetatum (fragmentum Nauck)

38	55n

Nomina aetatum (fragmentum Parisinum)

16	55n

Balbillus

Fragmenta

8.104.20	109

Cicero

De divination

2.4.12	28

De natura deorum

2.3	28

Diodorus Siculus
Bibliotheca Historica

20.84.2	57, 58
31.6	51

Dio Chrysostom
In Athens, About His Banishment

2–6	54

Diogenes Laertius
Epicurus

135	28

Dorotheus
Fragmenta Graeca

424.6	119

Epictetus
Dissertationes ab Arriano digestae

2.10.5–6	121
2.10.6	121–22

Erotianus
Fragmenta

33.27	108–9, 126

Erotianus
Vocum Hippocraticarum collectio

109	119–20, 129

Josephus
Against Apion

1.200–204	115
1.228	104
1.232	104
1.256	115

Jewish Antiquities

1.21	62
1.68–69	28
1.311	111
2.86	111
3.60	27
4.121	111–12, 129
4.122	112
5.86	62
5.358–359	112
6.49	103n
6.54	112
6.314	103n
6.344–350	112
6.348	112
7.57	112
7.335	56, 60
7.336	56
8.59	56
8.231–234	3
8.231	102
8.234	102–3
8.405–407	27
8.406–407	103
8.418	103, 113
8.419	103, 113
13.175	113
13.300	103
14.213	56–57, 60
15	103
15.373	103
16.214	113
17.43	103
17.211	88
18.195–201	103–104
18.199	104
18.201	104

18.217	113
18.218	113

Jewish War

1.55	113–14
1.608	114
2.159	114
3.484	114
4.220–236	114
6	114–15
6.8	115, 129

Life

103–106	115
106	88

Longinus

De sublimitate

9.12	120–21, 129

Philo

Agriculture

65	62

Cherubim

120–121	56

On Dreams

1.2	115–16

On the Confusion of Tongues

76	62
77–80	55
78b	55–56

79	56
82	55

Special Laws

3.103	119–20

Who Is the Heir of Divine Things

260–261	27

Plutarch

Bravery of Women

255.C	117

The 'E' at Delphi

386.D	105
386.A	105

Fragmenta

21–23	106–7

Lives: Alcibiades

24.4	116, 117, 129

Lives: Comparison of Pericles and Fabius Maximus

2.3	116

Lives: Dion

21.8	116

Lives: Pyrrhus

10.3	57, 57n, 60

Lives: Sulla

37.1	116, 129

On Being a Busybody

519.F (10)	117, 118, 129

On Exile

2–12	54

On the Delays of the Divine Vengeance

567.D (31)	117–18

On the Malice of Herodotus

41	55n

The Obsolescence of Oracles

8–9	29
40–41	29
431.E (39)	117

The Oracles at Delphi No Longer Given in Verse

339D	105
396–399	29

Other Fragments (Fragments)

216c	118, 129
217a	118, 129

Whether Land or Sea Animals Are Cleverer

979.A	106
979.E	106
982.C	106

Polybius

Histories

6.52	51
32.6.4	55, 58

Rufus of Ephesus

Quaestiones medicinales

20–21	122, 129
21	122, 129

~

Early Christian Writings

Augustine

On Baptism, Against the Donatists

4.3	19

Catachising of the Uninstructed

18	19

Index of Scripture and Other Ancient Works   217

City of God

5.9–10	18
5.9	18
5.10	18
20.10 (1.2432)	14

Enchiridion

104	19

Expositions on the Psalms

87.3 (1.8421)	14
122.4 (8.593–94)	14

Homilies on the Gospel of John

53.4	18–19

Reply to Faustus

22.89 (4.309)	14

Bede the Venerable

Commentary on the Seven Catholic Epistles

70	16
89	16

Clement of Alexandria

Fragments

12.3 (2.585)	13

Clement of Rome

1 Clement

42	104

43–44	104
43.6	104
44.1	104
44.2	17

Clementine Homilies

3.11–15	17
3.43–44	17

Constitution of the Holy Apostles

2.7 (4.222)	14
3.2 (7.431)	14

Cyril of Jerusalem

Catechetical lectures

19 (7.144–46)	14

Didymus the Blind

Epistolam S, Petri Primam Enarratio

1.2	16

Gregory of Nazianzen

Orations

43.41 (7.409)	15

Gregory the Great

Book of Pastoral Rule

2.3 (12.11)	15

Ignatius

Epistle to the Ephesians

9 (1.53)   13

Epistle to the Philadelphians

4 (1.81)   13

Jerome

Dialogue against the Luciferians

3-4 (6.321)   14

John Chrysostom

In Primam S. Petri Epistolam

1   15-16

John of Damascus

Exposition of the Orthodox Faith

21   17

Leo the Great

Letters

29.5 (12.42)   14

Sermons

82.1 (12.195)   14

Methodius

Oration Concerning Simeon and Anna

3.392-93   13-14

Shepherd of Hermes

31.4   17
66.5   17-18

Tertullian

An Answer to the Jews

3 (3.155)   13

Origin

Against Celsus

2.20 (4.440)   17
4.96 (11.1173d)   17
5.10 (4.546-47)   13
8.19 (4.646)   13

Index of Subject Matter

Concept and word, distinction of, 85–90
Context and semantic range, interrelation of, 90–97

First Peter, general, 7–12
First Peter, suffering of the recipients , 163–66
Foreknowledge and hope, 72–73, 166–69, 177–78
Foreknowledge, defined, 6
Foreknowledge, discussed in Jewish and Greco-Roman literature, 26–29
Foreknowledge, relation to foreordination, 3–4, 6n, 97, 135–36, 184
Foreknowledge, relation to prophecy, 3, 26–29, 153–58, 160–61
Foreknowledge, views of Augustine on, 18–20

John H. Elliott's *A Home for the Homeless*, critical reception, 43n, 45–48
John H. Elliott's *A Home for the Homeless*, defense of, 64–71
John H. Elliott's *A Home for the Homeless*, significance, 39, 43–45

Κατά with the accusative, use of, 139–42, 145–49

Language, social nature of, 75, 89–94, 96

παρεπίδημος, use in Koine Greek, 55–56, 58–61
παροικία, use in Koine Greek, 57–58
πάροικος, use in Koine Greek, 56–61
προγινώσκω, use in Koine Greek and the LXX, 110–25, 127–30
πρόγνωσις, use in Koine Greek and LXX, 101–10, 125–27

Relevance theory, 75–77, 86

Social Identity, 39, 170–77, 185
Social Identity, defined, 7
Social scientific criticism, application to NT studies 32–36
Social scientific criticism, defined, 30
Social scientific criticism, history of, 30–32
Stranger, concept of, 50–54

Index of Modern Authors

Abernathy, David, 148
Achtemeier, Paul J., 8, 12, 31, 43, 46, 48, 67, 68, 134, 154, 161, 173
Adams, F. A., 146
Agnew, Francis H., 23, 151

Badilita, Smaranda, 61
Baker, Coleman A., 185
Bandy, Alan S., 11
Barr, James, 81-83, 89, 93
Barrow, R. H., 28
Bartlett, David L., 22, 135, 160-61
Barton, Stephen H., 36
Baugh, S. M., 21, 83, 109-10, 124, 135, 159
Baxter, Benjamin J., 84
Beale, G. K., 167
Beare, Francis Wright, 23-24, 93, 137, 156
Bechtler, Steven Richard, 59-60, 67-69, 178
Berding, Kenneth, 30, 35-36
Best, Ernest, 137
Black, David Alan, 78-79, 81-82, 88-89, 187
Blackburn, Perry L., 175
Bloom, Paul, 76, 87, 92-93
Boman, Thorleif, 89
Boring, M. Eugene, 143-44
Brandis, Christian A., 121
Bréal, Michael   , 82, 89
Beilby, James K., 191
Brox, Norbert, 22, 24, 40-41, 158, 161
Burge, Gary M., 53

Buswell, James Oliver, Jr., 136-37, 148, 159
Butler, Jim, 72-73

Caird, G. B., 48, 75, 89, 96
Calvin, John, 20
Campbell, Barth L., 165
Caragounis, Chrys C., 81
Carroll, Lewis, 74-75
Carson, D. A., 168, 176
Carston, Robyn, 77, 86-87
Charles, J. Daryl, 22
Chester, Andrew, 163, 169, 174
Chevallier, Max-Alain, 12, 40-41, 44, 67, 170
Chin, Moses, 47, 56, 58, 61, 68-69, 71
Chomsky, Noam, 76
Christiansen, Ellen Juhl, 135
Church, Alonzo, 85
Cobb, John W., 21
Cohick, Lynn H., 53
Cook, L. Stephen, 27
Corritore, Alfio, 67-68
Cothenet, Abbé Edouard, 169
Cotterell, Peter, 81, 83-84, 88, 92
Craffert, Pieter F., 32-33, 35
Crook, Zeba A., 34
Cruse, D. A., 87

Dana, H. E., 146
Davids, Peter H., 22, 24, 27, 42, 84, 135, 155, 159
Davidson, A. B., 27
Davidson, Donald, 84
De Clorivière, Pierre-Joseph Picot, 68

221

De Saussure, Ferdinand, 74-75, 81, 96
Deissmann, Adolf, 78, 79, 99
Den Bok, Nico, 19
Deterding, Paul E., 68
Donelson, Lewis R., 133, 155, 161
Dryden, J. De Waal, 45-46, 63-65, 172-73
Du Buit, F. M., 22
Dummett, M. A. E., 76, 84
Dunning, Benjamin H., 26, 60
Dupont-Roc, Roselyne, 149
Dvorak, James D., 36

Eddy, Paul R., 191
Elliott, John H., 1-2, 4-5, 7-8, 11-12, 22, 24-25, 31, 33-34, 36-37, 39, 43-50, 58-59, 63-72, 131-33, 137, 150, 158, 162, 165, 167, 170-71, 176-78, 180-81, 183-84, 186-88
Erasmus, 20
Esler, Philip F., 32, 34-35

Fagbemi, Stephen Ayodeji, 7-8, 26, 42, 46, 50, 66-67, 69, 143-44, 151-52
Fanning, Buist M., 174
Feldmeier, Reinhard, 22, 24, 42, 52, 56-58, 60, 133, 154, 161
Filson, Floyd V., 40
Furnish, Victor Paul, 41

Gager, John G., 67
Gibson, Arthur, 92
Glenny, W. Edward, 174, 177
Goldstein, Horst, 25-26, 172
Goppelt, Leonhard, 1, 12, 22, 24, 187
Gréaux, Eric James, 26
Green, Gene L., 8, 27-29, 53, 78, 86-87, 90, 155, 165, 168, 174
Green, Joel B., 162, 165-66, 169-70
Greenhill, William Alexander, 109
Grice, H. P., 84
Grubel, James, 96
Grudem, Wayne A., 22-24, 42, 132-34, 138, 142, 145, 150, 152, 157, 182
Guthrie, Donald H., 164
Gutt, Ernst-August, 75, 77

Hale, Edward Everett, 38
Harink, Douglas, 23, 163, 167, 188
Harmon, G. M., 8
Harris, Murray J., 145-47
Harrison, Everett Falconer, 157
Harrison, Gessner, 146-47
Hauerwas, Stanley, 187-88
Helyer, Larry R., 172-73
Hemer, Colin J., 8, 43, 70
Hill, David, 81, 100
Hillyer, Norman, 131-32, 154-55
Himes Paul A., 152
Hirsch, E. D., Jr., 91-92
Holden, James Herschel, 100, 109, 119
Hope, Edward, 146
Horrell, David G., 7, 31-32, 34-36, 164-65, 174-75, 177, 185
Hort, F. J. A., 22-24, 131, 134, 137-38, 145
Howard, Douglas A., 9

Jaillard, Dominique, 28-29
James, Edgar C., 21, 110, 125, 131, 159-60
Jobes, Karen H., 7, 12, 22, 24, 49-50, 61-62, 65, 68, 71, 134-35, 137, 150-51, 154-55, 157, 170-71, 173, 178-79, 184
Jones, C. P., 29
Jorgenson, James, 19
Joseph, Abson Prédestin, 133, 152, 163-64, 170-71
Judge, E. A., 7

Katz, Jerrold J., 85
Kellum, L. Scott, 163
Kelly, J. N. D., 12, 22, 24, 132, 134, 137, 154-55, 160
Kempson, Ruth, 193
Kendall, David W., 168
Kilpatrick, G. D., 156-57
Kirk, Gordon E., 164
Kirkpatrick, William David, 3
Kistemaker, Simon J., 22, 24
Kolden, Marc, 72
Köstenberger, Andreas J., 163
Knopf, Rudolf, 158

Index of Modern Authors 223

Lea, Tommy, 12
Lee, Clarence L., 52
Lee, John A. L., 101
Leighton, Robert, 24
Lescelius, Robert H., 21
Levick, Barbara, 10
Liddell, Henry George, 57, 108, 119–20, 122
Liebengood, Kelly, 8, 71, 132
Lloyd, Seton, 10
Louw, Johannes P., 84–86, 88, 91, 93–95
Love, Julian Price, 25, 153, 155
Luraghi, Silvia, 146–47
Lyons, John, 81–82, 93, 95

Malherbe, Abraham J., 31–33
Malina, Bruce J., 30, 34, 52
Mantey, Julius R., 146
Marrow, Stanley B., 43
Marshall, I. Howard, 22, 24
Martin, Ralph P., 163, 169, 174
Martin, Troy, 165–66, 186
Mbuvi, Andrew M., 71
McCall, Tom, 21, 124
McKnight, Scot, 12, 22, 24, 48, 62, 70
Meinertz, Max   , 163–64
Metzger, Bruce M., 12
Michaels, J. Ramsey, 12, 22, 24, 42, 58, 102, 132–34, 157
Mitchell, Stephen, 8–10, 52
Moffett, Samuel Hugh, 10
Moo, Douglas, 83, 123–24
Moore, Carey A., 102
Morris, Leon, 92, 123
Moule, C. F. D., 11
Moulton, James Hope, 78, 80
Mulholland, M. Robert, Jr., 36

Neyrey, Jerome H., 28
Nida, Eugene A., 84, 86, 91, 93–94

Obermann, Andreas, 58
Olson, C. Gordon, 21, 102, 123
Ortwein, Gudrun Guttenberger, 60
Osiek, Carolyn, 34

Page, Sydney H. T., 151

Pervo, Richard I., 109
Peterson, David G., 110
Philipps, Karl, 50, 52, 178
Picirilli, Robert E., 135
Pierpont, William G., 141
Piper, John, 72, 95–96
Poh, C. L. E., 26, 42, 46, 66–67
Porter, Stanley E., 146
Prasad, Jacob, 160, 167
Price, S. R. F., 51–52

Quarles, Charles L., 163

Radermacher, Ludwig, 79
Ramsay, Sir William Mitchell, 51
Reed, Jeffrey T., 78
Reicke, Bo, 24, 51
Richard, Earl J., 11, 169
Robertson, A. T., 79–80, 100, 146–47
Robinson, Maurice A., 141
Rohrbaugh, Richard L., 52
Roy, Steve C., 185

Sawyer, John F. A., 82
Scharfe, Ernst, 68
Schelkle, Karl Hermann, 12, 23–24, 134, 148, 160
Schmid, Josef, 10
Schmitz, Leonhard, 100, 118
Schrage, Wolfgang, 23–24
Schreiner, Thomas R., 7–8, 22, 24, 42, 83, 124, 169
Schröger, Friedrich, 3, 25, 44, 133, 150, 169
Schutter, William L., 46, 66, 152, 157
Schweizer, Eduard, 24
Scott, Robert, 57, 108, 119–20, 122
Seland, Torrey, 48–49, 58, 61, 63, 67
Selwyn, Edward Gordon, 7–8, 12, 22, 24, 58, 137, 150, 153–56
Sharp, Granville, 109
Silva, Moisés, 80–82, 92
Smith, Craig A., 79–80
Smith, Kevin Gary, 77
Smith, William, 100
Soucek, Josef B., 25
Sperber, Dan, 75, 77
Spicq, Ceslas, 12, 24, 163

Spörri, Theophil, 2, 25, 41
Staden, P. van, 33
Stanglin, Keith, 21, 124
Starwalt, Ervin Ray, 11-12
Steenberg, Pierre Francois, 26, 67
Steiger, Wilhelm, 22, 24, 134
Stewart, Alexander E., 178
Stover, Michael, 100

Taber, Charles R., 76
Talbert, Charles H., 42
Tånberg, K. Arvid, 89
Thomas, Robert L., 76, 81
Thompson, James W., 11, 164
Thurén, Lauri, 148, 160, 170, 178
Trebilco, Paul, 175
Trobisch, David, 80
Turner, Max, 81, 83-84, 88, 92

Ubieta, Carmen Bernabé, 51, 53, 58
Usteri, Johann Martin, 12, 22, 24

Van Aarde, Andries G., 31, 33
Van Rensburg, Fika J., 47-48, 176-77

Vance, Laurence M., 147
Verhaar, W. M., 76
Volf, Miroslav, 71
Vrede, Wilhelm, 163-64

Wallace, Daniel B., 109, 146-48
Warden, Preston Duane, 8, 11, 25, 153-54, 156
Whitaker, Richard E., 93
Wilckens, Ulrich, 123
Wilkenhauser, Alfred, 10
Williams, Jocelyn A., 170
Williams, Martin, 143, 167
Williams, Travis B., 164-65
Willimon, William H., 187-88
Wilson, Deirdre, 75, 77
Winer, George Benedict, 79
Winston, David, 111
Witherington, Ben, III., 12, 22, 25, 135, 151, 158, 160
Wolff, Christian, 41, 43-44, 53, 72
Wright, F. A., 100
Wright, N. T., 95-96

www.ingramcontent.com/pod-product-compliance
Lightning Source LLC
Chambersburg PA
CBHW051639230426
43669CB00013B/2368